Before Brass Tacks

Basic Skills in English

Lynne Gaetz
Collège Lionel-Groulx

Prentice Hall Allyn and Bacon Canada
Don Mills, Ontario

To Diego and Rebeka, the loves of my life.

Canadian Cataloguing in Publication Data

Gaetz, Lynne, 1960–
  Before brass tacks : basic skills in English

(Brass books series)
ISBN 0-13-081823-2

1. English language—Textbooks for second language learners.* I. Title.
II. Series: Gaetz, Lynne, 1960–   . Brass books series.

PE1128.G3253 1999   428.2'4   C99-932376-5

Prentice-Hall, Inc., Upper Saddle River, New Jersey
Prentice-Hall International (UK) Limited, London
Prentice-Hall of Australia, Pty. Limited, Sydney
Prentice-Hall Hispanoamericana, S.A., Mexico City
Prentice-Hall of India Private Limited, New Delhi
Prentice-Hall of Japan, Inc., Tokyo
Simon & Schuster Asia Private Limited, Singapore
Editora Prentice-Hall do Brasil, Ltda., Rio de Janeiro

ISBN 0-13-081823-2

Vice President, Editorial Director: Laura Pearson
ESL Manager and Publisher: Jodie Blaney
Executive Developmental Editor: Marta Tomins
Art Director: Mary Opper
Production Editor: Matthew Christian
Copy Editor: John Sweet
Production Coordinator: Wendy Moran
Interior Design: Zena Denchik
Cover Design: Lisa LaPointe
Cover Image: Photo Disc
Page Layout: Hermia Chung

 4 5 IW 03

Printed and bound in Canada.

Table of Contents

Part 2 — Grammar

Preface

To the student

"Let's get down to brass tacks" is a Cockney expression, meaning "Let's get down to the basic facts." It describes the approach that this book takes. Interesting and very "readable" essays are combined with helpful hints for the structuring of your own opinion essays. Writing Tips are included in each chapter, with a focus on opinion-essay writing.

The Grammar Sections in this book cover the forms that may be problematic for you. Each grammar unit contains clear explanations, so the Grammar Sections could be used as a self-study manual. Your teacher may ask you to do the Grammar Sections for homework. If so, make sure that you read the explanations in each Grammar Section very carefully before attempting the exercises.

Each Grammar Section contains some "class exercises." The answers to these exercises are not in the separate answer key because sometimes the teacher may want to explain a concept or do an exercise with the students.

To the teacher

The book contains twelve chapters, which concentrate on reading, writing and speaking skills. There are also twelve Grammar Sections, containing basic grammar practice and communication activities. If you want the students to correct their own grammar exercises, request *Before Brass Tacks, Basic Grammar Answer Keys* with your book orders.

Reproducible listening exercises and the tape transcript can be found in the separate Instructor's Manual. This Manual also contains game ideas, writing test suggestions and marking grids, and corrections to all activities.

Good luck.

Acknowledgments

I would like to thank the following people for their help and support: my students and all of the teachers in the English Department at Collège Lionel-Groulx. I am indebted to the people at Prentice Hall Canada for getting after me to do these projects. In particular I would like to thank Jodie Blaney, Dominique Roberge, Marta Tomins, Matthew Christian and John Sweet. For their useful comments during the review process, I would like to thank Geraldine Ausbach and Suneeti Phadke. I would also like to thank Patti Holter for her editing of the Instructor's Manual and Answer Key. I appreciate the great support from Line Bechard. Finally, I would like to extend a special thanks to my parents, my husband and my children, who helped keep my spirits up and who put up with my long hours on the computer.

The Topic Sentence

Essays come in a variety of shapes and sizes. Unlike the short story, the essay deals with subject matter that is, for the most part, non-fiction. While the short story is developed in the imagination of the writer, the essay is born in reality.

This chapter's Writing Tip concentrates on the topic sentence, which is a fundamental building block to paragraph writing. The speaking activity is a simple "Who Is It?" game that permits you to practice forming questions. Review Grammar Section 1 for correct question forms of sentences containing the verb *be*.

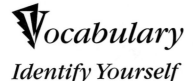

Vocabulary

Identify Yourself

Most of the following terms are commonly found on application forms.

maiden name	married woman's original family name
middle name	rarely used name that falls between the first and last name
nickname	a familiar form of a proper name. Example: Robert becomes Bob.
Mr.	title before the name of a man

Miss	title before the name of a single woman
Mrs.	title before the name of a married woman
Ms.	title before the name of all women, regardless of marital status
single	unmarried
celibate	original meaning from Latin was "unmarried," but currently used to mean "abstaining from having sex"
widowed	having lost a spouse through death
common law	the state of living together without formal marriage. The term "domestic partners" is also used.

VOCABULARY EXERCISE

Complete the following form. Refer to the previous list or the dictionary if any of the words are unfamiliar to you.

Personal Information

Last Name First Initial	Circle one Mr. Miss Ms. Mrs.	Maiden Name:
Marital Status (Circle one) Single Married Divorced Separated Common-law Widowed		
Current address (Street, City, Province or State, Country)	Nickname	
Height: Weight: Hair color: Eye color:	Distinguishing marks (moles, dimples, etc.)	

ℝeading

Reading Tip: Context Clues

Ideally, when you read a new and unfamiliar word, you should verify its meaning by looking the word up in the dictionary. However, in the real world, this is a very time-consuming process. It may also mean that instead of focusing on the message of a text, you are focusing on the meaning of individual words.

The meaning of many words and expressions can be guessed by looking at the context in which the word is being used. You can look at the sentence in which the word appears and try to find a synonym (word that means the same thing) or antonym (word that means the opposite). Sometimes the meaning of a difficult word can be guessed by looking at the sentences surrounding the word. By using logic, the meaning becomes clear.

For example: Look at the words *top-notch* in this context. The meaning of the words becomes obvious.

> This restaurant provides top-notch service. The waiters are polite and the service is prompt. I highly recommend this restaurant.

What does "top-notch" mean? _____

PRE-READING ACTIVITY

Before reading the essay "Meaningful Manners," answer the following questions to measure how polite you are. Beside each question, check off either true or false.

		True	False
1.	I rarely use swear words.	✓	
2.	I never swear in front of children.	✓	
3.	I always leave a tip for the waiter or waitress in a restaurant.	✓	
4.	I always tip the professional person who cuts my hair.	✓	
5.	I always offer my seat on the bus to the elderly or the obviously pregnant.	✓	
6.	I always hold the door open for the person immediately following me.	✓	
7.	I chew my food with my mouth closed.	✓	
8.	I don't speak when my mouth is full of food.	✓	
9.	I obey "no smoking" rules.	✓	
10.	I avoid gossiping.	✓	
11.	I send "thank-you" notes to relatives who send me gifts.	✓	
12.	When someone writes me a letter, I take care always to write back.	✓	
13.	I cover my nose and mouth when I cough or sneeze.	✓	
14.	I keep litter in my pocket until I find a garbage can.	✓	
15.	I always turn off my Walkman and remove my headphones when my teacher is speaking to the class, or I never bring a Walkman to class.	✓	

SCORE: If you answered twelve to fifteen questions with a "yes," then you are very polite. If you answered fewer than eleven questions with a "yes," then you definitely need to learn some manners!

Meaningful Manners
by Ellen Taeg

1   Once upon a time, women were treated like delicate flowers, unable to open a door or cross a street without assistance. We have all seen drawings of a man spreading out his beautiful cloak over a muddy road so that a lady won't dirty her feet. In the past, in times of disaster, women and children were saved first. In fact, when the great ship *Titanic* went down on a cold April night in 1912, some of the ship's crew believed that "women and children first" meant "women and children only." In one case, a lifeboat was less than half full with women, and many men were hovering nearby. The women in that lifeboat pleaded that their husbands be allowed in to help row, but their pleas were ignored. The lifeboat was lowered, and the men were left behind to drown.

2   On the other hand, the preferential treatment given to women had a dark side. While women were treated as if they were fragile creatures, women were also denied the right to vote, to study and enter universities, to practice medicine and midwifery, and to enter into a variety of other professions. Women were considered too fragile and foolish for the professional world.

3   Notions of "women first" have fallen by the wayside. Now, both men and women should practice civility or "politeness," and this civility should be extended towards all people, regardless of sex.

4   As our North American society becomes more casual, many people are left wondering just what the polite thing to do is. Here are some etiquette standards that should still be adhered to.

Introductions.

5   It is no longer necessary to introduce each person who enters a party to the rest of the crowd. There are some rules, however, that never go out of date. If you are with a friend and another person joins you, it is simply polite to inquire if they know each other. If the newcomer is known only by you, then you should politely say, "Sam, this is my friend Evan," or "I'd like you to meet Evan. Evan, this is Sam."

You have forgotten someone's name.

6   Some people are very good at remembering names; others have memories like a sieve. If you do forget someone's name, you could simply admit your lapse of memory. Just say, "I'm very sorry, but I've forgotten your name." You could even excuse yourself first by admitting, "I've got a terrible memory for names. What was your name again?"

7   If it's just too embarrassing to admit that you have forgotten the name of an ex-girlfriend, for example, you could just introduce that person by saying, "This is an old, close friend of mine." You could then hope that your friends introduce themselves to each other.

8   A good way to save everyone embarrassment when you are the newcomer to a group is to simply introduce yourself. "Hi, I'm Evan. And you're...?"

Who opens the door for whom?

9   Although women do not need to enter a room first, it is important that people of both sexes always hold the door open for the person following them. In fact, it is extremely rude to let a door slam shut on the person following you.

When to stand on buses and subways.

10   If you find yourself on a crowded subway or bus, it is simple human kindness to offer your seat to someone who is much older, or infirm, or pregnant, or burdened down with packages. If you see a man or woman standing and holding a baby, immediately offer your seat to that person. In short, if you are young and healthy, having to stand for a while will be no hardship.

Who pays?

11   While men used to automatically pick up the tab, today the rule is "each one pays his or her own way." If a female earns substantially more than her male date, there is nothing wrong with the female picking up the tab. However, the higher wage earner should not mention that he or she earns more; it could be perceived as boasting. Simply smile and pick up the bill.

12   Many couples take turns: she pays this week, he pays next. Another simple rule you could follow: the person who does the inviting could pay the bill.

Table manners.

13   Certain table manners are related to simple common courtesy. You probably don't like to see someone talk when their mouth is full of half-eaten food. Make sure you don't expose others to that disgusting sight. Also, take small- to normal-sized bites of food. Children often stuff their mouths, and this is not a pretty sight.

14   There are some other tips that are always useful to know. Never use a toothpick at the table when you have something between your teeth; use the toothpick in privacy. In the past it was considered rude to rest your elbows on the table, but now that is perfectly acceptable between courses. Finally, if you are at a fancy restaurant, a simple rule of thumb regarding silverware is this: always start with the cutlery on the outside of the place setting and work your way in.

Who should you tip?

15   The word "tip" was originally formed from the first letters of the words "to insure promptness." It is polite to always tip the waiter or waitress in a restaurant, *even if the service isn't top-notch*. Often that isn't the waiter's fault. Maybe the cook is slow or maybe the owner hired only one waitress when business is heavy enough for two.

16   And please, don't forget the pizza delivery person. You tip the person who walks across a room to deliver your meal. Why would you refuse to tip the person who drives through a snowstorm to deliver you a warm pizza?

17   There are some others that you should tip. Both men and women should tip the person who cuts their hair. Tip the taxi driver. Tip the bartender if you are just drinking. In some places, notably Quebec, it is common practice to tip the person behind the counter in an ice-cream parlour or a deli. If you're not sure, look to see if there is a tip jar on the counter.

18   What is considered proper and polite does change over the centuries. We now live in a time when there are relatively few rules regarding proper behavior. Although we live in a very individualistic society, and although many will say that it is what is inside that counts, how we act in public is a good indicator of what is inside. Finally, if you follow the golden rule and do to others what you would like others to do to you, you will probably do no wrong. Kindness is never out of fashion.

VOCABULARY

Try to guess the meaning of the following vocabulary words. Instead of looking up the word in the dictionary, try to guess its meaning from the context. In other words, read the word in its paragraph, and see if any words or phrases near the difficult word give you a hint as to its meaning.

1. The word *muddy* (para. 1), as it is used in the text, means:
   a. dull and cloudy.
   b. soil and water mixed, producing soft, wet earth.
   c. confused.

2. The word *hover* (para. 1), as it is used in the text, means:
   a. to float on air.
   b. to be between life and death.
   c. to wait nearby.

3. The word *plead* (para. 1), as it is used in the text, means:
   a. to beg or request earnestly.
   b. to admit or deny guilt.
   c. to argue or contradict.

4. Write a synonym (a word that means the same thing) for *tab*. (para. 11)
   bill   pay the bill or the check

5. What is the *golden rule*? (para. 18) _do to others what you_
kidness would like others to do to you

READING COMPREHENSION

For each of the following sentences, write T (for "true") or F (for "false") in the space provided.

1. You should introduce each person who enters your party to the rest of the crowd.   F

2. It is considered impolite to acknowledge that you no longer remember someone's name.

3. Women should hold the door open for the people following them.

4. Both young men and young women should stand on crowded buses if an elderly person needs the seat.

5. It is OK to leave no tip when the service you receive is very bad.

6. Pizza delivery people should receive no tip, or a very small tip.

DISCUSSION

1. Why are women no longer given special treatment regarding etiquette?

2. When you go out with the opposite sex, who pays? Who should pay?

3. What is your opinion about tipping? Should people who give poor service not be tipped? Do we have to tip too many people?

4. Should the government impose a 15-percent service charge? If they do, it means that the servers always gets their tip, and you don't have to decide to tip or not. Is that a good idea? Explain your answer.

Writing Tips

The Topic Sentence

A good topic sentence introduces the subject of the paragraph and gets the reader's attention. The point that you are trying to make in your paragraph should be clearly evident in an interesting topic sentence. Everything else in the paragraph should be a detail that supports your topic sentence.

A good topic sentence is not too broad. Don't make your topic sentence so general that you need several paragraphs to support it.

I'm going to tell you everything about soccer.

This is impossible to do in one paragraph.

A good topic sentence unifies the paragraph. A topic sentence should be general enough that all the details and examples in the paragraph relate back to it. Don't include facts in your paragraph that have nothing to do with the topic sentence.

Very little equipment is required in soccer. Some children don't like to play sports.

The second sentence doesn't relate to the first sentence, and should not be in the same paragraph.

WRITING TIPS EXERCISE 1

In the following paragraph about manners, put a check beside each sentence that could be included in the paragraph.

Topic sentence: It is very rude to speak when your mouth is full of food.

Details:

- Some parents don't like their children to hear bad language.   _____
- You should chew with your mouth closed.   _____
- Don't use bad language at the dinner table.   _____
- If you have something to say, finish chewing and then say it.   _____
- It is rude to sneeze without covering your mouth.   _____
- No matter how important your comment is, no one wants to see half-eaten chicken.   _____

WRITING TIPS EXERCISE 2

Read the following paragraph and identify the topic sentence (the sentence that unifies the paragraph). Then cross out any sentences that are not related to the topic sentence. Note that the first few sentences of a paragraph can introduce the reader to the topic, before the actual topic sentence appears.

Some people like to keep a diary because it helps them remember who they've seen and where they've been. Others keep diaries because they have a chance to express their emotions on paper. One of the most famous diary-writers of all time, Anaïs Nin, claimed that keeping a diary was her way of making every day life feel as exciting as fiction. If you want to be a writer, diary keeping is an ideal way to exercise your craft. The best writers practice their craft every day. Many writers, such as F. Scott Fitzgerald, were unhappy alcoholics. Writing in a diary is like practicing the scales on a piano: you express yourself in your given art without worrying about the final product. Some writers had terrible drug habits. Even simply recording your daily activities can help your writing ability. The author of *Naked Lunch* shot his wife in the head. According to Henry Miller, "to write each day is the thing. Not to turn out masterpieces."

Writing Suggestions

1. Write a paragraph about one of your hobbies. Make sure that your paragraph is unified and focused. Highlight your topic sentence.

2. Write a paragraph about manners. What is very impolite? In a paragraph describe an impolite act. Make sure that your paragraph is unified and focused. Highlight your topic sentence.

3. Write a paragraph about a topic of your choice. Make sure that your paragraph is unified and focused. Highlight your topic sentence.

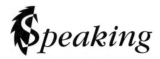

Speaking

SPEAKING EXERCISE ▪ WHO IS IT?

One student will be picked from the class; he or she comes before the group. Your teacher will give that student a paper with the name of a famous celebrity, politician, sports hero or artist. You must guess the name of the famous person by asking questions with yes/no answers. The student who correctly guesses the name of the famous person must then come to the front of the class. (Your teacher might ask you to play this game in teams.)

Example:	The famous person is Michael Jordan.	
Possible questions:	Is it a female?	No.
	Is he in movies?	Sometimes.
	Is he a famous musician?	No.
	Does he play sports?	Yes.
	etc.	

There is also a speaking activity at the end of Grammar Section 1.

In Sickness and In Health

Vocabulary   Body Parts and Illnesses

Reading   Reading Tip: Using a Dictionary

                      "Weighty Considerations" by S.D.D.

                      "I Am Not Free to Enjoy Food" by Dorothy Nixon

Writing Tips   More on Topic Sentences

Speaking   Medical games

Link to Grammar   Grammar Section 2: The Simple Present Tense

This chapter's health-related theme begins with a vocabulary exercise. This exercise allows you to verify your knowledge of English names for body parts and for some illnesses. Please note that in Grammar Section 2 there is a Vocabulary Boost that contains medical vocabulary.

The readings in this chapter focus on a truly contemporary issue: our obsession with weight. The first reading contains survey results: Canadian men and women of all ages were polled and asked about their attitudes regarding health issues. The second reading is an essay by Dorothy Nixon. Dorothy takes a humorous yet deadly serious look at our love-hate relationship with food and our bodies.

Like all chapters, this chapter contains a Writing Tip, this time about the writing of topic sentences. The ability to write and recognize topic sentences is fundamental in both reading and writing. The speaking section contains a game that will help you remember health-related vocabulary. There is also a suggested role-playing activity that allows you to assume the role of a patient or a doctor.

Vocabulary

Body Parts and Illnesses

These vocabulary activities could be done in pairs or teams. After each team has tried to match as many words as possible, the teacher could then explain the meanings of the most difficult terms. The answers to the following exercises are at the end of this chapter.

VOCABULARY EXERCISE 1

Label the body parts using the words provided.

forehead	cheek	eyelashes	eyebrow	chin	waist
thigh	hip	knee	toe	wrist	thumb
elbow	shoulder	ankle	heel	neck	knuckle

a. _____
d. _____
c. _____
b. _____
e. _____
f. _____
g. _____
m. _____
n. _____
j. _____
h. _____
i. _____
l. _____
k. _____
o. _____
p. _____
q. _____
r. _____

VOCABULARY EXERCISE 2

Write down the meaning, or a translation, for the following illnesses. Mention a few symptoms associated with each.

1. Flu _____

_____

2. Stomach flu _____

_____

3. Cold _____

_____

4. Chicken pox _____

_____

5. Mumps _____

_____

6. Measles _____

_____

Answer the following questions. You can write translations or synonyms for each word.

7. What does *pregnant* mean? _____

8. What are lice? _____

9. What is a bruise? _____

10. What is a scab? _____ A scar? _____

Reading

Reading Tip: Using a Dictionary

A dictionary is useful if it is used correctly. Use a dictionary that has been published or revised within the last fifteen years. Older dictionaries may contain terms or meanings that are no longer relevant. Also, be aware that dictionaries that translate words from one language to another may give simplified or inexact translations.

Tips for proper dictionary usage:

- **Use dictionaries when appropriate.** When you write, it is important to use a dictionary to check the spelling of difficult words. When you read, try to guess the meanings of most words. If you can't guess the meaning, then consult your dictionary.

- **Look at the preface and notes in your dictionary.** Find out what your dictionary has to offer. It may contain an irregular verb list. Many dual-language dictionaries indicate spelling of plural forms.

- **Be aware of word-break divisions.** Your dictionary may indicate (with a heavy black dot) recommended places for dividing words. This means that when you are writing and arrive at the end of a line, you can break the word at any place where a dot exists. Do not write the dots when you copy the word!

  Examples: mod•er•ate sub•ject

- **Be aware of stressed syllables.** Some dictionaries indicate which syllable should be stressed in spoken English. Often the mark is placed just before the stressed syllable.

  Examples: recla'mation ("ma" is the stressed syllable)
  o'riginal ("ri" is the stressed syllable)

- **Some words have many definitions.** Some dictionaries list the earliest meaning of the word first and the most recent meaning last; others put the most current meaning first. Most English words have many meanings. When you are looking up a word, *do not read only the first meaning!* Look for the meaning that best fits the context of your sentence.

PRE-READING ACTIVITY

Before reading the essay "Weighty Considerations," predict the answers to the following questions. After each question, circle either yes or no, or circle the letter of the best answer. After you have read the text, you can put the poll results at the end of the questions.

In your opinion: **Poll result**

1. Are the majority of Canadians overweight?   Yes   No   _____

2. Who are more overweight?   a) men   b) women   _____

3. Who are more likely to think they are overweight?   a) men   b) women   _____

4. Approximately what percentage of women are really overweight?
a) 20%   b) 40%   c) 60%   c) 80%   _____

5. Approximately what percentage of men are really overweight?
a) 20%   b) 40%   b) 60%   c) 80%   _____

6. About what percentage of Canadians have dieted in the past three months?
a) 15%   b) 33%   b) 66%   c) 90%   _____

Weighty Considerations
by S.D.D.

A poll was conducted in 1997 by Maclean's *magazine and CBC's "The National."*
Canadians from across the country and from all age groups were polled on a
variety of topics. In all, 1200 people were polled, and in a specific quest for
suspected generational differences, this poll asked questions to an additional 200
people in the 18- to 29-year-old age group, in an attempt to determine the mind-
set of the so-called Baby Busters.

1 The body images are almost as distorted as the reflections in a fun-house mirror. In this year's *Maclean's*/CBC News poll, 43 percent of women say they consider themselves overweight, and just 33 percent of men think the same way. At the same time, a solid majority of men—62 percent—say they are "about the right weight," while barely half of women—54 percent—say their weight is acceptable.

2 But a reality check and a set of scales paint a different picture—of the men, at least. In fact, 57 percent of men and 40 percent of women are overweight, according to Dalhousie University epidemiologist Michel Joffres, who helped collect national height and weight data for the recent Canada Heart Health Survey. "Men do not like to admit that they should lose weight," says Joffres. "But a lot of women in the normal range—and a significant number of women who are underweight—still want to lose weight."

3 The poll reveals one in three Canadians has been on a diet to improve their health—though not specifically to lose weight—in the past three months. And, not too surprisingly, more women than men are dieting. "Men tend in general to have a much better view of their bodies," says Marguerite Neri, general manager for Weight Watchers in southern Ontario. "Even if they are carrying extra pounds, it's OK. They don't put themselves down for it."

4 "I have a husband like that," says Lynn Merritt, 51, an executive secretary from Mississauga, Ont. "He is about 30 lb. too OK [overweight]." Merritt, now trimmed to 143 lb. on a five-foot, four-inch frame, decided to slim down a few years ago. "I was well over 200 lb. and starting to feel the health problems—bad knees, wheezing," she says. "I couldn't do a flight of stairs if my life depended on it." Her partner lost weight, too, when Merritt began to serve less fattening foods, but he soon gave up. "He lost 30 lb.," says Lynn. "But he decided he didn't like vegetables. He's in the same rut I was in."

5 In fact, many Canadians are stuck in a rut of too many calories, too little exercise. An overwhelming 93 percent of poll respondents say it is important to be physically fit. But only 40 percent say they played a sport, and just 18 percent worked out in a gym, in the previous month. Lori Beattie, a Calgary personal trainer, suspects that the 18 percent who went to a gym were also among those who participated in a sport. "There are extremists—people who go Roller-blading are also out hiking and biking," says Beattie, 27. "And there are people who have the remote control in their hand most of the time. They all know exercise is

important, but they say, 'I'm not comfortable putting on spandex and going to the gym.'"
Beattie earns her living by motivating the flabby to rise from their couches to join outdoor
fitness programs—everything from city-park walking, hiking, cross-country skiing to
snowshoeing in the Rockies. "I don't promote the spandex fitness club mentality," says
Beattie. "I try to promote a healthy lifestyle. It's about getting out there and doing things you
enjoy, not feeling bad because you don't have the right look."

VOCABULARY

1. The word *scales*, as it is used in paragraph 2, means: (circle one)
   a. small, rigid, flattened plates.
   b. instruments on which something can be weighed.
   c. a series of tones going up or down in pitch.

2. Try to guess the meaning of the word *flabby* from the context. Then look it up in
   the dictionary.

   Your guess: _____

   Dictionary definition: _____

3. Find a three-word expression in paragraph 5 meaning "a monotonous routine or
   fixed practice." _____

READING COMPREHENSION

1. Go back to the pre-reading activity. Write down the poll results after questions 1 to
   6, and compare your answers with the poll results. Which guesses of yours are not
   supported by the poll results? _____

   _____

   _____

2. In this opinion poll, more women than men think they are overweight. How is this
   perception inaccurate, according to Michel Joffres?

   _____

   _____

3. In your opinion, why do so many women *think* they are overweight when they are
   not? Why do fewer men than women worry about their weight?

   _____

   _____

   _____

DISCUSSION

1. Why do you think women, more than men, tend to be self-critical about their body image? Compare your answers to Reading Comprehension question 3.

2. Were your answers to the pre-reading questions 1 to 6 the same as the poll results? Did any of the poll results surprise you?

3. Do you get enough exercise each week? Why or why not? Does your college or school provide you with enough opportunities to play sports? Explain.

4. Why are most people at the present time less physically fit than other generations were?

PRE-READING VOCABULARY

Familiarize yourself with the following terms before reading the text. The number in parentheses indicates the paragraph where the word is found.

(1) *sustained*	supported
(3) *poring over*	looking through, with great interest
(5) *a bug*	a viral infection
(5) *implored*	begged, pleaded
(10) *bingeing and starving*	eating too much and then not eating enough
(12) *emancipated*	liberated
(15) *sleaze sheet shrieks*	cheap tabloid newspaper announces
(17) *burdened*	carrying something

Reading 2.2

I Am Not Free to Enjoy Food
by Dorothy Nixon

Dorothy Nixon writes about the media, culture and education, and is especially interested in new technologies and their effect—or potential effect—on women and children. She currently writes film reviews and general-interest columns for America Online.

1 My nephew, an 18-year-old into typical pursuits for his age like cars, computers and girls, came down with a life-threatening intestinal disorder and was hospitalized for a month. He

spent much of that time sustained by intravenous fluids. Before visiting him in the hospital, I phoned first to ask if there was anything I could bring him.

2   "Cookbooks," he replied, without hesitation. "Recipe books, pictures of food, anything to do with food."

3   In the hospital he tossed aside the *Sports Illustrated* Swim Suit Issue I had presented him with and began poring over the Bon Appetites. He then begged me to talk about what I had eaten that day. "When I get out of here," he told me in all adolescent earnestness, "I am going to enroll in chef's school."

4   But my nephew soon recovered. The next time I paid him a visit, I was pleased to see that he had gained back all of his weight, and then some. Now, the culinary arts were the farthest thing from his mind; he discussed the computer animation courses he wanted to take while munching on a dripping piece of pepperoni pizza.

5   Recently, my own son, Andrew, caught a bug and couldn't keep anything down for two days. On the morning of the third day he sat in front of the television, fully recovered but empty-bellied, and he saw a commercial for fishsticks. "Please, Mom," he implored. "I want some fishsticks. Please go to the grocery store and get me some. Now!"

6   Andrew normally hates fishsticks.

7   Now, if you are a woman, the odds are you can relate all too well to both these anecdotes. And, if you are a woman, chances are your experience with starvation was self-inflicted. At any given time, millions of women in North America are on diets, many of these diets of the silly and dangerous kind that make us so hungry we flip through magazines to salivate over pictures of canned peas we do not dare to eat.

8   I personally love food. No, I adore it. I love the symbolism of it, the nurturing life-giving aspect of it, the social aspect of it. I like the taste of good food, too. But like most women who buy, prepare and dole out food to their families, I am not always free to enjoy it. Not without guilt.

9   "Decadent Cake Recipes, Do You Dare?" blares a headline on the cover of a women's magazine at the supermarket checkout. Right under it, though, we find another conflicting headline. "How to Fight Those Thunder Thighs." And, sadly for us, this kind of thing is the rule, rather than the exception.

10   If women in our culture tend to alternate between bingeing and starving, it's certainly easy to see why.

11   Then again, we women buy most of the food in this society. Have you ever gone grocery shopping on an empty stomach? Hmmm. Maybe there is some marketing method to this editorial madness, after all.

12   A researcher in B.C. has other ideas. A few years ago he published data suggesting that it is natural for women to starve themselves if they do not want to procreate. This, and not advertising's mixed messages, is the reason modern emancipated woman are hard on themselves when it comes to food.

13   His is an intriguing argument, but I cannot see the logic here: we've had the pill since 1960. One would imagine that if this researcher's thesis was correct, women would have

eating Not

been stuffing their faces with wild abandon since that time. We have not. The ideal woman has only gotten skinnier and skinnier over the past few decades.

14   An acquaintance of mine who works in the fashion industry once told me that she, too, feels that women want to be skinny. The same person also made a suspect remark to me about Oprah Winfrey one day after looking at the cover story of a tabloid. "Why can't she keep her weight off?" she sneered with a level of condescension in her voice that Oprah, a trail-blazer and true female role model, clearly didn't deserve.

15   But then the tabloids are all about fat, aren't they. "Cher has a double chin," one sleaze sheet shrieks, making mock of a modern goddess of sveltitude. And here's a before snapshot of a "chubby" Lady Di and an after shot of Princess Diana as the elegant—and bulimic—role model to all.

16   The other day at my health club, I waited to take my turn at the step machine. "Please, please don't make me stop," pleaded a thin young woman as she pumped furiously at the pedals. "I have to wear off the huge meal I ate last night."

17   This woman was not burdened by excess pounds. But she did have some major self-loathing to sweat off.

18   As I waited my turn on the trendy torture device, I saw in my mind's eye a distant ancestor of Oprah, of us all, a beautiful big woman, generous hips swaying rhythmically as she walked the steaming African grasslands in her daily search for tubers and nuts and berries.

19   And I could only imagine that compared to that woman on the step machine, compared to most women in this culture, she must have felt as light as air.

VOCABULARY

1. Find a word in paragraph 3 that means "to throw lightly." ___tossed aside___

2. What are *thunder thighs*? Don't look in your dictionary. You can check the meaning of *thigh* by looking at the vocabulary at the beginning of this unit. Then, by looking at the word in context, guess what *thunder thighs* are. (para. 9)
   ___the part of the leg between the hip and the knee___

3. What is the meaning of *procreate*? (para. 12) ___reproduce, have a baby___

4. Find a word in paragraph 13 that means "engaging or interesting." ___intriguing___

5. What is an antonym (word that means the opposite) for the word *chubby*? (para. 15) ___slim thin___

6. Why is the word *chubby* in quotation marks (" ")? ___being sarcastic___

7. What is the meaning of the word *loathing*, in paragraph 17? Look at the sentences around it to guess the meaning. *hating* *strong dislike and disgust*

READING COMPREHENSION

1. What is the B. C. researcher's theory regarding female starvation? _____
   not to have baby

2. Why does the narrator disagree with the B. C. doctor's theory? _____
   _____ *there is pill and still want went costly skinny*

3. In the final paragraph, the narrator refers to a large African ancestor and states that "compared to most women in this culture, she must have felt as light as air." What does the narrator mean? Why would the large African woman feel lighter than the thin woman on the step machine? _____
   the African body do not bother her like the step machine woman

DISCUSSION

1. The author illustrates how, when people are hungry, they spend more time thinking about food. In your experience, does this make sense? If it is true, what does this say about dieting?

2. Why were our ancestors not concerned about weight?

3. Do you agree with the B.C. doctor's theory that women starve themselves in order to delay childbearing? Why or why not?

4. What can be done to help people accept their body weight?

Writing Tips
More on Topic Sentences

In the previous chapter you learned that a topic sentence unifies a paragraph around one subject, or "topic."

Like longer essays, paragraphs have an internal form. Generally, paragraphs start with a topic sentence that expresses the main idea of the paragraph. The topic sentence is then followed by other sentences that reinforce the main idea. The other sentences may provide examples, facts, statistics or anecdotal evidence. These all support the topic sentence. The paragraph generally concludes with a sentence that sums up the main points or expresses another notion about the topic.

WRITING TIPS EXERCISE 1

Read the following paragraph.

Major scientific breakthroughs are always made by scientists with university degrees, right? Wrong! In fact, many breakthroughs in math and science are made by amateurs. For example, in 1996, a 9-year-old schoolgirl designed an experiment that challenged the notion among the alternative-medicine community that there is "healing touch." After trying her simple experiment, the healers were correct just 44 percent of the time. In another case, a housewife from San Diego discovered new geometric shapes of non-repetitive patterns that could join, perfectly, on a surface. Scientists thought that all of the possibilities were known, but the housewife proved them wrong. The man who discovered oxygen was a minister. Benjamin Franklin was a statesman who discovered that lightning is electricity. Scientific breakthroughs can be made by amateurs with intense curiosity and a fresh approach to analyzing a problem.

1. Highlight the topic sentence.

2. How is the topic sentence supported? In point form, list the supporting ideas.

_____

_____

_____

_____

_____

WRITING TIPS EXERCISE 2

Look at each of the following combinations of words. Choose Group 1, 2 or 3 and write a topic sentence for a paragraph that could include those items. Remember that your topic sentence should not be too general, and it should be interesting. For example, a topic sentence for Group 3 could be: *This year's female runway models are dressing in men's formal wear.*

Group 1	*Group 2*	*Group 3*
lie	skill	tuxedo jacket
infidelity	speed	tie
trust	force	hat
fear	strength	suspenders
loneliness	passion	vest

Writing Suggestions

1. Choose one of the following words. Write a paragraph about that topic. To help with your writing, you could ask yourself questions to help focus your paragraph. Your paragraph could be about just one element (who does it) or about a combination of elements (what is done and why it is done).

Honesty   Happiness   Money   Fidelity   Soccer   Health

Who?   *You could list people who do it, or need it, or have it.*
What?   *You could look at what forms it takes.*
When?   *You could explore the evolution of the topic over time.*
Why?   *You could explain the reasons the topic is important.*
How?   *You could list ways that the topic is done.*

2. Write about illness or an accident. Have you ever been sick or injured? In a paragraph, describe the accident or illness. Make sure that your paragraph contains a topic sentence. Highlight your topic sentence.

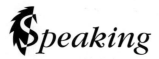

Speaking

SPEAKING EXERCISE 1

This activity provides an oral review of the vocabulary in this chapter. Your teacher will make a stack of cards, each card containing the name of a body part or an illness. "Illness" vocabulary is also in Grammar Section 2.

You will then be placed in teams of five or six. The cards will be placed, face down, in a pile. One student picks the top card and proceeds to describe the body part or illness. The student describing the body part must not point to the body part or mention the name of it. The student doing the description says only one sentence. The person next to him then guesses. If the guess is wrong, the student says another sentence. The next student guesses. In other words, team members guess, one at a time, clockwise, what the body part is. Team members must remember what the name of the body part is, and cannot look in their notes or in their books. Only the person picking up the card is allowed to refresh her memory.

When another team member guesses the word that was on the card, that team member gets to keep the card and it becomes that person's turn. When the time is up, the team member with the most cards wins.

SPEAKING EXERCISE 2

You will be asked to role-play the following scenarios. Some of you will be given the role of doctor and some will be the patients. You should read only your own role, and you should close your book after understanding your role.

Doctor

1. *1 or 2 students. One could be a doctor and one could be a nurse or medical student.*
Diagnose the patient. Prescribe heart pills and tests. It looks very serious.

2. *1 or 2 students. One could be a doctor and one could be a nurse or medical student.*
The patient(s) has chicken pox. There is nothing to do but wait. The patient(s) should not go to school. There is absolutely no medication that will really help the itching. The only medication is an expensive lotion, but it doesn't really work.

3. *1 or 2 students. One could be a doctor and one could be a nurse or medical student.*
Diagnose the patients. Ask the patients if they get dizzy or if they see spots. The patients have migraine headaches. Prescribe a potent new medication for migraines.

4. *1 or 2 students. You are both doctors.*
The patient has been complaining of back pain. There is no evidence of any back injury. It is likely that the patient is a hypochondriac. (A hypochondriac is someone who imagines that s/he is ill.) This patient often complains of pain for which there is no explanation. Refuse to sign the patient's form.

Patient

1. *1 or 2 students. One could be a man who suffers from chest pains, and one could be his wife.*
Wife: Your husband's chest hurts. He has complained a lot and you are very worried.
Husband: You have a little chest pain. It is nothing. You don't want any medication. You are in very good shape and you exercise every day.

2. *2 to 4 students. You are parents of one or two small children.*
The child (or children) has itchy red spots all over his or her body. The children complain constantly. You demand some medication for them. You will not leave until the doctor prescribes something.

3. *2 students. You are a married couple.*
You both have headaches on a regular basis. You don't believe in regular medication and will only take natural medication. Ask the doctor to prescribe herbs.

4. *2 students. You are a married couple.*
One of you has chronic back pain. Demand that the doctor sign a form so that you can miss work. Also tell the doctor about your sore foot. You also get blinding

headaches. Your job at a car factory requires concentration, and you can't concentrate because you feel so bad. If the doctor signs the forms, you will be paid to stay home. Your spouse supports what you are saying.

ANSWERS TO VOCABULARY EXERCISE 1:
a. forehead   b. cheek   c. eyelashes   d. eyebrow   e. chin   f. neck   g. shoulder   h. elbow   i. waist
j. wrist   k. hip   l. thigh   m. thumb   n. knuckle   o. knee   p. ankle   q. toe   r. heel

ANSWERS TO VOCABULARY EXERCISE 2:
Symptoms for the following illnesses: 1. sore throat, aching joints, fever and headache.   2. diarrhea, vomiting, fever.   3. coughing, sneezing, congestion.   4. raised, scab-like sores on the body, fever.
5. swollen glands in the throat, fever.   6. red spots all over the body, fever.   7. It means "with a baby in the womb; expecting a baby."   8. These are insects that nest in a person's hair.   9. This is a blue mark on the body   10. *Scab*: hardened blood that covers a wound. *Scar*: a mark remaining after tissue has healed.

Gestures

A gesture is a sign or signal done with the body in an attempt to communicate. In some languages, these gestures are described in spoken communication. For example, in French "cligner une oeil" means "close one eye." In English we have a short word that describes this gesture; the word is "wink." In this chapter you will learn short verbs that describe a variety of gestures. In the reading "Gesture This" you will learn about the meaning of common gestures in different countries.

This chapter's Writing Tip is a look at main opinion statements. It is important to be able to state your main opinion clearly and concisely when you write an opinion essay. The "gestures" theme continues in the speaking section, where there is a game that will allow you to practice your vocabulary. Notice that Grammar Section 3 also contains a Vocabulary Boost that focuses on gestures.

ocabulary

Gestures

These exercises may prove difficult for the students to do alone. Suggestion: The teacher could demonstrate the gestures. After, the students could have a few moments to complete the vocabulary exercises. The answers to the following exercises are at the end of this chapter. Some of these gestures are defined in Grammar Section 3, The Present Progressive.

 VOCABULARY EXERCISE 1

1. These gestures involve facial expressions. Match the expression with the emotion represented. (Hint: The famous singer Elvis Presley was known for his trademark "sneer.")

smile	*unhappiness*
frown	*disgust*
sneer	*happiness*

These gestures all involve sounds. Your teacher will act out the gestures, and you can write the meaning beside each word. (You can either describe the gesture or translate it.)

cough	_____	hum	_____	whisper	_____
sneeze	_____	snap	_____	whistle	_____
sniff	_____	tap	_____	snore	_____
clap	_____	yawn	_____		

In questions 2 to 5, fill in each blank with one of the above gestures. *Write each gesture once only.*

2. Which of the above gestures would you do when you have a cold?

_____   _____   _____

3. Which gestures are made when you are tired or sound asleep?

_____   _____

4. Which gestures would you make at a rock concert?

_____   _____   _____

_____   _____

5. Which gesture means "speak quietly"?

_____

VOCABULARY EXERCISE 2

These are gestures that we may do either instinctively or with the intention of sending a message.

wink	shrug	blink
nod	duck	pout

1. Which gesture is done with both eyes? _____

Which gesture is done with one eye only? _____

2. Someone is pointing a gun at you. Which action should you do? _____

3. Which gesture means *I don't know*? _____

4. Which gesture do you do to indicate *yes*? _____

5. What do children do when they don't get what they want? _____

Reading

Reading Tip: Finding the Main Idea

The main idea is the main point of a text. In a sentence of main idea, you must express the central thought of the piece. The rest of the reading develops this central idea.

In many texts, you can find a statement explaining the central idea in one of the first paragraphs. Subsequent paragraphs then develop that central idea.

Determine the type of text. To find the main idea of a text, you must first decide what type of text you have read.

Is the writer mainly just telling a story?	(Narrative Essay)
Is the writer trying to influence the reader?	(Opinion Essay)
Is the writer describing something?	(Descriptive Essay)
Is the writer giving information?	(Informative Essay)

If you have determined that the writer is expressing an opinion, then you will focus on looking for the opinion. If the writer is giving information, then you can focus on the reason for the information.

Sometimes a text does several things at once. An essay can describe something, tell a story and express an opinion at the same time. In these cases, look for the main message of the text.

Determine the central subject (main idea). If the text tells a story, you can determine the main idea by asking yourself who, what, when, where and why questions. If the text is an opinion or information essay, ask yourself the following questions:

Who or what is the subject of this text?

What aspect of the subject does the author develop?

Why is this topic important?

After you have answered these questions, combine the notions into one sentence. That sentence is the statement of the main idea.

PRE-READING VOCABULARY

Familiarize yourself with the following terms before reading the text. The number in parentheses indicates the paragraph where the word is found.

(1) *cringe*   shrink back
(1) *grimace*   face twisted in a frown
(3) *tuck*   to fold or gather
(5) *wave*   moving the hand back and forth
(9) *orifice*   hole
(9) *worthless* without value

Reading 3.1

Gesture This!
by Gaetan Allen

1   Human beings can communicate with much more than our voices; our bodies are wonderfully expressive. When we are disgusted, we cringe in horror. When we're happy, our bodies open, our backs straighten, and our faces light up in a smile. We could assume that all humans use the same gestures to indicate the same things, especially since spontaneous gestures and expressions are universally understood. A smile is a smile is a smile. And everyone worldwide understands what an angry grimace means. Deliberate gestures, however, can be as specific as languages.

2   Greetings change from one land to another. While Americans like to extend a hand and shake, using the right hand only, in many countries people do not touch hands. In India and parts of the Middle East, greetings are done by putting one's hands together in a prayer-like gesture, and there is no body contact. In some cultures, you kiss the person that you are greeting lightly on each cheek, and give the person a light hug. Obviously, these cultural differences in greetings can occasionally cause confusion and embarrassment.

3   Not only can gestures be misunderstood, but simple things like the placement of your hands or feet can gravely insult a host. In India, it is considered highly disrespectful to point your feet towards another person. As people often sit on carpets on the floor, it is important that you tuck your feet under you, away from the speaker, so as not to insult anyone.

your baby
d...

4   According to Desmond Morris, some gestures have their root in infancy. The baby's earliest activity is to suck at its mother's breast. This involves pursing the lips, and the expression survives into adulthood as a kiss. Something as basic as the yes or no gesture, however, is culture specific. While most people in the world nod their head up and down to indicate "yes," in Turkey and Greece an upward nod means "no." A head movement to the side means "yes" in that region of the world. This can be somewhat confusing for tourists.

different's each culture

5   In North America we indicate "come here" by waving the hand, palm up, towards the body. When we want someone to go away, we wave the hand, palm down, and fan the fingers out. During my stay in Thailand, I was often called (or rebuffed?) with a palm-down waving gesture that, to me, looked like "go away." I usually did, until someone pointed out that the gesture means "come here." In my case, my life didn't depend on an accurate reading of the gesture, but I was told of a circumstance where a misunderstanding cost a life. A Thai soldier indicated, by using the hand down gesture, that he wanted a foreigner to come for an inspection. When the foreigner ran in the opposite direction, he was shot. The story gave me pause, as I was confronted several times by machine-gun-toting soldiers during my time in Turkey. I realized that travel books should really include sections on gestures!

stop

6   Humans especially enjoy employing gestures as a form of insult. Some rude gestures are widely understood. For example, when you put your thumb on your nose and wave your fingers upwards, combined with sticking out your tongue, it is clear that you are making a disrespectful sign. A threatening fist means "watch it or I'll punch you." *Knuckle sandwich*

7   One of the oldest known gestures is when the middle finger is raised and the other fingers are curled. The person gesturing generally thrusts this middle finger up. This gesture can move people to murderous rage in North America, yet in some parts of the world it is not widely used and is not considered serious. This gesture is not recent. In fact, it was used in ancient Roman times and has survived for at least two thousand years.

8   In North America the "OK" sign is made by joining the thumb and forefinger together to make a circle. It is understood to mean that everything is fine. This can be interpreted as a rude insult, or an invitation, in Brazil. In that country, if you were to use this symbol and combine it with a smile, others could assume that you want a sexual encounter.

9   Many people in the Middle East see this sign as a foul obscenity, the circle imitating an orifice that both sexes share. An innocent Canadian could find himself in trouble if he uses this sign to signify that he is just fine. To his Middle Eastern hosts, it means the equivalent of "up yours." To add further confusion, in parts of southern Europe the symbol means "zero." If you use this sign after eating a tasty meal, the chef could think that you are calling the meal worthless.

hole

up your ass

10   Gestures both help and hinder human communication. It is useful to use hand signals when you don't share a common language with someone. Don't assume, however, that a gesture you often employ will be automatically understood by citizens of other cultures. Hand signals and body language can be misunderstood just as easily as badly pronounced words.

VOCABULARY

1. Write a synonym (another word with the same meaning) for the word *hug*. (para. 2)

embrace   عانق   ضمّ

2. Write down the meaning of *infancy* (para. 4). The sentence following the word gives you a clue about its meaning.

early childhood   _baby_

3. Using your own words, define the word *nod*. (para. 4)

move your head up and down

4. *Foul*, as it is used in paragraph 9, means: (circle one)
a. stormy or rough.
(b.) disgusting or offensive. قذر ، مقرف
c. unfair, against the rules.

READING COMPREHENSION

1. Who or what is this essay about? _Gesture_

2. What aspect is developed? _differences in gestures, they are_ specific language

3. Why is this topic important? _to avoid misunderstanding between_ people

4. The main idea is the most important or central idea of a text. To find out the main idea of the essay, combine the answers to questions 1 to 3 and restate them in one complete sentence.

Gestures, like words, can mean different things in different places, and can be the cause of misunderstandings.

DISCUSSION

1. Have you ever had a misunderstanding because of body language? Explain. What could be done to help people avoid "gestural" misunderstandings?

2. Invent a new gesture. Describe the gesture and explain its meaning.

Writing Tips

The Opinion Statement

The opinion statement (or "thesis" statement) identifies the main subject of your essay. It is unnecessary to refer to yourself in the opinion statement. Someone who reads your statement should know exactly what you think about a given topic.

In reports or research papers it is useful to let the reader know immediately what your arguments are going to be. However, in opinion-essay writing, this removes the punch from the other paragraphs. Therefore, in opinion essays, simply state your opinion and leave your main points for the body of the essay.

Opinion Statement Do's	Opinion Statement Don'ts
• Express an opinion as clearly as possible	• Say *I am going to talk about...* or *I think that...* or *I believe...* These types of phrases are unnecessary.
	• Give all of your reasons in your opinion statement. *

WRITING TIPS EXERCISE 1

Look at the following opinion statements. Make any possible improvements. Which statement is the best?

Essay subject: Skinny fashion models

1. I think that models should not be so skinny.
2. I am going to tell you about how skinny fashion models do not reflect reality.
3. Very thin fashion models set dangerous examples of beauty for young people because young girls try to copy them, some young girls get eating disorders and many of the models are unhealthy.
4. Magazines should stop using skinny models in their ads.

WRITING TIPS EXERCISE 2

Read the following introductions. Highlight the opinion statements.

Introduction 1: Katya is over six feet tall. She weighs 110 pounds. She is a very successful model. She earns over $2000 per day for a photo shoot. She is also ill.

---

* Some writing manuals disagree with this point. If your teacher wants you to present your main arguments in the introduction, then you should do it.

She is suffering from anorexia. Thin fashion models are a menace to both themselves and society.

Introduction 2: Hockey, which used to be a very entertaining sport, is now much too violent. In the past we could enjoy the skill and artistry of players like Wayne Gretzky and Mario Lemieux. Recently, however, more and more goons have been hired by the NHL. These goons are there to hurt, and possibly destroy, the best players on the ice.

Notice that the opinion statement can be anywhere in the introduction. It can be at the beginning, in the middle or at the end of the introduction.

Writing Suggestions

1. Look at the following topics. Alone or with partners, create interesting opinion statements for three of the topics. You could also create opinion statements for a topic of your choice.

Happiness	Legalize drugs
A famous Canadian	Ban smoking
Gun-control laws	Society's obsession with beauty
Violent video games	Violence in sports

Opinion statements:

a. _____

b. _____

c. _____

2. Write two paragraphs for homework. Go to one of your favorite public places (a café, a park, etc.) and observe what is going on around you. Write one paragraph describing, in detail, what is going on at that moment. (Use the present progressive.) Write the second paragraph describing your daily habits. (Use the simple present.) If you need help with your tenses, you could refer to Grammar Sections 2 and 3.

peaking

SPEAKING EXERCISE ▪ DRAW IT

Your teacher will divide the class into two groups. One at a time, you will be asked to go to the front of the class. You will then draw one of the gestures on the board that you learned at the beginning of this chapter. For example, a student draws a girl shrugging. His team, or his side of the class, must say, "She is shrugging." You are not allowed to look in your book and must guess the gestures from memory.

ANSWERS TO VOCABULARY EXERCISE 1:

1. frown–unhappy, sneer–disgust   2. cough, sneeze, sniff   3. yawn, snore   4. hum, snap, tap, whistle, clap   5. whisper

ANSWERS TO VOCABULARY EXERCISE 2:

1. blink, wink   2. duck   3. shrug   4. nod   5. pout

4 The Questionnaire

Vocabulary	Emotions
Reading	Reading Tip: Make a Plan
	"What's Your Emotional IQ?" by Daniel Goleman
Writing Tips	The Questionnaire
Speaking	Activity Questionnaire
Link to Grammar	Grammar Section 4: The Simple Past Tense:
	Regular Verbs

This chapter begins with a vocabulary exercise that contains words related to emotions. Emotions may be more important than we thought. Intelligence is measured by an "intelligence quotient," or IQ, test. But do IQ tests measure the type of intelligence that really helps us cope with the stresses of life? In the reading "What's Your Emotional IQ?" you will learn about a new type of IQ test.

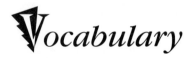

Vocabulary

Vocabulary Exercise: Emotions

Match the situation described in column 1 with the appropriate emotion from the list below. The answers to this exercise are at the end of the chapter.

disgusted	bored	annoyed	disappointed
scared/afraid	relieved	embarrassed	lonely
deceived	ashamed	enraged	thrilled

My Situation	**How I Feel**

1. I expect to pass, but then I fail a major exam. _____

2. I think that I have failed an exam, but then I find out that my mark is 85 percent. _____

3. I stand up and realize that my "fly" (the zipper on my pants) is open. _____

4. I am alone in the house, when suddenly I see someone climb into a window at the far end of the room. _____

5. I win a million dollars in a lottery. _____

6. It is another rainy day. No one is around. There is nothing to do. _____

7. I gossip about my best friend. I tell my boss a lie about her. Later, she confronts me. _____

8. My brother spits, and his spit lands on my bare foot. Yuck! _____

9. I go to a new college. I don't know anybody. I eat lunch alone. _____

10. I discover that my sister used my CD as a Frisbee. She ruined it. _____

Reading

Reading Tip: Make a Plan

Opinion essays generally have a main point. This point is developed with supporting ideas. When you want to determine main and supporting ideas of a reading, you can make a plan to help you. (It is also a good idea to make a plan when you do a listening test. Listen for the main opinion, and listen for supporting details.)

Sample plan format:

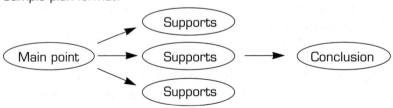

This is a plan for the reading in Chapter 3:

Main point: Gestures: not universal
                           may be misunderstood

Supports: Confusing gestures:
- greetings differ (handshake, kiss, etc.)
- hand and feet position
- nod for "yes" and "no"
- wave of "come here" or "go away"
- insult gestures: raised middle finger
- circle symbol

Conclusion: Gestures: as easily misunderstood as words

How you form your plan is not important. What is important is your ability to identify main and supporting ideas, and to illustrate your understanding in some type of plan.

PRE-READING ACTIVITY

Circle the letter of the answer that most closely resembles your typical reaction to the opening statement.

1. When someone is rude to you, do you:
   a. carry around your anger for a long time afterwards.
   b. find reasons why that person said the hurtful thing, and then try to forgive that person and forget about it.
   c. dismiss the rudeness and just get on with the next thing in your day.

2. When you feel angry, do you think it is best to:
   a. hold your anger in, because you dislike expressing angry feelings.
   b. vent your anger to get rid of it (scream or yell at somebody).
   c. try to reinterpret the situation in a more positive light, or go away (e.g. for a drive) and try to cool down.

3. When you have a challenge in front of you that requires a lot of work (such as to quit smoking or to study for a goal), do you:
   a. try to avoid the challenge.
   b. do the work involved, but without much enthusiasm.
   c. have a "can do" attitude and clear goals, and work towards your goals as enthusiastically as possible.

4. When faced with a failure or rejection (e.g. failed exam, job loss, etc.) do you:
   a. interpret the rejection as meaning *I'm no good, I'm a failure.*
   b. blame the failure on someone or something else: it wasn't your fault.
   c. try to see the positive side; reframe the situation in a more positive light.

5. When something you really want to eat is in your pocket (e.g. a chocolate), but you should really wait to eat it (e.g. wait until class is over), do you:
   a. just eat the snack even if the time isn't appropriate.
   b. try to avoid eating the snack, but at the end of class open it and eat it rapidly.
   c. try to ignore the snack and concentrate on the class, knowing that you will enjoy it more if you eat it later.

6. When you have a personal problem and you feel low, do you:
   a. keep the problem to yourself, and probably show your bad mood to others.
   b. talk about the problem until someone else feels low too.
   c. talk about the problem and work towards solutions so that your bad mood will lift.

There are no "right" answers to this quiz. However, if your answers were predominantly "c," then you are probably emotionally healthy. Read the following essay and then look at your answers again. Remember, even if you have a negative outlook, you can work on your emotional health.

PRE-READING VOCABULARY

Familiarize yourself with the following terms before reading the text. The number in parentheses indicates the paragraph where the word is found.

(1) *steamy*	hot and humid
(1) *sullen*	sadly serious
(4) *in jeopardy*	at risk
(8) *gut feelings*	feelings that are deep inside (feelings we often ignore)
(8) *sweat*	perspiration
(9) *oblivious*	not aware
(13) *stew*	to worry
(13) *reckless*	unsafe, negligent
(17) *alleviate*	ease, lessen
(18) *marshal*	to assemble
(23) *run an errand*	do a task

Reading 4.1

What's Your Emotional IQ?
by Daniel Goleman

Daniel Goleman questions the usefulness of traditional IQ tests. Goleman's theories have become so acceptable that many companies now use "emotional intelligence" tests in order to screen candidates. The following text has been adapted from Goleman's book Emotional Intelligence *by the writers at* Reader's Digest.

1 It was a steamy afternoon in New York, the kind of day that makes people sullen with discomfort. I was heading to my hotel, and as I stepped onto a bus, I was startled to be greeted by the driver, a middle-aged man with an enthusiastic smile.

2 "Hi! How're you doing?" he said. He greeted each rider in the same way. As the bus crawled through the gridlock, the driver gave a lively commentary: there was a terrific sale at that store ... a wonderful exhibit at this museum ... had we heard about the movie that just opened down the block? By the time people got off, they had shaken off their sullen shells. When the driver called out, "So long, have a great day!" each of us gave a smiling response.

3 That memory has stayed with me for close to 20 years. I consider the bus driver a man who was truly successful at what he did.

4 Contrast him with Jason, a straight-A student at a Florida high school who was fixated on getting into Harvard Medical School. When a physics teacher gave Jason an 80 on a quiz, the boy believed his dream was in jeopardy. He took a butcher knife to school, and in a struggle the teacher was stabbed in the collarbone.

5 How could someone of obvious intelligence do something so irrational? The answer is that high IQ does not necessarily predict who will succeed in life. Psychologists agree that IQ contributes only about 20 percent to the factors that determine success. A full 80 percent comes from other factors, including what I call emotional intelligence.

6 The following are some of the major qualities that make up emotional intelligence and how they can be developed:

7 **1. Self-awareness.** The ability to recognize a feeling as it happens is the keystone of emotional intelligence. People with greater certainty about their emotions are better pilots of their lives.

8 Developing self-awareness requires tuning in to what neurologist Antonio Damasio, in his book *Descartes' Error*, calls somatic markers—literally, gut feelings. Gut feelings can occur without a person being consciously aware of them. For example, when people who fear snakes are shown a picture of a snake, sensors on their skin will detect sweat, a sign of anxiety, even though the people say they do not feel fear. The sweat shows up even when a picture is presented so rapidly that the subject has no conscious awareness of seeing it.

9 Through deliberate effort we can become more aware of our gut feelings. Take someone who is annoyed by a rude encounter for hours after it occurred. He may be oblivious to his continued irritability and surprised when someone calls attention to it. But if he stops and evaluates his feelings, he can change them.

10 Emotional self-awareness is the building block of the next fundamental of emotional intelligence: being able to shake off a bad mood.

11 **2. Mood management.** Bad as well as good moods spice life and build character. The key is balance.

12 We often have little control over *when* we are swept by emotion. But we can have some say in *how long* that emotion will last. Psychologist Dianne Tice of Case Western Reserve University in Cleveland asked more than 400 men and women about their strategies for

escaping foul moods. Her research, along with that of other psychologists, provides valuable information on how to change a bad mood.

13   Of all the moods that people want to escape, rage seems to be the hardest to deal with. When someone in another car cuts you off on the highway, your reflexive thought may be *That jerk! He could have hit me! I can't let him get away with that!* The more you stew, the angrier you get. Such is the stuff of hypertension and reckless driving.

14   What should you do to relieve rage? One myth is that ventilating will make you feel better. In fact, researchers have found that expressing anger is one of the worst strategies. Outbursts of rage pump up the brain's arousal system, leaving you more angry, not less.

15   A more effective technique is "reframing"—consciously reinterpreting a situation in a more positive light. In the case of the driver who cuts you off, you might tell yourself *Maybe he had some emergency*. This is one of the most potent ways, Tice found, to put anger to rest.

16   Going off alone to cool down is also an effective way to defuse anger, especially if you can't think clearly. Tice found that a large proportion of men cool down by going for a drive—a finding that inspired her to drive more defensively. A safer alternative is exercise, such as taking a long walk. Whatever you do, don't waste the time pursuing your train of angry thoughts. Your aim should be to distract yourself.

17   The techniques of reframing and distraction can alleviate depression and anxiety as well. Add to them such relaxation techniques as deep breathing and meditation, and you have an arsenal of weapons against bad moods. "Praying," Tice also says, "works for all moods."

18   **3. Self-motivation.** Positive motivation—the marshalling of feelings of enthusiasm, zeal and confidence—is paramount for achievement. Studies of Olympic athletes, world-class musicians and chess grand masters show that their common trait is the ability to motivate themselves to pursue relentless training routines.

19   To motivate yourself for any achievement requires clear goals and a can-do attitude. Psychologist Martin Seligman of the University of Pennsylvania in Philadelphia advised the MetLife insurance company to hire job applicants who tested high on optimism but failed the normal aptitude test. Compared with salesmen who passed the aptitude test but scored high in pessimism, this group made 21 percent more sales in their first year and 57 percent more in their second.

20   A pessimist is likely to interpret rejection as meaning *I'm a failure; I'll never make a sale.* Optimists tell themselves *I'm using the wrong approach* or *That customer was in a bad mood*. By blaming failure on the situation, not themselves, optimists are motivated to make that next call.

21   A predisposition to a positive or negative outlook may be inborn, but with effort and practice, pessimists can learn to think more hopefully. Psychologists have documented that if you can catch negative, self-defeating thoughts as they occur, you can reframe the situation in less catastrophic terms.

22   **4. Impulse control.** The essence of emotional self-regulation is the ability to delay impulse in the service of a goal. The importance of this trait to success was shown in an

experiment begun in the 1960s by psychologist Walter Mischel at a preschool on the Stanford University campus in California.

23   Children were told they could have a single treat, such as a marshmallow, right now. However, if they'd wait while the experimenter ran an errand, they could have two marshmallows. Some preschoolers grabbed the marshmallow immediately, but others were able to wait. To sustain themselves in their struggle, they covered their eyes so they wouldn't see the temptation, talked to themselves, sang, even tried to sleep.

24   The interesting part of this experiment came in the follow-up. The children who as four-year-olds had been able to wait for the two marshmallows were, as adolescents, still able to delay gratification in pursuing their goals. They were more socially competent and self-assertive, and better able to cope with life's frustrations. In contrast, the kids who grabbed the one marshmallow were, as adolescents, more likely to be stubborn, indecisive and stressed.

25   The ability to resist impulse can be developed with practice. When you're faced with an immediate temptation, think of your long-term goals—whether they be losing weight or getting a medical degree. You'll then find it easier to keep from settling for the single marshmallow.

26   *5. People skills.* The capacity to know how another feels is important on the job, in romance and friendship, and in the family. We transmit and catch moods from one another on a subtle, almost imperceptible level. The way someone says thank you, for instance, can leave us feeling dismissed, patronized or genuinely appreciated. The more adroit we are at discerning the feelings behind other people's signals, the better we control the signals we send.

27   The importance of good interpersonal skills was demonstrated by psychologists Robert Kelley and Janet Caplan in a study at Bell Labs in Naperville, Ill. The labs are staffed by engineers and scientists who are all at the apex of academic IQ tests. Some of those studied emerged as stars, while others languished.

28   What accounted for the difference? The standout performers had a network with a wide range of people. When a nonstar encountered a technical problem, Kelley observed, "he called various technical gurus and then waited, wasting time while his calls went unreturned. Star performers rarely faced such situations because they built reliable networks *before* they needed them. So when the stars called someone, they almost always got a faster answer."

29   No matter what their IQ, once again it was emotional intelligence that separated the stars from the average performers.

VOCABULARY

1. The bus "crawled through the gridlock." (para. 2) Rewrite this phrase in more simple English.

2. What does the author mean by *reframing*? (para. 15) _____

[margin note: في موقف] reinterpreting a situation in a more positive light

3. Find a two-word expression in paragraph 16 that means "to calm yourself."

_____ cool down _____

4. Find a word in paragraph 27 that means "failed or declined." *languished*

languished

[handwritten Arabic: ما جرى والتي !]

READING COMPREHENSION

1. Why has the writer remembered the New York bus driver for close to twenty years?

Because he smiled with the passenger good attitude, positive, friendly, make everybody happy made himself happy

2. Why did the Florida high-school student stab his teacher?

Because she gave him 80 on a quize the boy believe that his dream was in jeopardy *he was so stress, he couldn't deal with stress*

3. According to the author, is it a good idea to express your anger? Why or why not? You can refer to paragraph 14.

[margin note: he react like aggressive]

[margin note: No,] makes you anger, distract because it's causing your angrier not less

4. Make a plan for this essay. What is the main point, and what are the five supporting details?

Main point: success in life are more to do with how you manage your emotion then how good *re lou*

Supporting details: (Beside each element of emotional intelligence, briefly explain what it means.)

a. Self awareness
The ability to recognize a feeling as it happens

b. Mood management
bad as well as good moods spice life and build character the key is balance.

c. self-motivation
The marshalling of the feelings enthusiasm, real confidence is paramount for achievement

the most

d. _Impulse control_
The essence of the emotional self-regulation is the ability to delay impulse in the service of a goal

e. _People skills_
the capacity to know how another feels is important in job, in romance, in the family

Concluding point: _That this emotional intelligence that seperate the stars from average performers._

5. Put an *X* next to the sentence that best sums up the main idea of this essay.

_____ Not all people with a high IQ succeed in life.

_____ Psychologists agree that 80 percent of our intelligence comes from our emotions.

_____ The ability to recognize a feeling as it happens is the keystone of emotional intelligence.

___X___ Success in life has much more to do with how we manage our emotions than with a high IQ.

_____ Some people with high IQs are unable to communicate effectively with others.

DISCUSSION

1. Have you ever met anyone like that New York bus driver? What quality does that bus driver have that is so special?

2. Do you believe that negative, emotionally unhealthy people can improve their emotional health? How could they do this?

3. Do you think that emotional health is genetic? Do you notice that you, or your brothers or sisters, resemble a parent or relative in the way that you react emotionally?

Writing Tips

The Questionnaire

With a classmate (or in a small team) you are going to prepare a questionnaire. You have seen examples of questionnaires in Chapters 1 and 2, as well as in this chapter. There are questionnaires before the readings "Meaningful Manners," "Weighty Considerations" and "What's Your Emotional IQ?"

Your team must prepare a questionnaire. Your teacher will set the number of questions. (There could be between five and ten questions.) In order to complete your questionnaire, follow the guidelines below.

1. **Goal.** Determine your goal. What do you want to discover?

    Examples:

    a) How happy are college students with their lives?

    b) Do students give money to beggars?

2. **Make a guess.** Make a guess, or tentative assumption, about the outcome of your questionnaire.

    We believe that students in our class are satisfied with their lives.

3. **Plan your questions.** Do not ask open-ended, essay-style questions. Instead, ask yes/no questions, or give the people questioned a choice of answers.

    Sample questions:

    Choice   *1. Choose one of the following answers: In general, you feel*
    a) not at all happy.
    b) not very happy.
    c) quite happy or very happy.

    Yes/No   *2. Do you have a part-time job?*   *YES*   *NO*

4. **Prepare an answer sheet.** Prepare an answer sheet for your questionnaire, or if you question many students orally, leave adequate space for your answers on the questionnaire. You could also just make one question sheet and photocopy it for distribution.

    Choose one of the following answers: In general, you feel

    a) not at all happy.
    b) not very happy.
    c) quite happy or very happy.

    a) ✓✓✓   *b)* ✓✓   *c)* ✓✓✓✓✓

Writing Suggestions

1. With your team, create a questionnaire about one of the following topics. You could also choose your own topic. Make sure that you define your goal clearly.

Honesty	Charity	Happiness
Disciplining	Pets	Fears
Money or spending habits	Part-time jobs	Study habits
Swearing habits	Manners	Dreams

    Each student in your team should have a list of the questions, and each student should leave a space under each question where the results could be recorded.

Make sure that your questions follow the proper question form.

Question word	Auxiliary	Subject	Verb
Why	*do*	*you*	*have a part-time job?*
How many hours	*do*	*you*	*work each week?*

2. After distributing the questionnaire, or after doing the speaking activity (see next section), each team member can write a short essay about the questionnaire. The essay should include:
   - the goal
   - the initial guess
   - a summary of the results
   - a conclusion in which the difference between the initial guess and the results is explained.

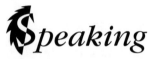peaking

Speaking Exercise: Questionnaire Activity

After your team has developed the questionnaire, the team should split up. In each team, one member remains seated while the others go to other teams. Each student asks his or her questions to the others in the new group. After all students have asked their questions, they return to their original teams.

The original team should examine and compile results. Are there any surprises? Does the original guess reflect reality?

Teams can present their results to the class in the form of an oral presentation.

ANSWERS TO VOCABULARY EXERCISE 1:
1. disappointed   2. relieved   3. embarrassed   4. scared or afraid   5. thrilled   6. bored   7. ashamed
8. disgusted   9. lonely   10. enraged or annoyed

5 The Introduction

This chapter provides information about the animal world. The vocabulary section contains terms for animal lovers. The Writing Tips deal with the writing of introductions. Pay particular attention to the manner in which the subject is introduced in "Puppy Love."

Vocabulary

Vocabulary Exercise: Animal Life

Name two animals that have the following body parts. Then write a brief definition of the body part or draw it. Use your dictionary if necessary. The Vocabulary Boost in Grammar Section 5 will reinforce your understanding of these terms. *Note:* The answers to this exercise are at the end of the chapter.

1. fin _____

2. paw _____

3. claw _____

4. horns _____

5. hoof _____

6. beak _____

7. gills _____

8. antler _____

You could buy the following four items when you have a dog. Either describe the items or explain what they are used for.

9. collar _____

10. leash _____

11. pooper scooper _____

12. dog license _____

13. muzzle _____

Reading

PRE-READING VOCABULARY

Familiarize yourself with the following terms before reading the text. The number in parentheses indicates the paragraph where the word is found.

(1) *shreds*   fragments
(1) *chewed up*   bitten and ruined
(4) *set aside*   to reserve
(5) *to heel*   to walk beside the owner (at the owner's heels)

Reading 5.1 # Puppy Love

1   When Marnie got home after an extra-long day at work, she was greeted by a house that looked like a tornado had just swept through. Newspapers torn to shreds littered the kitchen floor. Children's plastic toys were chewed up and tiny plastic arms and legs were left behind. The arm of the sofa was torn, the padding inside yanked out. To add insult to injury, there was a large pee stain on the living-room carpet. Marnie's puppy, Zeke, was unhappy about

being left alone, and he let her know it in no uncertain terms. It's very exciting to get a new dog, but it is important to properly train and care for your new pet.

2   Puppies, like children, don't do well in an over-permissive environment. If a puppy isn't taught who is boss, she may decide that she is the master of the house. Dogs, like most other mammals, prefer to be leaders. Animals, in social units, invariably have a hierarchy or rank. If you are not clearly positioned as the master, and if you feel a little insecure in the role, a puppy can become a dog who bites, attacks others and destroys property simply because the dog thinks that she is the boss.

3   How can you demonstrate that you are the master? First of all, you must take a certain authority with the animal. Confidently assert your dominance. Don't be afraid to pet your pup and to play with him. Let your puppy know, with your gentle but firm tone and handling, that you are secure in your role as his master. If he is on the sofa or your bed, make him get off of it. Eat before your dog eats. If the animal jumps up on you, order him to get down. When outdoors, make sure the animal is always on a leash. In other words, make sure the dog knows that you are the boss and that you make the rules.

4   Your dog cannot be the boss. She needs to know, however, that she has her own space in your house. Give your dog a corner, with her own bed and her own toys. Let your dog know that when she is in her bed, you will respect her privacy and her space. Encourage your kids to leave the dog alone when she is resting. It is even a good idea, if possible, to set aside a small room for the dog; that way, if you need to leave the puppy alone for long periods, she can have what she needs, yet she won't be able to get to the parts of the house where she could destroy your things. If you don't give the dog her own space, she may try to make the sofa, or your bed, her space.

5   If you have a difficult, overactive pet, it may be necessary to take him to obedience school. Some pets just never learn to heel or to obey commands. Marnie's dog, Zeke, never did learn to stop urinating in the house. After a course of obedience training, Marnie reported that her animal was like a new dog. Not everyone is familiar with training methods, and not everyone is assertive enough and consistent enough to train their own animal.

6   When a film about Dalmatians was popular, pet stores reported a run on these animals. Unfortunately, a Dalmatian is not an easy-going, relaxed breed of dog; they have high energy levels and require a lot of attention. Many families have given up on their "hard to handle" pets, and SPCAs have reported a dramatic increase in the numbers of Dalmatians left to them. If you are unfamiliar with dogs, you should check in libraries or on the Internet before buying a pet. Find out the names of reputable dog breeders and phone them. Talk with other dog owners. It is always a bad idea to buy a dog just because it looks cute. Different dogs have been bred for different purposes. Find out the type of dog most suited to your personality before you invest in a pet.

7   Finally, make sure that *you* have the time to devote to your dog. Many parents buy dogs for their children, honestly thinking that a small child will do the work of caring for the dog. When the child doesn't prove up to the task of cleaning and walking the dog, these animals end up being sent off to the SPCA. Dogs don't bathe themselves; someone has to do it. Dogs

need to be taken for walks daily, in good weather and bad. And remember, it is cruel and inhumane to keep a large dog locked up in a city apartment all day. Dogs aren't ornaments. They have needs. They need fresh air and adequate exercise.

8   Dogs make great pets. Dogs, unlike cats, are always happy to see you. They are almost always ready to be your comfort and your friend. Just make sure that your dog knows his place, and you and your dog can have a happy, productive coexistence. And please, only get a dog when you are ready to give it time and companionship.

VOCABULARY

1. The word *litter* (para. 1), as it is used in the text, means: (circle one)
   a. the young ones of an animal.
   b. garbage left on the ground.
   c. straw or hay used as bedding for animals.

2. What is a *puppy*? _____

3. The word *assert* (para. 3), as it is used in the text, means: (circle one)
   a. to emphasize firmly.
   b. to decide to fix.
   c. to give evidence of an association.

READING COMPREHENSION

The following sentences may accurately reflect what is in the text or they may be inaccurate. For each, write *T* (for "true") or *F* (for "false") in the space provided.

1. Dogs like to be the boss.   _____

2. You should hit your animal to show that you are dominant.   _____

3. One way to show dominance is to keep the dog off the furniture.   _____

4. Dalmatians are easy-going, relaxed dogs.   _____

5. Marnie's dog, Zeke, was never properly trained.   _____

6. What is the opinion statement in the introduction? _____

   _____

7. What does the writer mainly do in the introduction? (circle one)
   a. tell a story about something
   b. give background or historical information about the topic
   c. give a detailed description of something

DISCUSSION

1. How many of you have pets? Do you take care of your dog, including the feeding and walking of the dog? Have you ever sold a pet because it was too much work?

2. Are dogs better pets than cats? Why or why not?

3. What should be done about dangerous dog breeds (e.g. pit bulls)?

4. What are the topic sentences in paragraphs 2 to 7? If you just read the topic sentences, do you have a good idea of what the essay is about?

riting Tips

The Introduction

Introductions should arouse the reader's interest in the topic. In reports, it is appropriate to give the reader a road map, and to let the reader know exactly where you are going. However, in a less formal opinion essay, it is a little boring for the reader to know all of your arguments before he has even begun the body of the essay.

For example, let's change the introduction to the essay about puppies. Imagine that the essay begins like this:

> It's very exciting to get a new dog, but it is important to properly train and care for your new pet. For example, you should make sure the dog knows that you are the master, but you must also give the dog his own space, make sure you know about dog breeds before you pick out your pet, and make sure that you have the time to devote to your pet.

An introduction like this gives away too much. It does not make the reader want to read on. The reader already knows everything that the writer has to say. Therefore, in the introduction, don't give away all of your reasons for your opinion.

Introduction Do's	Introduction Don'ts
— Get the reader's attention. You can do this by: • telling a story • giving background information • making a surprising statement	— Don't write: *I'm going to talk about... I will convince you...* — Don't state your reasons for your opinion in the introduction.*

---

* As was stated in Chapter 3's Writing Tip, some writing manuals disagree with this point. If your teacher wants you to present your main arguments in the introduction, then you should do it.

Introduction Styles

A good introduction should attract the reader's attention. You can do this in several ways. Imagine that you were asked to write an essay on the following topic:

Dogs are better pets than cats.

You could begin with:

1. *An Anecdote*

Tell a brief anecdote that relates, in some way, to your topic.

One day, after an especially hard day at the office, I got to my door. My cat was on the porch. I looked at the cat and it just lay there, limp. Lifeless. Suddenly there was slow movement. The cat lifted its head, and a cool green eye observed me, not amused. The cat's eyes seemed to say, "You are an annoying creature. Please get lost." It then slid its head down and tucked it under its paws. When I turned the doorknob, I could see that my dog, Wizzer, was at the door. I opened the door and Wizzer ran in circles around me, absolutely ecstatic that I was home. My bad mood lifted. It had to. How could I stay grumpy in the face of so much joy? If you want a pet that has a little joie de vivre, *avoid cats like the plague and buy a dog.*

2. *Historical or Background Information*

Begin an essay by discussing the history of your topic.

Dogs are man's (and woman's) best friend. From the working dogs who pull sleighs up north, to the heroic dogs like Lassie and Rin Tin Tin, dogs have been our companions and our saviors. Although no monuments have been erected to the dog, dogs remain unsung heroes. The best pet you can possibly own is a dog.

If you don't know the history of your topic, you could give background information. For example, you could explain what types of dogs exist, where dogs can be bought, etc.

WRITING TIPS EXERCISE

Highlight the opinion statements in the two introduction examples above.

Writing Suggestions

1. Think of any topic about which you have a strong opinion. After you have found your topic, write two introductions for an essay about that topic. You do not have to write the entire essay; just write two different introductions, using the following methods:
a) tell a story
b) give historical or background information

Make sure that each of your introductions contains an opinion statement. You may use the same opinion statement for both introductions.

2. Write an essay about the best type of pet. Explain how this pet is better than all other pets. Write an introduction, two reasons for your opinion and a conclusion.

3. Write a short essay about one of the following topics:
   - why pit bulls should be muzzled
   - why we need to preserve endangered species, regardless of the cost
   - why we need to learn more about nature in school
   - why women are more weight-obsessed than men
   - why knowing more than one language is important

You can write about your own experiences to support your points. Write an introduction, two reasons for your opinion and a conclusion.

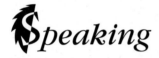

Speaking

SPEAKING EXERCISE ▪ LIE DETECTOR ORAL PRESENTATION

Your teacher will divide the class into groups of six to eight students. You must come up with one true statement and two lies, and tell other group members the three statements. The other members must then question you to determine what is true and what are lies.

For this oral, you must find just one interesting thing that you have done; you make up the other two things. For example, Bob says the following; only the second statement is true.
   1. I took a trip to France.
   2. I won a tennis trophy.
   3. I got lost in a forest for one night.

For a few minutes, others in the group question Bob in an attempt to discover which two statements are lies.

SUGGESTED ANSWERS TO VOCABULARY EXERCISE 1:
1. whale, goldfish (extension used by fish for propelling)   2. cat, dog (the foot)   3. cat, bear (the long, sharp nail)   4. bull, goat (an animal's bony outgrowths on the head)   5. horse, deer (hard covering that encloses an animal's foot)   6. parrot, canary (hard nose and mouth adapted for tearing and probing)
7. goldfish, trout (flaps near head used for breathing)   8. deer, caribou (a solid, branch-like horn)
9. piece of leather looped around an animal's neck   10. a long line for leading and restraining an animal
11. a small shovel used for collecting animal excrement   12. an identification tag on an animal's collar
13. a covering for the mouth of an animal, to prevent biting

The Life Lesson

A narrative essay is a non-fiction composition that tells a story. The purpose in telling the story may be to illustrate a point or just to entertain the reader. Some people tell stories about events in their lives in the hope that they will better understand that event. The form of the narrative essay is consistent, however. All narrative essays arise out of the writer's desire to express *what happened*. In this chapter you will read a narrative essay about a life-changing experience.

Vocabulary

VOCABULARY EXERCISE • SCHOOL AND OFFICE SUPPLIES

Working in pairs, describe the following items, explain what they are used for, or draw a picture of them. Use your dictionary if necessary. (There are no answers at the end of this chapter.)

1. binder _____

2. stapler _____

3. staple _____

4. tack _____

5. pin _____

6. needle _____

7. thread _____

8. paper-clip _____

9. ruler _____

10. pencil-case _____

11. tape _____

12. glue _____

Find three more items in your pencil-case, purse or book bag. Write down the English name of the item and explain its use.

1. _____

2. _____

3. _____

Reading

PRE-READING VOCABULARY

Familiarize yourself with the following expressions before reading the text. The number in parentheses indicates the paragraph where the word is found.

(1) *money was tight*	there was very little money
(3) *chat*	speak about light subjects
(4) *afield*	away from home
(5) *trembling*	lightly shaking or vibrating
(5) *pushover*	easy target
(6) *jumbled*	confused; mixed up

Hitchhiker

Anonymous

1   In my first year away from home I was just 17. I was sent to study in a nearby city, and I was given enough money to pay for a shared apartment and school fees. Money was tight, however, and so I decided to economize by avoiding public transport. I would just hitchhike everywhere. Something about being 17, I don't know. But I thought that I was invincible.

2   The first times I hitchhiked I felt free and so alive out there on the streets. It was actually exciting to imagine what stranger would give me a lift. And, being a girl alone, I never had to wait long.

3   The first few times it was easy. I hitchhiked to the university campus in the morning, and back to my apartment in the late afternoon, rather than take two buses. The drivers were on their way to work, and chatted amiably. However, on one occasion, a driver implied that he wanted something "extra" for the lift. I simply turned cold and I firmly asked him to stop the car. He accepted my refusal, and took me to my destination. On that occasion I felt very brave and in control of the situation. I didn't show any signs of fear, but instead let the driver know that I would not be intimidated. I truly believed that I was a strong enough woman to deal with those situations.

4   During the spring break, I decided to go farther afield. I decided to hitchhike alone to New York. On this trip I was picked up on the outskirts of town by a young man in a pickup truck. Unlike most drivers, he didn't engage in small talk. Rather, he looked ahead at the road and then back at me, nervously, but he didn't speak.

5   The driver was neatly dressed, and his truck was old but very clean. The driver appeared like a normal guy, but his attitude began to scare me. I tried to engage him in conversation but he didn't speak, yet he would turn and stare at me. We were on the highway going about 120 km per hour when he removed one hand from the steering wheel and unzipped his pants. I started to panic. How would I get my backpack, which was in the back of the truck, and get out? The man then said "Touch me," and his face was sweaty and his body was trembling. I had prided myself at being strong and assertive with other men, and simply making it clear that I was no pushover. This guy was different, though. On the other occasion when the man had propositioned me, I knew that the man was basically moral and could be reasoned with. Now, however, I sensed, as an animal would, that there was no reasoning with this truck driver. I knew that I would not be able to communicate with this man. I would not be able to talk him out of anything.

6   He stopped watching the road even though we were going very fast and he just kept looking at me with an empty stare. I was squished against the door, as far from him as possible. My thoughts were jumbled. What if he turns off this main road? What if he hurts me? In a moment of panic, I told him that if he didn't stop I would jump. The car was going

very fast but I just had a sense, quite clear, really, that I would rather jump out than stay any longer in the truck with this crazy person.

7   He then pulled over, grim-faced, and let me get out. I was very, very relieved. However, now I had another problem. I was now stuck on a highway, very far from any town, and with no easy place for another driver to pick me up. Eventually someone else did stop and take me to the next city. I was shaken by the incident with the truck driver, but amazingly I was not yet deterred from hitchhiking. In fact, my successful way out of the truck just reinforced my belief that I was tough.

8   My destination was still New York City, in the U.S.A., where I planned to visit an old friend. I decided to continue hitchhiking there, thinking that I wouldn't have such bad luck again. Luckily, I did make it to New York in one piece. Several long-distance truckers gave me silent but safe rides.

9   That first night in New York, while waiting for my friend to finish work, I went to a small restaurant. I entered into a conversation with a man in his thirties. When he found out that I was Canadian and that I had just hitchhiked to New York, he asked me why I had hitchhiked. I told him about the thrill of standing on the roadside, and about how money was tight. He then said quietly, "You must not care very much about your life." He didn't lecture me, and he didn't mention it again. I wanted to be able to say that I loved my life and cared very much about it. I wanted to justify my risk taking. I wanted to insist that hitchhiking is safe. But I knew it was all a lie.

10   For some reason, at that moment, I was ready to really think about his words. If a parent or friend had implied that hitchhiking was dangerous, I probably would have decided that they were overprotecting me. Here was a total stranger saying it, though, and somehow the words resonated. It hit me: I was playing Russian Roulette with my life!

11   After a few days in New York, I gathered my remaining money and took the train home. I decided that I did care about my life. About three years later, a murder case hit the local newspaper: a man, with his female companion, had abducted a woman from a parking lot and abused and murdered her. I looked at the face of the man in the paper and recognized that truck driver who had scared me. In three years the man had become a murderer.

12   I suppose all teenagers think that they are invincible. Adolescence is a time of risk taking. I am in my twenties now, and I have come to realize that this life is precious, and if I want it to last, I had better take care of it.

VOCABULARY

1. What is hitchhiking? Describe it in your own words. _____

_____

2. In paragraph 2, find another word that means "a ride." _____

3. Define "outskirts." (para. 4) Look at the context clues. _____

4. The word *engage* (para. 5), as it is used in the text, means: (circle one)
   a. to plan to get married.
   b. to hire.
   c. to occupy or keep busy.

5. Find a word in paragraph 5 that means "to fix your eyes on something." _____

6. Find a word in paragraph 6 that means "crushed or flattened." _____

7. The word *lecture* (para. 9), as it is used in the text, means: (circle one)
   a. to read.
   b. to scold or reprimand.
   c. a speech given in front of an audience.

READING COMPREHENSION

1. Why does the narrator hitchhike? _____
   _____

2. What does the narrator learn? _____

3. How does the narrator learn that lesson? _____
   _____
   _____

DISCUSSION

1. In your opinion, is hitchhiking really dangerous? Do you hitchhike? Why or why not?
2. What other dangerous things do young people do?
3. Why do young people generally take more physical risks than older people?

Writing Tips

Supporting the Opinion Statement

In the previous chapter you were given examples of opinion statements. You were also given a sample introduction.

Introduction

Hockey, which used to be a very entertaining sport, is now much too violent. In the past we could enjoy the skill and artistry of players like Wayne Gretzky and Mario Lemieux. Recently, however, more and more goons have been hired by the NHL. These goons are there to hurt, and possibly destroy, the best players on the ice.

It is important to be able to support your opinion. An opinion essay contains an introduction, several supporting paragraphs and a conclusion.

Before you write an essay, brainstorm supporting reasons for your opinion statement.

Opinion Statement

Hockey, which used to be a very entertaining sport, is now much too violent.

Supporting Arguments

More and more people are losing their careers to the violence.

Games are not as interesting.

There are more life-threatening injuries.

Transitional Words: Chronology

Any of the following words can be used to introduce a new supporting paragraph.

First/Second/Third	Furthermore
Additionally	Clearly
Also	Then
Next	Equally important
Finally	Another example

WRITING TIPS EXERCISE

Choose two of the following opinion statements, or create your own. Brainstorm at least two supporting arguments for two opinion statements.

1. We are (or are not) a beauty-obsessed culture.

2. Capital punishment should (or should not) be reinstated.

3. Pit bulls should (or should not) be banned from cities.

4. Cigarette companies should (or should not) be allowed to advertise.

5. Smoking should (or should not) be banned in public.

Opinion statement 1: _____

_____

Supporting arguments:

1. _____

2. _____

Opinion statement 2: _____

Supporting arguments:

1. _____

2. _____

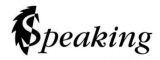

Writing Suggestions

1. Write two more opinion statements. Write two or three supporting arguments for each opinion statement.

2. Write an essay about an experience that changed your life in some way. The experience could have happened to you, or it could have happened to someone else and yet affected you.

For example, have you ever been caught cheating? Stealing? Has somebody you care about been involved with drugs? Have you insulted a friend? Was there a kid in your school that everyone made fun of? Have you ever done anything really nice for someone, and then been changed by the experience?

In your essay, describe the following:

When, where and how did the incident happen? How old were you?

What were your thoughts and feelings in connection with the incident?

How are you different today?

Speaking

SPEAKING EXERCISE ▪ LIFE-CHANGING EXPERIENCE

Prepare an oral presentation about a life-changing experience. What life-changing incident happened to you? Follow the directions in "Writing Suggestions" (above). You should include the following:

- **Introduction.** Where were you when the incident happened? How old were you?
- **Body.** What happened? How did you feel about it?
- **Conclusion.** How are you different now? How did the incident change you?

This life-changing experience could be presented to a group of five or six other students. The other students in the group could question the speaker after the presentation.

Crime and Punishment

Vocabulary	Crime
Reading	"Moonshine, Brightly" by Joe Fiorito
	"Witches" by Monique Polak
Writing Tips	The Conclusion
Speaking	Crime Role-Playing
Link to Grammar	Grammar Section 7: Prepositions and Plurals

This chapter takes a look at the world of crime. The vocabulary section contains crime-related terms. Both readings focus on crimes of the past. "Moonshine, Brightly" is about Joe Fiorito's memories of his family's illegal booze-making. "Witches" will tell you something about these maligned women who were tried and punished for their "crimes." The Writing Tip contains information about how to write a successful conclusion.

Vocabulary

VOCABULARY EXERCISE ▪ CRIME

Match the crime in column A with the description in column B. Write the letter of the correct description in the space beside each crime term. The answers to this exercise are at the end of this chapter.

A. Crime Terms		**B. Descriptions**
1. *mug*	_____	a. illegal alcohol
2. *stab*	_____	b. an accidental killing

3.	*strangle*	_____	c. to abduct and confine another person
4.	*assault*	_____	d. to rob someone on the street
5.	*manslaughter*	_____	e. to crash into something and then drive away
6.	*hit and run*	_____	f. the creation of false documents or writing of bad checks
7.	*moonshine*	_____	g. to bring contraband items over international borders
8.	*fraud*	_____	h. the intentional setting of a fire
9.	*rob*	_____	i. to physically attack someone
10.	*pickpocket*	_____	j. to kill by placing a rope tightly around someone's neck
11.	*purse snatcher*	_____	k. to create fake money
12.	*kidnap*	_____	l. a person who grabs the handbag out of someone's hand
13.	*smuggle*	_____	m. to attack with a sharp, knife-like object
14.	*counterfeit*	_____	n. someone who steals items from others' pockets
15.	*arson*	_____	o. to steal

Reading

PRE-READING VOCABULARY

Familiarize yourself with the following expressions before reading the text. The number in parentheses indicates the paragraph where the word is found.

(2) *bootleg*	illegal; contraband
(4) *roadster*	an open automobile
(4) *hollowed out*	with all obstructions removed
(7) *the jig is up*	the gamble is over
(12) *slosh*	to splash liquid
(13) *rum-running*	illegal transfer of alcohol
(15) *trip me up*	harm me
(17) *got my eye on*	interested in something

Reading 7.1

Moonshine, Brightly
by Joe Fiorito

Joe Fiorito has written for newspapers and magazines, and he has published collections of his articles. The story "Moonshine, Brightly" was published in Fiorito's book Comfort Me With Apples. *In this story Fiorito describes his family's history of making illegal moonshine. To understand this story, you must remember that the United States prohibited the production and sale of alcohol in the 1920s. This period of time was known as Prohibition and many people, including Sam Bronfman and Joe Kennedy, made their fortunes by selling illegal alcohol.*

1 There's a bottle of home-made grappa in my cupboard. It looks like tapwater, and it tastes like grape kerosene, but a weakness for home-made booze runs in the family. It's a tradition that goes back a long way.

2 My relatives were poor when they came to Canada a hundred years ago. To survive, they cut a bit of wood, they did a little hunting, they grew a little food. They lived on a farm in the bush. To make some extra cash, my uncle Tony made bootleg whiskey.

3 You might call him a moonshiner. I prefer to think of him as a boutique distiller. He grew his own high-quality ingredients. His still was custom-built according to traditional specifications. He even made his own deliveries, just like the Bronfmans. But unlike Mr. Sam, my uncle Tony wasn't in it to get rich. He was simply trying to earn a bit of off-farm income.

4 Tony ran his booze to the hotels in town once a week down a network of narrow back roads. He used his cousin's Chalmers touring car, a huge roadster whose front seat had been hollowed out and custom-fitted with a secret tank.

5 During the height of the summer season sometime in the early Twenties, Tony heard that the cops were onto him. He had a run to make, so he asked my father to come for a ride. My father was five years old at the time.

6 A ride in the car was a treat, but Tony made it paradise—he gave my little dad a whole pack of gum to chew. Tony said, "Put all of this gum in your mouth. If anybody makes me stop the car, you stop chewing. And if anybody asks you anything, you just nod yes or no. Got that?" My five-year old dad stuffed his cheek and nodded happily, and off they drove.

7 Sure enough, the provincial police were waiting for them on a little cowpath of a road. The cops smiled and put their hands on their guns. They said, "We got you now, Tony. The jig is up. We want to search the car."

8 "Hey, you got it wrong," said Tony. "I'm taking my little brother to the dentist. He's got a bad tooth. Take a look at him."

9 The cops peered closely at my little dad, who was sitting scared in the front seat of the car. One of the cops said, "Jesus will you take a look at this."

10 My little dad's jaw looked swollen. "Does it hurt, sonny?" My dad nodded. "Are you going to the dentist, sonny?" My dad nodded. "Is he going to pull your tooth?" My dad nodded again.

11 "That's a brave little kid," said the cops, smiling kindly. "Tony, you better get him to town right away."

12 Tony took off, laughing to himself as moonshine sloshed in the hidden tank.

13 That was my old man's introduction to rum-running. He's over seventy now, and while it's fair to say that booze did him more harm than good over the years—in the final analysis, all my relatives are better consumers than producers—the old man did teach me how to drink.

14 We could have a glass of anything when we were kids. It was never a big deal. There was no moralizing. We learned to drink it, just as we learned to make it.

15   I discovered moderation at home where it was safe. The taste of liquor didn't trip me up when I got old enough to do my first stupid things.

16   Oddly, in recent years my old man's grown allergic to drink. It makes him sneeze, and he swells up. This may be a cosmic balancing of the books, but I think it's sad. It means the loss of one more pleasure, at an age when he needs all the pleasure he can get.

17   And it's sad for another reason. I've got my eye on some copper coils. If I decide to make a little moonshine of my own, I want an experienced palate to judge the final product. And maybe to help me rig my Honda with a secret tank.

VOCABULARY

1. Find a slang word in paragraph 1 that means "alcohol." _____

2. Find a word in paragraph 4 that means "not wide." _____

3. As it is used in paragraph 10, the word *swollen* means: (circle one)
    a. enlarged or distended.
    b. painful.
    c. small.

4. The word *rig* (para. 17), as it is used in the text, means: (circle one)
    a. tractor-trailer.
    b. to manipulate by dishonest means.
    c. to equip.

READING COMPREHENSION

1. How did Uncle Tony fool the police? _____

    _____

    _____

DISCUSSION

1. Why did prohibition not work? When something like drugs or alcohol are illegal, who makes money from them?

2. In your opinion, should alcohol be made illegal again? Should drugs be legalized? Does it make sense to ban drugs yet sell alcohol? Explain your answer.

Witches
by Monique Polak

Once upon a time it was considered a crime for a woman to practice medicine, act as a midwife, or simply live alone and own property. In the following text, the history of witches is examined.

1   Wearing ratty black capes, pointy hats, painted moles on their faces, sporting long green plastic nails, many little witches will be out this Halloween, trick or treating up a storm. Their goal: to look as hideous as possible. Once a year, North American girls revel in the rare opportunity to escape the tyranny of what feminist thinker Naomi Wolf calls *The Beauty Myth*.

2   In our time, witches are objects of scorn. Unfortunately, our daughters, many of whom annually adorn themselves in witch costumes, are unaware of the historic battles so-called witches, who were really early feminists, fought on behalf of future generations of women.

3   From the 14th to the 18th century, first in Europe, and later in America, women who threatened patriarchal society were routinely accused of being witches. Many were executed. Rosalind Miles, author of *The Women's History of the World*, uses the term "gynocide" to describe this systematic massacre of women.

4   Since women during this period were denied university educations, those who wished to study fields such as medicine were forced to go underground. Many women accused of being witches were actually exploring botany, pharmacology and alchemy.

5   Midwives, familiar with methods to facilitate child-bearing, were also prime targets of the witch-craze. Interestingly, the French term *sage-femmes* refers both to witches and midwives. Its literal meaning, "wise-women," undoubtedly reveals the characteristic of these women which most threatened male-dominated society.

6   Non-conformist women who dared to reject traditional female lifestyles also faced the threat of being denounced as witches. In Salem, Mass., in 1692, the height of American witch trials, single mothers like Sarah Good and Sarah Osburn were hanged as witches. Good and her three children were reduced to poverty after her husband abandoned the family. Town gossip accounted for the husband's departure by saying he suspected his wife of being a witch. Sarah Osburn, a wealthy widow, had the audacity to get married again, to the young Irish farmhand who managed her property.

7   In Carol Karlsen's exploration of New England witchcraft, *The Devil in the Shape of a Woman*, she demonstrates that witches were considered seductresses, women "who made no attempt to restrain their sexual impulses." During the Salem witchhunt, both Good and Osburn served as convenient scapegoats for their neighbors' venom and sexual repression.

8   Older women were also vulnerable targets. Ironically, the word "hag," a derogatory word used in our culture to describe an old, unattractive woman, originally referred to a woman who had "sacred knowledge."

9   Like women who possessed unorthodox healing skills, or who rejected conventional female roles, "hags"—in the earliest meaning of the word—threatened male-dominated

society. Better to debase these women by ridiculing their aging appearances than to respect their wisdom and experience. Feminist author Erica Jong found that the contemporary image of the witch as a warty old crone "bespeaks our terror of aging—more terrifying, as usual, in women than in men."

10   In ancient cultures, women were revered for their knowledge, their wisdom and above all for their ability to give life. Great goddesses included Isis of Egypt, Astarte of Asia Minor, Ishtar of Assyria, and Demeter and Persephone of Greece.

11   As women's power began to threaten patriarchal society, these goddesses were demoted in their various pantheons. Later, witchhunts effectively terrorized and controlled assertive women. Jong speculates that "when the witch craze died out . . . a new form of male patriarchal social control replaced it: . . . romantic love."

12   So perhaps this Halloween is time to tell our daughters about the rich history of witches, an essential chapter in women's history. Time, too, to reclaim for females the power these wise women possessed.

VOCABULARY

1. What is a *midwife?* (para. 5) Guess the meaning of the word by reading the sentence in which it appears. Also read the sentences after the word for clues to its meaning. _____

2. The word *audacity* (para. 6), as it is used in the text, means: (circle one)
   a. intelligence.
   b. boldness and fearlessness; impudence.
   c. greed; hunger for money.

3. The word *scapegoat* (para. 7), as it is used in the text, means: (circle one)
   a. someone who is the object of ridicule.
   b. the butt or focus of everyone's joke.
   c. the person unfairly punished because of the acts or attitudes of others.

4. A *hag* (para. 8) currently means "an old and unattractive woman." What did the word originally refer to? _____

READING COMPREHENSION

Some of the following sentences are true and some are false. Put *T* (for "true") or *F* (for "false") beside each sentence.

1. Many women accused of being witches were university educated.   _____

2. Many so-called "witches" were really scientists.   _____

3. The term *witch* literally means "wise-women." _____

4. Sarah Good was killed in 1692. _____

5. The wealthy Sarah Osborn's second marriage was to a poor man. _____

6. Only young single women were called witches in Salem, Massachusetts. _____

DISCUSSION

1. Have you been told about the repression of witches? Was it part of your grade-school curriculum? Should it be?

2. Why has the image of the evil, ugly witch endured when it is far from the reality of witches?

riting Tips

The Conclusion

A good conclusion should bring an essay to a satisfactory close. Your essay should end by giving the readers something to think about. Read the following do's and don'ts.

Conclusion Do's	Conclusion Don'ts
• Repeat the main idea of the essay. • Restate, in a few short phrases, your main supporting points. • Make a final suggestion or prediction.	• Introduce new ideas. • End with a question. • Contradict your earlier statements.

Transitional Words: Conclusions

Any of the following words can be used in a conclusion.

Finally	To conclude
In conclusion	In short
To sum up	Consequently
Therefore	Thus

WRITING TIPS ▪ CLASS EXERCISE

Read the following opinion essay. Highlight the thesis statement and the topic sentences in each paragraph, and then write an effective conclusion.

Hockey Violence

by Diego Pelaez Gaetz

Hockey, which used to be a very entertaining sport, is now much too violent. In the past we could enjoy the skill and artistry of players like Wayne Gretzky and Mario Lemieux. Recently, however, more and more goons have been hired by the NHL. These goons are there to hurt, and possibly destroy, the best players on the ice.

Hockey players are now able to get away with grabbing, hooking (when the end of the stick is used to trip the player) and nasty checking (when an elbow or stick gets involved in the ramming of someone against the boards). This violence has meant that the games are no longer as interesting as they were in the past. Almost every week one of the better players gets injured and has to sit out the game. This means that the elite players can't demonstrate their skill on the ice.

Some very good hockey players in recent history have lost their careers due to hockey violence. Brett Lindros has had several hockey-related concussions. Mario Lemieux has had many back injuries due to nasty checking against the boards. Paul Kariya, a left-wing player for the Anaheim Mighty Ducks, was cross-checked in the head and was unable to attend the 1998 Winter Olympics. In Kariya's case, the player who injured him simply got a four-game suspension, yet this player put Kariya's career in jeopardy. On the street, such an assault would be a crime and would be punishable by law. On the hockey rink, these crimes are accepted and even encouraged.

Add Your Own Conclusion

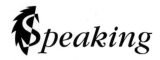

Speaking

SPEAKING EXERCISE ▪ CRIME ROLE-PLAYING

You will be asked to role-play the following scenarios. You will be given either the "police" role or the "civilian" role. You should read only your own role, and you should close your book after understanding your role.

Police

1. *2 students. You are both police officers.*
   A driver is speeding. The driver was going about 150 km per hour (or 110 miles per hour). Stop the car and give a ticket to the driver. Don't let the driver talk you out of it.

2. *2 students. You are both police officers.*
   A couple were robbed earlier today. Try to get a detailed description of the suspects.

3. *2 students. One is a "nice" police officer and one is a "mean" officer.*

A bank machine was robbed. You have four suspects. Separate the suspects and try to get them to *snitch* (tell) on each other. Offer freedom to the one who snitches. Also, see if the suspects have the same story. Where were they Saturday at 8 p.m.? Try to get details from them.

You can send three of the suspects out of the class while you interrogate one suspect. Classmates can help you think of questions for the interrogation!

Example: *What were you doing at 8 p.m. last Saturday?*
Why were you there?
etc.

Civilians

1. *1 or 2 students.*

You were driving a little bit over the speed limit. You were going about 120 km per hour (or 80 miles per hour). Tell the police that you have an emergency. Also remind the police officers that other drivers are going faster than you were. If the police officers try to give you a ticket, offer them some money. If you get a speeding ticket, you will lose your driver's license, and you really need your car!

2. *2 students. You are a married couple.*

You are tourists. Earlier today you were robbed in the street. Describe the suspects to the police. The suspects were both wearing ski masks. The person playing the husband should read only his role. The person playing the wife should skip immediately to the wife's role.

Husband (Don't read the wife's role.) This is what you remember: The three robbers were white. They were very tall. They were all wearing blue ski masks, but you are quite sure they were male. One of them was very strong. The tallest man had a gun. They overpowered you. You were very frightened.

Wife (Don't read the husband's role). This is what you remember: The two robbers were white. They were wearing green ski masks, but you are quite sure they were female. You could tell this because you smelled a familiar perfume and one of them had a ponytail. The two women were quite strong, but they were not very tall. They spoke in deep, female voices. The two robbers didn't have a gun, but you are quite sure that one of them had a knife. You were very frightened.

3. *4 students.*

All of you robbed a bank last Saturday at 8 p.m. The police suspect the four of you. All of you must come up with a good alibi. Tell the officer you were all at a restaurant or sports bar, or some other public place. Before the role-playing, *take some time to prepare a story for the police.* You were all together, so you should all remember the same details. It is possible that the police will separate you during the interrogation.

ANSWERS TO VOCABULARY EXERCISE 1:

1. d   2. m   3. j   4. i   5. b   6. e   7. a   8. f   9. o   10. n   11. l   12. c   13. g   14. k   15. h

Personal History

Vocabulary   Family Tree
Reading   "One Day in the Flats" by Adele Berridge
Writing Tips   The Essay Plan
Speaking   Oral presentations
Link to Grammar   Grammar Section 8: Comparisons

Everyone has a story. What seems commonplace to us now will be fascinating to our grandchildren. In thirty or forty years the world will have changed, and some things we use every day will be considered valuable antiques. An appreciation of our history is important, and it gives us perspective on our present time. This chapter focuses on families, the stories of family members, and the places we come from.

The vocabulary section contains "family" vocabulary and includes terms that are relevant for our new, mixed families. Use your dictionary if some terms are not familiar to you. Please note that in Grammar Section 8 there is a "relationship" vocabulary exercise.

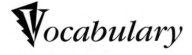

Vocabulary

VOCABULARY EXERCISE ▪ FAMILY TREE

Working in pairs, fill in the blanks using the words in the box, and put the names of the family members on the chart. Answers to this exercise are at the end of the chapter.

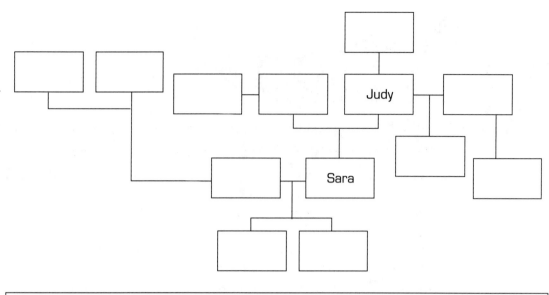

great-grandmother	son	stepsister	half-brother	father-in-law
grandmother	mother-in-law	half-sister	daughter	husband
brother-in-law	father	brother	stepmother	wife
sister-in-law	sister	stepbrother	stepfather	

My name is Sara and I was born on January 2, 1980.
My mother's name is Judy and she was born on March 8, 1956.
My mother married a man named Harvey. Harvey was born on September 2, 1956.
Together, my mom and Harvey created me.

1. Harvey is my _____.

My parents divorced when I was eight years old. My dad is now married to a woman named Maria. My mother is now married to a man named Paulo.

2. Maria is my _____ and Paulo is my _____.

3. Paulo had a child called Tayo before he married my mother. Tayo is my

_____.

4. Paulo and my mother had a daughter named Jade in 1995. She is my

_____.

5. I am married to a man named Pierre. Pierre is my _____ and I am

Pierre's _____.

6. Pierre's parents live with us because his mother is ill. Pierre's mother is named Monice.

Monice is my _____. Pierre's father, Luc, is my _____.

7. Pierre and I have two children. Alice is our _____. Roberto is our

_____.

8. My grandmother's name is Irene. Irene is the _____ of my children.

eading

PRE-READING VOCABULARY

Familiarize yourself with the following expressions before reading the text. The number in parentheses indicates the paragraph where the word is found.

(1) *peel*	to remove or strip off something that is stuck to a surface
(3) *biffy*	toilet
(3) *outhouse*	enclosed toilet situated outdoors
(3) *reek*	terrible odor
(5) *fall in*	get in line
(7) *rasping*	heavy, noisy breathing
(7) *clutch*	to grasp or hold tightly
(10) *jaunty*	free and easy, confident

Reading 8.1

One Day in the Flats
by Adele Berridge

The following story is about a day in the life of a young boy. His family were immigrants from Russia who had traveled over land and sea and ended up in a small town in the province of Alberta, Canada. It was the 1930s, a time when people got accustomed to coping with hardship.

1   When I was seven years old, my family lived in a tiny two-room house. Every morning I raised my head from the mattress and watched my father get ready. He didn't own a suit, but he owned a clean red shirt, and pants with invisible stitching on the patches. He wore those pants while he went work hunting. My father would pick up the cardboard, the scissors glinting, as he cut himself soles for his shoes. He would then gently fit the cardboard soles into the bottoms of his well-worn shoes. Every day he went out and walked all over the flats asking anyone, even people in trucks, if they needed any help, and every evening he came home with his head hanging low. Every night he sat at the table, untied his shoelaces and took off his shoes. Then he peeled the cardboard off the soles of his feet.

2   One morning my dad whistled and beckoned me to come along. A small boy was company. We walked through the flats, past the tiny houses, past the kids whose dads worked at the flour mill. Everyone recognized the kids of those mill workers: they wore the flour sack clothing—checked red, blue or green gingham from the bags of Ogilvy's mill. My mom got the torn sacks from my Uncle Tony, and I wore the flour sack clothing too. Even underwear. But I wasn't a flour sack kid; my dad had no job.

3   I walked past the flour mill and past the house of the honeyman. Archie Greenstein's son, Nick, was the honeyman. Nick was tall and thin. His blond hair always hung over one eye, and I looked up to him. Every few days Nick came around with a truck, went into our outhouse, picked up the fifteen-gallon can under our biffy and replaced it with an empty can. The back of his truck had two layers; the empty cans went on top and the full cans on the bottom. After Nick filled the bottom layer with the cans weighing 150 pounds each, he would drive down to the Saskatchewan River, remove the hefty, filthy, stinking cans and pour them out, into the water. The reek stuck to Nick's pants. It stuck to his shirt. His hands.

4   At that moment Nick was starting his day's work and was getting into his truck. We nodded "hello" to Nick and then my father and I continued walking side by side. My dad murmured that Nick Greenstein was lucky. I listened solemnly and wondered if I could be a honeyman one day.

5   We kept walking until the road curved and we got to the buildings with the smokestacks. The sign *Alberta Clay Products* was clean and new. Hanging on the fence was a smaller, hand-printed sign saying "Englishmen need not apply." People around here, especially the Eastern Europeans and the Russians, thought that the English were lazy. We saw the line-up and we fell in. The men in front murmured in the smoke and sucked on cigarette butts, and I heard shouting in a familiar language.

6   Through the fence in the yard we saw men running. They were thin as coat-hangers and they ran pushing the big gray wheelbarrows full of cement. They ran without stopping, dust rising behind them. But then one tall fellow staggered drunkenly and leaned over low.

7   All the men in the line-up stopped talking to look at the tall fellow. His cheeks were so hollow you could see the outline of his cheekbones. We heard the fellow breathing hard, rasping. His back rose and fell as he gasped for air, and one hand clutched at his ribcage while he leaned on the wheelbarrow handle with the other. He took off his cap. There was a dividing line where the dirt on his face reached the clean, white, wet skin that had been under his cap. Then I heard the shout. In front of everyone, the foreman fired the man and pointed towards the exit.

8   The other workers kept running and we heard their pounding feet and the spinning wheels, and the sound of the tall fellow rasping, his back heaving as he gasped for air.

9   The fellow stood up almost straight and put his cap on and walked towards the exit. He walked slowly past me, past my dad and all the other men, but he didn't look at any of us. He just looked straight ahead. He was barely at the corner when all the men started talking and laughing again.

10   When the next man's name was called, the new guy ran in all jaunty and smiled at the foreman. A wheelbarrow full of cement sat empty in the middle of the courtyard. The new man ran up to it and grabbed the handles. He hurried to the dumpsite to unload it. His face was wired in a wide grin the whole time.

11   My dad and I waited. When the sun was high and hot in the late afternoon, there were still about forty people in front of us in the line, standing and waiting for a job that might last a day or two. Inside the courtyard the feet were still pounding and the wheels were still spinning. I was seven years old and fidgety, and my father told me to get myself back home.

12   When the sun was down and the air had cooled off and my two brothers and I had settled down on the mattress in the corner, the door opened and my father came in, his head hanging low. My mother stood up and went to put on the kettle. I raised my head and from my spot in the corner I could see my father. I watched through the table legs and saw him untie his shoelaces. He took off his shoes and peeled the cardboards, one by one, from the soles of his feet and dropped them, softened like tissue, onto the floor.

VOCABULARY

1. What are *cardboard soles?* (para. 1) _____

2. What does a *honeyman* do? (para. 3) _____
   _____

3. A *wheelbarrow* (para. 6) is: (circle one)
   a. a small truck.
   b. a large sack.
   c. a small vehicle with one wheel, used for carrying small loads.

4. The foreman fired a fellow. What is *fired?* (para. 7) _____

READING COMPREHENSION

1. Why did the narrator's father put cardboard soles in his shoes?_____
   _____

2. Why did the father think that the honeyman was lucky?_____
   _____

3. Why was the thin man fired from his job at Alberta Clay Products? (para. 7) _____
   _____
   _____

4. What kind of clothing did the narrator wear when he was a child?_____
   _____

5. In about five sentences, briefly summarize what happens in this story. _____
   _____
   _____
   _____
   _____
   _____

DISCUSSION

1. Is this an ordinary story today? What makes the story interesting or unusual?

2. Have you ever interviewed an older member of your family about his or her childhood? If you have, what have you found out?

Writing Tips

The Essay Plan

Before writing an essay, you should make an essay plan (outline). Your plan should have the following form:

Introduction   Anecdote or background information
                    Opinion Statement

Body 1   **Topic Sentence** _____
                   Supports: facts, examples, statistics or personal experiences
                   a. _____
                   b. _____

Body 2   **Topic Sentence** _____
                   Supports: facts, examples, statistics or personal experiences
                   a. _____
                   b. _____

Body 3   **Topic Sentence** _____
(Optional)   **Supports:** facts, examples, statistics or personal experiences
                   a. _____
                   b. _____

Conclusion   **Sum up** main points.
                   Give a **final suggestion**, prediction or solution.

Sample Essay Plan

Violence in Hockey

Opinion Statement		Hockey, which used to be a very entertaining sport, is now much too violent.
Body 1	**(Topic Sentence)**	Hockey games are no longer as interesting as they were in the past.
	(Supporting facts)	a. Almost weekly, one of the better players gets injured and sits out the game.
		b. The violent players dominate the game, and the skilled players must fear them.

Sample Essay Plan (continued)

Body 2	**(Topic Sentence)**	Some very good hockey players in recent history have lost their careers due to hockey violence.
	(Supporting facts)	a. Paul Kariya, a left-wing player for the Anaheim Mighty Ducks, was cross-checked in the head and was unable to attend the 1998 Winter Olympics.
		b. Brett Lindros has had several hockey-related concussions.
Body 3	**(Topic Sentence)**	Young children are influenced by the violent behavior of the adults.
	(Supporting facts)	a. Kids, emulating their heroes, are slashing and tripping each other.
		b. In the last two years, over six hundred severe injuries have occurred in minor hockey.
Conclusion	**(Sum up)**	Violence in hockey has made the sport less interesting. It has also meant the end to the careers of some of the NHL's best players. Worst of all, children are influenced by the violent behavior of their hockey heroes.
	(Final suggestion)	Those wanting to see violence could tune in to boxing matches.

WRITING TIPS EXERCISE

Make an essay plan for an opinion essay on one of the following topics:
- Old people are not respected enough in our society.
- Alcohol should/should not be illegal.
- Children should learn about real witches.
- Your choice.

Writing Suggestions

1. Interview an older person (it could be a family member or someone that you meet in a nursing home). Write a short essay about that person's childhood, or share the information about that person orally. Your essay could have the same structure as the presentation listed in the following speaking section.

2. Find an interesting name of a city, town, street, province, state or country, and try to find out how that place got its name. Ideally, choose the name of a place that you know well. Write a short essay explaining how that place got its name.

 # Speaking

 ## SPEAKING EXERCISE 1 ▪ INTERVIEW ABOUT THE PAST

When we are young, we often forget or ignore the incredible amount of life experience that older people in our culture have. It could be claimed, convincingly, that our culture tends to undervalue the wisdom of the elderly. This activity will provide you with an opportunity to connect, even briefly, with someone who has a great deal of life experience.

Interview a family member who is older than you. If possible, choose a grandparent or an older aunt or uncle. If you do not have any older relatives, you could interview a neighbor; you could also go to a nursing home and ask to speak to someone. Ask the interviewee some questions about any of the following topics. Please be sensitive during the interview, and stop questioning about a topic if the person you are interviewing is uncomfortable talking about it.

History

- When and where were you born?
- What was your birthplace like when you were young?
- What activities did you do for entertainment? (Remember, television has only been widely available since the 1950s.)
- What was your family situation?
- What kinds of jobs did you do? What were the salaries like in the past?
- What was your most interesting occupation?
- How was the world different in the past?
- What is better in the world now?
- What is worse in the world now?

Values

- What are the most important things in life?
- What would you change about your life?
- What is your biggest regret?
- What is your greatest achievement?
- What has been your greatest source of happiness?
- What advice do you have for young people today?

After you complete the interview, present your findings in an oral presentation lasting a few minutes. Include the following:

Introduction: The name, age and current status of the person. How do you know the person?

Body: State the most interesting information that you learned from the person you interviewed. Did any of the information surprise you?

Conclusion: What do you know about the past that you didn't know before?

These presentations could be done before the class, or they could be done in small groups of students. This activity could also provide the background information for a writing assignment.

 ## SPEAKING EXERCISE 2 ▪ HOW A PLACE GOT ITS NAME

Find an interesting name of a city, town, street, province, state or country, and try to find out how that place got its name. Ideally, choose the name of a place that you know well. Prepare an oral presentation explaining how that place got its name.

ANSWERS TO VOCABULARY EXERCISE 1:
1. father   2. stepmother / stepfather   3. stepbrother   4. half-sister   5. husband / wife   6. mother-in-law / father-in-law   7. daughter / son   8. great-grandmother

 Heroes

Vocabulary	Physical Descriptions
Reading	"My Brother" by Rick Theis
	"Rosa Parks" by Kai Friese
Writing Tips	Transitional Words
Speaking	Oral Presentation: Someone I Admire
Link to Grammar	Grammar Section 9: The Past Progressive

This chapter focuses on heroes. In the essay "My Brother," a boy awaits the arrival of his brother who is coming home from the war. "Rosa Parks" is the story of a woman who was fed up with being pushed around because of her colour. Rosa's defiance and determination inspired many to follow her example.

The vocabulary includes terms relating to physical descriptions. In Grammar Section 9 there is vocabulary related to physical and psychological characteristics. These vocabulary words should help you when you do the speaking activity: you must describe someone that you admire. The Writing Tip includes transitional expressions that you can use to emphasize something or compare and contrast several things.

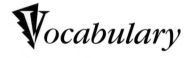 *Vocabulary*

 ## VOCABULARY EXERCISE ▪ PHYSICAL DESCRIPTIONS

Write each term below in the appropriate place in the drawing. Answers are at the end of this chapter.

sideburns	balding	cuff	dimple	bow tie
mole	checked	dots	stripes	wrinkles
collar	sleeve	whiskers	buttons	

b. _____
n. _____
c. _____
l. _____
a. _____
e. _____
d. _____
m. _____
k. _____
j. _____
f. _____
i. _____
g. _____
h. _____

Reading

PRE-READING VOCABULARY

Familiarize yourself with the following terms before reading the text. The number in parentheses indicates the paragraph where the word is found.

(3) *grip*	to hold tightly
(3) *hurtling*	tumbling, falling at great speed
(6) *tinged*	lightly touched
(6) *dread*	fear, apprehension
(6) *slap*	strike across the face
(6) *nightmare*	terrifying dream
(7) *slot*	space
(9) *nil*	nothing
(10) *duped*	fooled; taken advantage of
(11) *casket*	box for dead bodies

My Brother
by Rick Theis

In the following essay, Rick Theis describes his hero. Rick's hero is his older brother who chose to go to war during the years of America's involvement in Vietnam.

1   For a long time I'd planned to go out to the highway overpass and spraypaint a greeting to my brother: "Hi, Roger!" Now he'd be arriving the very next morning; back after three long years at war. He'd sent letters now and then, but I hadn't seen him since I was fourteen. It was dawn. The sky was clear, the sun bright. The air was cool and clean.

2   I leaned over the rail and was struck by the neat four-laned highway below. It was deserted except for a tiny car far in the distance. The dead grasses on either side were colored golden brown by the new sun. This beautiful solitude was itching to blossom into an exciting spring. And I would get to be with my brother again.

3   I carefully scrawled my message, upside down, across the bridge. Suddenly I lost my grip and slid forward. The hard concrete below flew up toward my face, taking my breath away. I grabbed the metal rail and barely stopped my body from hurtling over the edge. I finished the sign and hurried back to my car. The radio blasted as I raced down the expressway toward home. My brother would be back tomorrow.

4   I was up before the sun again the next morning. Dad and Mom were awake soon thereafter and we left for the airport by seven. Each mile of the trip seemed like a million until the airport was in view. Then I became ecstatic. The time had finally come to be with my brother again.

5   Driving up the long airport road I remembered playing baseball with him. He was young and strong. His hair flew wildly about his head as he rounded the bases and slid into home plate. He was my hero. He was everything I wanted to be. It's hard to believe that then he was only as old as I am now. When he graduated from high school it was off to the army with plenty of his friends. By now he would have been finishing up college ready to begin an adult life. But that would have to wait until after the service, he had said.

6   I couldn't understand him going to war. He had said he had to do it—it was the law, it was his duty, it was the way things were done. But the reality of war was something else altogether. His letters were so sad, tinged with dread and insanity. The darkest side of human nature slapped him across the face again and again. It demeaned him. He was the vehicle for a great evil but he could find no escape. His only solace was in believing that his family was safe, far from the nightmarish world he had to inhabit. I watched the death and destruction on TV and wondered if I'd be as brave as my brother when it was my time to go. He was my hero.

7   We pulled up to the parking lot and my Dad paid the attendant fifty cents. We searched through the rows and rows of cars until we found an empty slot. The anticipation had now gripped me completely. I wanted to run and meet him, throw my arms around him, hug him so tightly and never let him go.

8   There was something very important torn from my life—and my Mom's and Dad's, too—when he left. And what's to be said about his own life? He was so young when he had to make the decision: whether to go or not. He was idealistic and trusting. He was strong and invincible.

9   As we walked into the terminal his flight was landing. We found the proper gate and waited. I knew I would not go to war. And was sure he wouldn't go if he had it all to do over again. I knew by his letters. He never said it—he was too brave—but I knew it anyway. He was degraded, taught to inflict pain, hate and kill. He was forced to undertake a torturous journey and face bloody battlefields, burning towns and frightened children. He learned to act on command and suppress his instinctual conscience and humanity. He learned that the value of human life was nil, that politics was a black magic and that evil gathered momentum until it swallowed up everything in its path. He knew that he could have slowed that momentum had he been smarter, less headstrong, and more brave at age seventeen.

10   But to me he was still a hero. He had been required to make decisions that men twice his age and wisdom could make only with the greatest care. I think he was duped. I think he was chosen because he was young and wanted to be a man; young and unattached; young and inexperienced in life; young and available for war. I think he was stolen, used and discarded. I would like to tell him this, but I know he already knows.

11   My Mom and Dad are crying now as Roger is the last one off the plane. The day is bright and clear, the beginning of Spring and the beginning of a new understanding. The shiny black casket is rolled slowly down the long runaway. Soon my brother's body will pass under the concrete bridge with the spraypainted plea, "Stop War." Perhaps soon, we will.

VOCABULARY

1. *I carefully scrawled my message, upside down, across the bridge.* What is the meaning of *scrawled*? (para. 3)
    a. to autograph
    b. to scrape with the fingernails
    c. to write or draw quickly

2. Find a word in paragraph 6 that means "to degrade or lower." _____

3. Find a word in paragraph 6 that means "comfort or consolation."_____

4. Find a word in paragraph 9 that means "subdue or repress; hold in." _____

READING COMPREHENSION

1. Why was the narrator on the highway overpass? _____

_____

2. What did the narrator write on the overpass? _____

Why did he write that? _____

_____

_____

3. What did the narrator's brother learn at war? _____

_____

_____

4. What is the main message of this story? _____

_____

DISCUSSION

1. Did you think the brother was alive until the end of the story? How does the narrator manipulate the reader?

2. Why do armies recruit young boys of 18 years old? Why don't they recruit older men and women?

3. Does this story successfully illustrate the futility and stupidity of war?

4. Why does war exist, in your opinion? Is it possible to have a world without war? Why or why not?

 # PRE-READING VOCABULARY

Familiarize yourself with the following terms before reading the text. The number in parentheses indicates the paragraph where the word is found.

(1) *trundled*	moved on spinning wheels
(4) *quirk of fate*	peculiar turn of chance
(8) *she was booked*	she was charged with a crime
(14) *file an appeal*	register with the court a non-acceptance of the verdict
(15) *din*	commotion
(16) *storm the courthouse*	rush in a group towards the courthouse

Rosa Parks
by Kai Friese

Rosa Parks's refusal to "move to the back" of the bus on the evening of December 1, 1955, marked a historic moment: the start of a movement that would bring an end to a tradition of legal segregation in the United States. Parks certainly never suspected her gesture would turn a new page in the history of American race relations. She didn't move, she later explained, because she was just suddenly fed up with being pushed around. The following text describes that day in Rosa Parks's life.

1   It was Thursday, December 1, 1955. The workday was over, and crowds of people boarded the green-and-white buses that trundled through the streets of Montgomery. Rosa Parks was tired after a full day of stitching and ironing shirts at the Montgomery Fair department store. She thought she was lucky to have gotten one of the last seats in the rear section of the Cleveland Avenue bus that would take her home.

2   Soon the back of the bus was full, and several people were standing in the rear. The bus rolled on through Court Square, where African-Americans had been auctioned off during the days of the Confederacy, and came to a stop in front of the Empire Theater. The next passenger aboard stood in the front of an aisle. He was a white man.

3   When he noticed that a white person had to stand, the bus driver, James F. Blake, called out to the four black people who were sitting just behind the white section. He said they would have to give up their seats for the new passenger. No one stood up. "You'd better make it light on yourself and let me have those seats," the driver said threateningly. Three men got up and went to stand at the back of the bus. But Rosa Parks wasn't about to move. She had been in this situation before, and she had always given up her seat. She had always felt insulted by the experience. "It meant that I didn't have a right to do anything but get on the bus, give them my fare and then be pushed around wherever they wanted me," she said.

4   By a quirk of fate, the driver of the bus on this December evening was the same James F. Blake who had once before removed the troublesome Rosa Parks from his bus for refusing to enter by the back door. That was a long time ago, in 1943. Rosa Parks didn't feel like being pushed around again. She told the driver that she wasn't in the white section and she wasn't going to move.

5   Blake knew the rules, though. He knew that the white section was wherever the driver said it was. If more white passengers got on the bus, he could stretch the white section to the back of the bus and make all the blacks stand. He shouted to Rosa Parks to move to the back of the bus. She wasn't impressed. She told him again that she wasn't moving. Everyone in the bus was silent, wondering what would happen next. Finally Blake told Rosa Parks that he would have her arrested for violating the racial segregation codes. In a firm but quiet voice, she told him that he could do what he wanted to do because she wasn't moving.

6   Blake got off the bus and came back with an officer of the Montgomery Police Department. As the officer placed Rosa Parks under arrest, she asked him plainly, "Why do you people push us around?"

7   With the eyes of all the passengers on him, the officer could only answer in confusion. "I don't know. I'm just obeying the law," he said.

8   Rosa Parks was taken to the police station, where she was booked and fingerprinted. While the policemen were filling out forms, she asked if she could have a drink of water. She was told that the drinking fountain in the station was for whites only. Then a policewoman marched her into a long corridor facing a wall of iron bars. A barred door slid open. She went inside. The door clanged shut, and she was locked in. She was in jail.

9   Rosa Parks's decision to challenge her arrest in court led Montgomery's black community to organize a bus boycott as a show of support.

10   Rosa Parks woke up on the morning of Monday, December 5, thinking about her trial. As she and her husband got out of bed, they heard the familiar sound of a City Lines bus pulling up to a stop across the road. There was usually a crowd of people waiting for the bus at this time. The Parkses rushed to the window and looked out. Except for the driver, the bus was empty and there was no one getting on either. The bus stood at the stop for more than a minute, puffing exhaust smoke into the cold December air as the puzzled driver waited for passengers. But no one appeared, and the empty bus chugged away.

11   Rosa Parks was filled with happiness. Her neighbors were actually boycotting the buses. She couldn't wait to drive to the courthouse so that she could see how the boycott was going in the rest of Montgomery. When Fred Gray arrived to drive her to the trial, she wasn't disappointed. Rosa Parks had expected some people to stay off the buses. She thought that with luck, maybe even half the usual passengers would stay off. But these buses were just plain empty.

12   All over the city, empty buses bounced around for everyone to see. There was never more than the usual small group of white passengers in front and sometimes a lonely black passenger in back, wondering what was going on. The streets were filled with black people walking to work.

13   As Rosa Parks and her lawyer drove up to the courthouse, there was another surprise waiting for them. A crowd of about five hundred blacks had gathered to show their support for her. Mrs. Parks and the lawyer made their way slowly through the cheering crowd into the courtroom. Once they were inside, the trial didn't take long. Rosa Parks was quickly convicted of breaking the bus segregation laws and fined ten dollars, as well as four dollars for the cost of her trial. This was the stage at which Claudette Colvin's trial had ended seven months earlier. Colvin had had little choice but to accept the guilty verdict and pay the fine.

14   This time, however, Fred Gray rose to file an appeal on Rosa Parks's case. This meant that her case would be taken to a higher court at a later date. Meanwhile, Mrs. Parks was free to go.

15   Outside the courthouse, the crowd was getting restless. Some of them were carrying sawed-off shotguns, and the policemen were beginning to look worried. E.D. Nixon went out to calm them, but nobody could hear him in the din. Voices from the crowd shouted out that

they would storm the courthouse if Rosa Parks didn't come out safely within a few minutes. When she did appear, a great cheer went up again.

16   After seeing the empty buses that morning, and this large and fearless crowd around her now, Rosa Parks knew that she had made the right decision. Black people were uniting to show the city administration that they were tired of the insults of segregation. Together, they could change Montgomery. They could do some good.

VOCABULARY

1. Find a word in paragraph 2 that means "corridor." _____

2. Find a word in paragraph 3 that means "in an intimidating or menacing way."

_____

3. What is the meaning of "fare" as it is used in paragraph 3?
   a. money in payment for transportation
   b. to travel
   c. to succeed at doing something

READING COMPREHENSION

1. This story took place in 1955, in Montgomery, Alabama. What was considered the "white" section of the bus, according to this text?

_____

2. What happened on the bus? What was the sequence of events? Number these events in the correct order.
   _____   Rosa got one of the last seats in the rear section of the bus.
   _____   The bus driver ordered Rosa to stand at the back of the bus.
   _____   A white man entered the bus.
   _1._   Rosa, tired after a long day of work, boarded the bus.
   _____   An officer placed Rosa under arrest.
   _____   Rosa refused to move from her seat.
   _____   The bus filled up, and some people stood at the back.

3. What offense was Rosa charged with? _____

DISCUSSION

1. Why did Rosa fight her case instead of just paying the fine? How did her simple act of refusing to move to the back of the bus change the United States?

2. Both "My Brother" and "Rosa Parks" have powerful messages. Which essay is more effective? Explain why.

3. Is it possible to stop racism and discrimination? Explain your answer. What can be done to create a racist-free society? List some steps.

Writing Tips

Transitional Words

When writing, it is important to signal your intentions. Transitional words serve as markers: the reader is given a signal that the sentence is concluding, contrasting, emphasizing or clarifying a point.

Below is a list of useful transitional words that can be used to emphasize a point or to contrast and show differences between ideas.

 ## WRITING TIPS EXERCISE

Read the following story and add one of the transitional words from the preceding chart in each space. There may be more than one choice.

Transitional Words: Contrast and Emphasize	
Useful words to show differences:	**Useful words when emphasizing something:**
but	in fact
yet	certainly
however	clearly
on the other hand	beyond a doubt
whereas	truly
on the contrary	to emphasize
still	surely
although	for example
in spite of (despite)	
even though	

1. Some criminals are experts in their field. Others, _____, are one card short of a full deck. _____ , there are literally hundreds of stupid criminal stories. _____ , read on about a pair of stupid criminals.

2. One day two fellows from Kentucky decided to rob a bank machine. _____ the bank machine was very large and heavy, and _____

they didn't have appropriate equipment, they decided to go ahead with the robbery. They would pull the front off the bank machine. _____ both you and I know that this is a risky operation, _____ these fellows decided to give it a try anyway.

3. First, they found a large iron chain. They threw the chain into the back of their pick-up truck. Then they drove to the bank when the sun had set. Under the cover of darkness, they took the large chain and placed the hook firmly on the bank machine. Then they attached the other end of the chain to their rear bumper. They got into the truck and hit the accelerator. There was a loud grinding noise: instead of removing the front of the cash machine, the bumper of their truck was pulled off. _____ this was a moment that required quick thinking, _____ these fellows simply panicked. They drove off, leaving the chain still attached to the bank machine, their bumper still attached to the chain, and their vehicle license plate still attached to the bumper.

Writing Suggestion

1. Write a paragraph or short essay about your personal hero. Try to use some transitional words.

2. Fill in the following missing person report. Write information about another student, but do not ask that student questions; simply observe him or her. This could also be done for homework, and the report could be made about a friend or family member. Use your dictionary if you are not sure about certain vocabulary.

Missing Person Report

_____	_____	_____
Family name	First name	Nickname
_____	_____	_____
Eye Color	Hair Color	Sex
_____	_____	_____
Height	Weight	Distinguishing features (mole, dimple, etc.)

Description of Clothing

_____

_____

_____

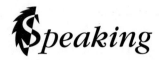 # *S*peaking

 ## SPEAKING EXERCISE ▪ SOMEONE I ADMIRE

Make a two- to three-minute presentation about someone you admire. It could be about a famous person or simply about a friend or relative. Structure your presentation in the following way, and use transitional words when appropriate.

Introduction (background information): Who is that person and where is he or she from? What is that person's history? What admirable qualities does that person have?

Body: Give one or two reasons for admiring that person. What specifically has that person done to deserve your respect? Give examples.

Conclusion: How has that person influenced your life? Make a suggestion to your audience, or make a prediction about that person.

If you present this to a group, other group members could ask you questions about the person that you admire.

ANSWERS TO VOCABULARY EXERCISE 1:

a. sideburns b. balding c. dimple d. mole e. collar f. stripes g. sleeve h. cuff i. checked
j. buttons k. dots l. whiskers m. bow tie n. wrinkles

10 Tabloid Culture

Modals are terms used for expressing ability (*can*), giving advice (*should*), making suggestions (*could*) and so on. Grammar Section 10 contains modals practice, and the ability to give advice and make suggestions is reinforced in this chapter. This chapter begins with a vocabulary exercise in which you are expected to come up with some polite telephone conversation sentences.

The main reading, "Tabloid Culture," is a little more difficult than previous readings, so it will provide you with a challenge. Note that there is a vocabulary list before the reading that you can consult. The Writing Tip contains guidelines on how to write a summary.

Vocabulary

The Telephone

VOCABULARY EXERCISE 1

With a partner, write down useful phrases in the spaces provided. Some suggested answers to this exercise are at the end of the chapter.

What should you say when:

1. you answer the phone and the speaker asks to speak to you? _____
   _____

2. you want to speak to someone? (Be polite.) _____
   _____

3. you want to leave a message? _____
   _____

4. you want to take a message? _____
   _____

5. you want the other speaker to wait? _____
   _____

VOCABULARY EXERCISE 2

Your teacher will leave some telephone messages for you. Write the message in the space provided.

Message 1. _____

_____

Message 2. _____

_____

Reading

PRE-READING VOCABULARY

Familiarize yourself with the following terms before reading the text. The number in parentheses indicates the paragraph where the word is found.

(1) *flee*	to run away from
(1) *come to grips with*	understand and accept
(3) *paparazzi*	tabloid photographers and writers
(3) *muttering*	speaking in a low voice
(4) *scope*	extent, reach, orbit
(5) *ironic, arched eyebrow way*	superior attitude
(6) *the fray*	the rest (referring to tabloid publications)

(7) *up to its neck in it*	completely immersed in it
(9) *gossip*	to divulge the secrets of others
(9) *creeping up*	slowly but surely progressing
(13) *feeble*	ineffective

Tabloid Culture

Reading 10.1 ## by Charles Gordon

In this reading, Charles Gordon explores our tabloid culture. This reading is slightly more difficult than previous readings.

1. Among the many unsettling images arising from the death of Diana is the image of us, reading the tabloids, looking at the pictures taken by men just like the men she was fleeing when her car crashed. Among the good things that may come out of the whole unhappy mess is an attempt by our society to come to grips with the nature and power of the media. While it is facile to say, as many did, that "we all killed her," because we all look at the tabloid headlines at the checkout counter, even if we don't actually buy the tabloids, it is true that our attitude towards those publications has been a lot more tolerant than it could have been.

2. At many levels. The week of Diana's funeral was also the week that the American shock specialist Howard Stern began broadcasting in Canada, heard on private radio stations in Toronto and Montreal, doing his own version of doo-doo and ca-ca jokes, with some anti-French remarks thrown in to mark the occasion.

3. Stern has an audience in the United States, probably one that overlaps substantially with the circulation of the tabloids for whom the paparazzi toil. There were a few halfhearted cries for government intervention and some muttering about the value systems of Canadian private broadcasters who give their best talk time over to American talk.

4. The story continues to play out. For the moment, its main contribution has been to further raise the profile of what might be called tabloid culture. All of a sudden, we are forced to take notice of the scope of the tabloids, the trashy talk shows on afternoon television, some of them moving into prime time with their sad panels of the colorfully dysfunctional and their angry finger-pointing audiences, the trash-talkers on radio and who knows what next?

5. The "we-are-all-guilty" argument owes something to the fact that there is a crossover of tabloid culture into the mainstream media. So-called respectable media keep the public informed, in an ironic, arched-eyebrow way, about what the tabloids are up to. When necessary, the irony is dropped in favor of a tut-tutting tone, the voice adopted when our newspapers displayed the silly headlines attacking the Royal Family's alleged failure to grieve properly.

6. This goes way back. When the wife of a Canadian prime minister dared consort with a known rock 'n' roll band back in the '70s, the story was reported by Canadian media mostly

in terms of what foreign media were saying. Since then, the so-called respectable media's flirtations with tabloid culture have become more overt. Not long ago, the respectable media adopted professional wrestling, a staple of tabloid culture, as just too cute for words, despite its closer resemblance to cheap theatre than to sport. In publications like *Spy* and *Vanity Fair*, polite society has its own elevated versions of the supermarket tabs. In Canada, we have *Frank* magazine, which at least does not pretend to be above the fray.

7   The point is that polite society is up to its neck in it. To an extent, this is nothing new. Gossip is not a new creation. That's a point made by people who are not particularly alarmed about what we have seen in the past few weeks. Gossip has always been with us; celebrities, from kings to movie stars to whatever Madonna is, have always been fascinating to the people of the world.

8   Even if you concede the truth of this argument, the hard fact is that there is simply a lot more of it around now. Writing about and photographing celebrities is big business now in a way that it never has been before. Anyone with the inclination and a TV set can know everything about every movie before it comes out, plus the complete romantic history, real or fabricated, of each of the main actors. Anybody with a couple of spare dollars at the supermarket checkout could learn, until a brief dawn of restraint broke over the tabloid world, every move Diana made and a lot she didn't.

9   We may have always had gossip, but we have not always had this. It has been creeping up gradually, until we suddenly wake up to find tabloid culture in full flower, if flower be the word for it.

10   Is there any significance that the creation of two cultures in our society parallels the development of two economies? By now we are aware that millions can be unemployed and thousands homeless, while others prosper as never before and build walls from behind which they are not compelled to view the less fortunate. They live, as we now know, in "gated communities," a less offensive way of saying that they have decided that walls can insulate them from responsibility for, and any contact with, people who are not like them.

11   So far the people behind the walls have more influence, and even command more votes, than those outside, which explains why nothing changes. Is it a stretch to see a parallel in the consumers of the respectable media taking refuge in the gated community of the CBC or PBS and the "quality" press, while all hell breaks loose on private television every afternoon, fake wrestling matches fill the halls and the paparazzi chase every face that looks vaguely familiar?

12   Do we, in other words, have a responsibility to come out from behind our walls and take a good look? Or can we simply laugh it off as something "other people" do?

13   Well, we are the other people, as the great philosopher Frank Zappa once said, his own way of saying what another great man once said, namely, that no man is an island. Having agreed upon that, the next step is harder. Regulation looks like a dead end. To say that our schools (the trainers of media consumers of the future) need to do better is true, but feeble. Maybe we can make a start by looking at tabloid culture and ceasing to be amused.

VOCABULARY

1. The word *unsettling* (para. 1), as it is used in the text, means: (circle one)
   a. disturbing and upsetting.
   b. puzzling or confusing.
   c. exciting, thrilling.

2. What is *tabloid culture?* (para. 4) _____
_____
_____

3. *The wife of a Canadian prime minister dared consort with a known rock 'n' roll band.* (para. 6) The "wife of a Canadian prime minister" is Margaret Trudeau, and the "known rock 'n' roll band" is the Rolling Stones. The phrase *dared consort with* means: (circle one)
   a. to carefully help.
   b. to boldly associate with.
   c. to easily leave with.

4. Find a word in paragraph 13 that means "stopping."_____

READING COMPREHENSION

1. Why does the narrator say that we all killed Princess Diana? How are we responsible for her death?
_____
_____

2. *So-called respectable media keep the public informed, in an ironic, arched-eyebrow way, about what the tabloids are up to.* (para. 5) Rewrite this sentence in simple English.
_____
_____

3. In paragraphs 10 to 12, the author compares the rich, in their gated communities, and the media. What is the author trying to say with this comparison?
_____
_____
_____
_____
_____

4. In the conclusion, what does the author suggest that we do?

_____

_____

_____

DISCUSSION

1. What should we all do to prevent journalists from harassing celebrities?

2. Why are people so interested in the tabloid press? Is it possible to stop "tabloid-style" reporting?

riting Tips

The Summary

When you summarize a text, you select only the most important points and restate them in your own words. In fact, an ability to summarize is important in both spoken and written English.

How to Summarize:

1. State the source. Always state the source of the information, preferably in the first sentence. If you are summarizing a text, identify the author and the title of the work that you are summarizing.

2. Select only the main, essential ideas. Your summary should mention points in the order in which they occurred. In other words, preserve the order and emphasis of the original work. Details that you consider insignificant can be excluded. Remember, a summary is an overall, global view of an article, a story, etc. Essential ideas include:
- the reason the article was written or the event occurred.
- repetitions of the same idea or theme.
- the most important ideas and events.
- the most important problems and/or solutions.

3. In summaries of written texts, use your own words! If you summarize an article, put any borrowed phrases in quotation marks. Not attributing quotes to the author is considered plagiarism.

4. Do not include your personal opinions. Strictly speaking, a summary is an overall view of an event or a text; personal opinions and observations should not be included. However, additional paragraphs with personal observations can be included if required for the assignment.

Find a text of about one page that interests you and then summarize it.

peaking

SPEAKING EXERCISE ▪ THE "SHOULD" GAME

Your teacher will assign you one of the following scenarios. With a partner, write a sentence explaining what you *could* do. (There are many possibilities for what you could do.) Then, explain what you *should* do; this should be something different than what you could do. Finally, write down what you really *would* do. After you and your partner have formulated and written down three sentences, your teacher will ask you to tell the class what your situation is and what you could, should and would do. (If necessary, refer to Grammar Section 10: Modals.)

For example, if the scenario is "Your best friend drives up and tells you that the car s/he is driving is stolen," a group of students might write:

> *We could go for a ride in the car.*
> *We should call the police and report our friend.*
> *We would probably tell our friend to stop acting crazy and get out of the car.*

The Scenarios

a. You have bicycled to a lake. You are skinny-dipping (swimming with no bathing suit) in a small lake. When you get out of the lake, you discover that someone or something has taken your clothing. There is a small town about one kilometer away.

b. A famous rock singer asks you to join his band. You really have no great musical ability, but you would love to work with this singer.

c. You are offered a fantastic, well-paying job on a small island near Indonesia. You must sign a five-year contract, and cannot return to visit your family and friends for those five years.

d. A rich person offers you $2 million to sleep with him or her.

e. You are walking along a frozen river-bank when you see a child in the distance scream and fall through the ice. There is no one else around.

f. You are in a bank when a man in disguise robs the bank. You recognize the man. He is a decent, but desperately poor, father.

g. You are in your girlfriend or boyfriend's house. Your friend leaves the room. His or her diary is lying on the desk and it is open. You notice that your name is written on the page.

h. You are in an expensive store when you accidentally knock over a very expensive glass sculpture. The sculpture shatters into hundreds of tiny pieces. There is a sign near the sculpture that says, "You break it, you pay for it." The store owner doesn't notice because he is just outside the front door. No one else sees you.

i. Your lover says that s/he is faithful to you. Your best friend tells you that your lover is a liar and is really dating other people.

j. You win a million dollars in a lottery and many of your friends ask you for money.

k. You are totally in love. Just before your wedding, your fiancé(e) mentions that s/he never wants children. You have always wanted to have at least two children. Somehow, this is a topic that you have never discussed with your partner before.

l. You are in an expensive restaurant. When you get the bill, you discover that the waiter forgot to include the fifty-dollar bottle of wine that you drank.

m. You find a white bag on the ground. The bag has no identification in it, but it is filled with about $5000 in small bills.

n. You go to a hairdresser. The hairdresser accidentally burns off a thick piece of your hair. You love your long hair.

o. You are driving on a highway, alone, when you see a man hitchhiking. The man is bleeding.

p. You are in a movie theater. You hate the smell of cigarette smoke. The person next to you lights up a cigarette. No one else complains.

ANSWERS TO VOCABULARY EXERCISE 1: (SUGGESTIONS)

1. Speaking.   2. May I please speak to ...   3. I would like to leave a message for ... *or* Could I please leave a message for ...   4. Could I take a message please? *or* Would you like to leave a message?   5. Could you please hold for a moment?

11 What We Need

Vocabulary	The Forces of Nature
Reading	"How Much Land Does a Man Need?" by Leo Tolstoy
Writing Tips	Correcting Writing Errors
Speaking	Role-Playing
Link to Grammar	Grammar Section 11: The Future Tenses

We live in a period of erratic and extreme weather conditions. Global warming, scientists say; the end of the world, doomsday believers shout. The vocabulary section of this chapter should expand your knowledge of weather-related terms. The next time you read an English paper, you will understand what a drought is.

The major essay in this chapter is a powerful story about human desire, written by the great author Leo Tolstoy. The Writing Tip gives you hints about correcting writing errors. This chapter ends with a speaking section.

Vocabulary

VOCABULARY EXERCISE ▪ THE FORCES OF NATURE

Match the vocabulary in column A with the definitions in column B. Write the letter of the correct definition next to the vocabulary word. Answers to this exercise are at the end of the chapter.

A. Weather Terms	B. Descriptions
1. *blizzard* _____	a. water that rises and spreads over land
2. *earthquake* _____	b. the entire sky is covered with clouds. The sun is not visible.
3. *drought* _____	c. mist in the air, like a cloud that is on the ground
4. *fog* _____	d. a flashing of light caused by atmospheric electricity
5. *flood* _____	e. a destructive whirling wind
6. *forecast* _____	f. hot and humid
7. *frost* _____	g. a loud sound that follows a flash of lightning
8. *hail* _____	h. a giant rise of water due to strong winds
9. *icicle* _____	i. a covering of ice crystals on a surface
10. *lightning* _____	j. a hanging piece of ice made from frozen dripping water
11. *muggy* _____	k. a movement of the earth's crust
12. *overcast* _____	l. a long period of dry weather
13. *thunder* _____	m. small balls of ice that fall from the clouds
14. *tidal wave* _____	n. prediction of weather conditions
15. *tornado* _____	o. a storm of blowing snow

Reading

PRE-READING VOCABULARY

Familiarize yourself with the following terms before reading the essay. The number in parentheses indicates the paragraph where the word is found.

(1) *peasant*	simple, poor farmer
(4) *colt*	a baby horse
(6) *5 cuts of a sickle made a sheaf*	5 cuts with a cutting tool makes a bunch
(9) *bustle*	busy atmosphere
(9) *to sow*	to plant
(31) *pasture cattle*	take cattle to grazing or feeding land
(32) *the dawn was breaking*	the sun was rising
(38) *spade*	digging tool
(43) *girdle*	wide belt
(59) *hillock*	rising piece of land

How Much Land Does a Man Need?
by Leo Tolstoy

The great Russian writer Leo Tolstoy wrote the masterpieces War and Peace *and* Anna Karenina. *Tolstoy, who lived from 1828 to 1910, wrote this story in 1886. In this tale, Tolstoy cleverly illustrates the necessity of setting boundaries on our own desires.*

1 There once was a peasant named Pahom who worked hard and honestly for his family, but who had no land of his own, so he always remained as poor as the next man. "Busy as we are from childhood tilling mother earth," he often thought, "we peasants will always die as we are living, with nothing of our own. If only we had our own land, it would be different."

2 Now, close to Pahom's village there lived a lady, a small landowner, who had an estate of about three hundred acres. One winter the news got about that the lady was going to sell her land. Pahom heard that a neighbor of his was buying fifty acres and that the lady had consented to accept one half in cash and to wait a year for the other half.

3 "Look at that," Pahom thought. "The land is being sold, and I shall get none of it." So he spoke to his wife. "Other people are buying it, and we must also buy twenty acres or so. Life is becoming impossible without land of our own."

4 So they put their heads together and considered how they could manage to buy it. They had one hundred rubles laid by. They sold a colt, and one half of their bees, hired out one of their sons as a laborer, and took his wages in advance. They borrowed the rest from a brother-in-law, and so scraped together half the purchase money. Having done this, Pahom chose a farm of forty acres, some of it wooded, and went to the lady and bought it.

5 So now Pahom had land of his own. He borrowed seed, and sowed it, and the harvest was a good one. Within a year he had managed to pay off his debts to the lady and his brother-in-law. So he became a landowner, plowing and sowing his own land, making hay on his own land, cutting his own trees, and feeding his cattle on his own pasture. When he went out to plow his fields, or to look at his growing corn, or at his meadows, his heart would fill with joy. The grass that grew and the flowers that bloomed there seemed to him unlike any that grew elsewhere. Formerly, when he had passed by that land, it had appeared the same as any other land, but now it seemed quite different.

6 Then one day Pahom was sitting at home when a peasant, passing through the village, happened to stop in. Pahom asked him where he came from, and the stranger answered that he came from beyond the Volga, where he had been working. One word led to another, and the man went on to say that much land was for sale there, and that many people were moving there to buy it. The land was so good, he said, that the rye sown on it grew as high as a horse, and so thick that five cuts of a sickle made a sheaf. One peasant, he said, had brought nothing with him but his bare hands, and now he had six horses and two cows of his own.

7   Pahom's heart was filled with desire. "Why should I suffer in this narrow hole," he thought, "if one can live so well elsewhere? I will sell my land and my homestead here, and with the money I will start fresh over there and get everything new."

8   So Pahom sold his land and homestead and cattle, all at a profit, and moved his family to the new settlement. Everything the peasant had told him was true, and Pahom was ten times better off than he had been. He bought plenty of arable land and pasture, and could keep as many head of cattle as he liked.

9   At first, in the bustle of building and settling down, Pahom was pleased with it all, but when he got used to it he began to think that even here he was not satisfied. He wanted to sow more wheat, but had not enough land of his own for the purpose, so he rented extra land for three years. The seasons turned out well and the crops were good, so that he began to lay money by. He might have gone on living comfortably, but he grew tired of having to rent other people's land every year, and having to scramble to pay for it.

10   "If it were all my own land," Pahom thought, "I should be independent, and there would not be all this unpleasantness."

11   Then one day a passing land dealer said he was just returning from the land of Bashkirs, far away, where he had bought thirteen thousand acres of land, all for only one thousand rubles.

12   "All one need do is to make friends with the chiefs," he said. "I gave away about one hundred rubles' worth of dressing gowns and carpets, besides a case of tea, and I gave wine to those who would drink it, and I got the land for less than twopence an acre."

13   "There now," thought Pahom, "out there I can get more than ten times as much land as I have now. I must try it."

14   So Pahom left his family to look after the homestead and started on the journey, taking his servant with him. They stopped at a town on their way, and bought a case of tea, some wine, and other presents, as the tradesman had advised him. On and on they went until they had gone more than three hundred miles, and on the seventh day they came to a place where the Bashkirs had pitched their tents.

15   As soon as they saw Pahom, they came out of their tents and gathered around their visitor. They gave him tea and kumiss, and had a sheep killed, and gave him mutton to eat. Pahom took presents out of his cart and distributed them, and told them he had come about some land. The Bashkirs seemed very glad, and told him he must talk to their chief about it. So they sent for him and explained to him why Pahom had come.

16   The chief listened for a while, then made a sign with his head for them to be silent, and addressing himself to Pahom, said:

17   "Well, let it be so. Choose whatever piece of land you like. We have plenty of it."

18   "And what will be the price?" asked Pahom.

19   "Our price is always the same: one thousand rubles a day."

20   Pahom did not understand.

21   "A day? What measure is that? How many acres would that be?"

22   "We do not know how to reckon it out," said the chief. "We sell it by the day. As much as you can go round on your feet in a day is yours, and the price is one thousand rubles a day."

23   Pahom was surprised.

24   "But in a day you can get round a large tract of land," he said.

25   The chief laughed.

26   "It will all be yours!" said he. "But there is one condition: if you don't return on the same day to the spot whence you started, your money is lost."

27   "But how am I to mark the way that I have gone?"

28   "Why, we shall go to any spot you like, and stay there. You must start from that spot and make your round, taking a spade with you. Wherever you think necessary, make a mark. At every turning, dig a hole and pile up the turf; then afterward we will go round with a plow from hole to hole. You may make as large a circuit as you please, but before the sun sets you must return to the place you started from. All the land you cover will be yours."

29   Pahom was delighted. It was decided to start early next morning. They talked a while, and after drinking some more kumiss and eating some more mutton, they had tea again, and then the night came on. They gave Pahom a featherbed to sleep on, and the Bashkirs dispersed for the night, promising to assemble the next morning at daybreak and ride out before sunrise to the appointed spot.

30   Pahom lay on the featherbed, but could not sleep. He kept thinking about the land.

31   "What a large tract I will mark off!" thought he. "I can easily do thirty-five miles in a day. The days are long now, and within a circuit of thirty-five miles what a lot of land there will be! I will sell the poorer land, or let it to peasants, but I'll pick out the best and farm it. I will buy two ox teams, and hire two more laborers. About a hundred and fifty acres shall be plow land, and I will pasture cattle on the rest."

32   Looking round he saw through the open door that the dawn was breaking.

33   "It's time to wake them up," thought he. "We ought to be starting."

34   He got up, roused his man (who was sleeping in his cart), bade him harness; and went to call the Bashkirs.

35   "It's time to go to the steppe to measure the land," he said.

36   The Bashkirs rose and assembled, and the chief came too. Then they began drinking kumiss again, and offered Pahom some tea, but he would not wait.

37   "If we are to go, let us go. It is high time," said he.

38   The Bashkirs got ready and they all started: some mounted on horses, and some in carts. Pahom drove in his own small cart with his servant, and took a spade with him. When they reached the steppe, the morning red was beginning to kindle. They ascended a hillock and, dismounting from their carts and their horses, gathered in one spot. The chief came up to Pahom and stretched out his arm toward the plain.

39   "See," said he, "all this, as far as your eye can reach, is ours. You may have any part of it you like."

40   Pahom's eyes glistened: it was all virgin soil, as flat as the palm of your hand, as black as the seed of a poppy, and in the hollows different kinds of grasses grew breast high.

41   The chief took off his fox fur cap, placed it on the ground and said:

42   "This will be the mark. Start from here, and return here again. All the land you go round shall be yours."

43   Pahom took out his money and put it on the cap. Then he took off his outer coat, remaining in his sleeveless undercoat. He unfastened his girdle and tied it tight below his stomach, put a little bag of bread into the breast of his coat, and tying a flask of water to his girdle, he drew up the tops of his boots, took the spade from his man, and stood ready to start. He considered for some moments which way he had better go—it was tempting everywhere.

44   "No matter," he concluded, "I will go toward the rising sun."

45   He turned his face to the east, stretched himself, and waited for the sun to appear above the rim.

46   "I must lose no time," he thought, "and it is easier walking while it is still cool."

47   The sun's rays had hardly flashed above the horizon, before Pahom, carrying the spade over his shoulder, went down into the steppe.

48   Pahom started walking neither slowly nor quickly. After having gone a thousand yards he stopped, dug a hole, and placed pieces of turf one on another to make it more visible. Then he went on; and now that he had walked off his stiffness he quickened his pace. After a while he dug another hole.

49   Pahom looked back. The hillock could be distinctly seen in the sunlight, with the people on it, and the glittering tires of the cart wheels. At a rough guess Pahom concluded that he had walked three miles. It was growing warmer; he took off his undercoat, flung it across his shoulder, and went on again. It had grown quite warm now; he looked at the sun, it was time to think of breakfast.

50   "The first shift is done, but there are four in a day, and it is too soon yet to turn. But I will just take off my boots," said he to himself.

51   He sat down, took off his boots, stuck them into his girdle, and went on. It was easy walking now.

52   "I will go on for another three miles," thought he, "and then turn to the left. This spot is so fine, that it would be a pity to lose it. The further one goes, the better the land seems."

53   He went straight on for a while, and when he looked round, the hillock was scarcely visible and the people on it looked like black ants, and he could just see something glistening there in the sun.

54   "Ah," thought Pahom, "I have gone far enough in this direction, it is time to turn. Besides I am in a regular sweat, and very thirsty."

55   He stopped, dug a large hole, and heaped up pieces of turf. Next he untied his flask, had a drink, and then turned sharply to the left. He went on and on; the grass was high, and it was very hot.

56   Pahom began to grow tired: he looked at the sun and saw that it was noon.

57   "Well," he thought, "I must have a rest."

58   He sat down, and ate some bread and drank some water; but he did not lie down, thinking that if he did he might fall asleep. After sitting a little while, he went on again. At

first he walked easily: the food had strengthened him; but it had become terribly hot, and he felt sleepy; still he went on, thinking: "An hour to suffer, a lifetime to live."

59   He went a long way in this direction also, and was about to turn to the left again, when he perceived a damp hollow: "It would be a pity to leave that out," he thought. "Flax would do well there." So he went on past the hollow, and dug a hole on the other side of it before he turned the corner. Pahom looked toward the hillock. The heat made the air hazy: it seemed to be quivering, and through the haze the people on the hillock could scarcely be seen.

60   "Ah!" thought Pahom, "I have made the sides too long; I must make this one shorter." And he went along the third side, stepping faster. He looked at the sun: it was nearly halfway to the horizon, and he had not yet done two miles of the third side of the square. He was still ten miles from the goal.

61   "No," he thought, "though it will make my land lopsided, I must hurry back in a straight line now. I might go too far, and as it is I have a great deal of land."

62   So Pahom hurriedly dug a hole, and turned straight toward the hillock.

63   Pahom went straight toward the hillock, but he now walked with difficulty. He was done up with the heat, his bare feet were cut and bruised, and his legs began to fail. He longed to rest, but it was impossible if he meant to get back before sunset. The sun waits for no man, and it was sinking lower and lower.

64   "Oh dear," he thought, "if only I have not blundered trying for too much! What if I am too late?"

65   He looked toward the hillock and at the sun. He was still far from his goal, and the sun was already near the rim.

66   Pahom walked on and on; it was very hard walking, but he went quicker and quicker. He pressed on, but was still far from the place. He began running, threw away his coat, his boots, his flask, and his cap, and kept only the spade which he used as a support.

67   "What shall I do," he thought again. "I have grasped too much, and ruined the whole affair. I can't get there before the sun sets."

68   And this fear made him still more breathless. Pahom went on running, his soaking shirt and trousers stuck to him, and his mouth was parched. His breast was working like a blacksmith's bellows, his heart was beating like a hammer, and his legs were giving way as if they did not belong to him. Pahom was seized with terror lest he should die of the strain.

69   Though afraid of death, he could not stop. "After having run all that way they will call me a fool if I stop now," thought he. And he ran on and on, and drew near and heard the Bashkirs yelling and shouting to him, and their cries inflamed his heart still more. He gathered his last strength and ran on.

70   The sun was close to the rim, and cloaked in mist looked large, and red as blood. Now, yes now, it was about to set! The sun was quite low, but he was also quite near his aim. Pahom could already see the people on the hillock waving their arms to hurry him up. He could see the fox fur cap on the ground, and the money on it, and the chief sitting on the ground holding his sides.

71   "There is plenty of land," thought he, "but will God let me live on it? I have lost my life, I have lost my life! I shall never reach that spot!"

72   Pahom looked at the sun, which had reached the earth; one side of it had already disappeared. With all his remaining strength he rushed on, bending his body forward so that his legs could hardly follow fast enough to keep him from falling. Just as he reached the hillock it suddenly grew dark. He looked up—the sun had already set! He gave a cry: "All my labor has been in vain," thought he, and was about to stop, but he heard the Bashkirs still shouting, and remembered that though to him, from below, the sun seemed to have set, they on the hillock could still see it. He took a long breath and ran up the hillock. It was still light there. He reached the top and saw the cap. Before it sat the chief laughing and holding his sides. Pahom uttered a cry: his legs gave way beneath him, he fell forward and reached the cap with his hands.

73   "Ah, that's a fine fellow!" exclaimed the chief. "He has gained much land!"

74   Pahom's servant came running up and tried to raise him, but he saw that blood was flowing from his mouth. Pahom was dead!

75   The Bashkirs clicked their tongues to show their pity.

76   His servant picked up the spade and dug a grave long enough for Pahom to lie in, and buried him in it. Six feet from his head to his heels was all he needed.

VOCABULARY

1. *Tilling* (para. 1), as it is used in the text, means: (circle one)
   a. a drawer for money.
   b. to destroy the land.
   c. to work the land by planting, raising and plowing crops.

2. *Acre* (para. 2), as it is used in the text, means: (circle one)
   a. a measurement.
   b. a piece of land that is about 2047 square meters.
   c. the land that a house sits on.

3. What is a *ruble*? (para. 4) _____

4. Find a word in paragraph 5 that means "the act of turning over soil using a large farming tool." _____

5. Find a word in paragraph 8 that means "many cows." _____

6. What is a *grave*? (para. 76)
   a. something serious
   b. a dangerous game
   c. a burial hole (for dead bodies)

READING COMPREHENSION

What happens to Pahom? Summarize the story in about ten sentences. Use a separate sheet of paper. (See rules for summarizing in Chapter 10's Writing Tips.)

DISCUSSION

1. How much land did Pahom really need?

2. What is the moral of this story?

 # Writing Tips

Correcting Writing Errors

Keep a copybook or duotang with your most common writing errors. After each writing test, you should add to the copybook. During subsequent tests, you should consult your Writing Errors copybook during the editing process. The hope is that you will not continue to repeat the same errors.

The book should have the following elements.

Part 1: Spelling list

On the first few pages of your copybook, list all your spelling errors. Indicate how you usually spell the word and then write the correct spelling of the word. You can add words to this list after each writing assignment. In some cases, if you are unclear about the meaning of a misspelled word, you could add the meaning too, or you could write a short sentence where the word is used correctly.

If you persist in misspelling some words even after they have been included on this list, highlight those words in yellow.

	SPELLING LIST	
INCORRECT SPELLING	CORRECT SPELLING	MEANING OR EXAMPLE
whut	with	
realy	really	
	their	That is their car.
	they're	they are
shure	sure	

Part 2: Rules and examples

Look at the type of error you make most frequently, and write a rule, in your own words, that explains what the problem is. Then add example(s) from your text to illustrate the error. If you don't know why something is wrong, you could ask your teacher. You could also look in the Grammar Section of this book; each Grammar Section contains rules and examples.

After your teacher corrects and returns each writing assignment, add at least one grammar rule (with examples) to your errors copybook.

> _Sept. 11_
>
> Problem: SV (subject-verb agreement)
> Rule: Always add "s" to simple present tense verbs that refer to he, she or it.
> Examples: ⇒ She always complains about her schedule.
>   ⇒ The woman has several children.
>
> _Sept. 30_
>
> Problem: More SV agreement
> Rule: Do not add "s" to verbs that follow plural subjects!
> Example: They (wants) more money. ⇒ They want
>
> Problem: Verb tense (ing)
> Rule: When an action is a fact, do not use the "ing" form. Use the simple present.
> Example: I (am always trying) to finish the work. ⇒ I always try to ...

Speaking

SPEAKING EXERCISE ▪ ROLE-PLAYING

Role-play the following scenarios. Some of you will be given the A roles and some will be given the B roles. For example, the student who reads the A3 role is paired up with someone who reads the B3 role.

You should read only your own role, and you should close your book after understanding your role.

A1. (2 students) You are a couple. You love your car. It is new, and you both have worked for years in order to buy this car. You do not like to lend it.

A2. (2 students: one is a shoe salesperson and one is the manager) You work in a shoe store. A customer wants to return some shoes, but the customer bought the shoes two months ago. All shoes must be returned within thirty days. You refuse to exchange the shoes or refund the money.

A3. (2 or 3 students) You have mice in your apartment. Demand that the landlord (the building owner) remove them!

A4. (2 students) You lost your dog a month ago. While walking on the street, you notice some people walking your dog! Politely ask the people to give you back your dog. (Plan a name for your dog.)

B1. (1 or 2 students) You need to drive 100 kilometers to get your parents. Your father is old and he wants to visit you, but he can't walk, so you have offered to pick him up in a car. Ask your dearest, best friends if you can borrow their car.

B2. (2 students: a woman who wants to return shoes, and her mother) You bought an eighty-dollar pair of shoes. The leather is changing color. Demand a refund. The leather is becoming yellow.

B3. (2 students) You are the owners of a building. The tenants in one apartment complain about mice, but your building is perfectly clean. You think that the tenants brought in the mice; they just want their rent to be reduced. Be firm. Do not let the tenants take advantage of you!

B4. (3 students: two humans and one dog) You are walking your dog. You bought your dog from a pet store two months ago. You love your dog.

ANSWERS TO VOCABULARY EXERCISE:
1. o   2. k   3. l   4. c   5. a   6. n   7. i   8. m   9. j   10. d   11. f   12. b   13. g   14. h   15. e

12 The Magic Thread

Because this is the last chapter in the book, the writing and speaking sections will provide you with a review of the opinion essay and oral presentations.

The reading in this chapter is an interesting old fairy tale. This fairy tale is not only an interesting story, but it has a simple and powerful message. Because this tale is the last story in the book, you will not be given a pre-reading vocabulary list. Instead, try to understand the reading as best you can, and answer the questions that follow it. Good luck!

 Reading

Reading 12.1 ## The Magic Thread

Too often we are impatient. We plan for the future without fully appreciating the present. Benjamin Franklin said, "He that can have patience, can have what he will." This old fairy tale illustrates the truth of those words. Before reading this story, make sure that you understand the meaning of the word thread.

1   Once there was a widow who had a son called Peter. He was a strong, able boy, but he did not enjoy going to school and he was forever daydreaming.

2   "Peter, what are you dreaming about this time?" his teacher would say to him.

3   "I'm thinking about what I'll be when I grow up," Peter replied.

4   "Be patient. There's plenty of time for that. Being grown up isn't all fun, you know," his teacher said.

5   But Peter found it hard to enjoy whatever he was doing at the moment, and was always hankering after the next thing. In winter he longed for it to be summer again, and in summer he looked forward to the skating, sledding, and warm fires of winter. At school he would long for the day to be over so that he could go home, and on Sunday nights he would sigh, "If only the holidays would come." What he enjoyed most was playing with his friend Liese. She was as good a companion as any boy, and no matter how impatient Peter was, she never took offense. "When I grow up, I shall marry Liese," Peter said to himself.

6   Often he wandered through the forest, dreaming of the future. Sometimes he lay down on the soft forest floor in the warm sun, his hands behind his head, staring up at the sky through the distant treetops. One hot afternoon as he began to grow sleepy, he heard someone calling his name. He opened his eyes and sat up. Standing before him was an old woman. In her hand she held a silver ball, from which dangled a silken golden thread.

7   "See what I have got here, Peter," she said, offering the ball to him.

8   "What is it?" he asked curiously, touching the fine golden thread.

9   "This is your life thread," the old woman replied. "Do not touch it and time will pass normally. But if you wish time to pass more quickly, you have only to pull the thread a little way and an hour will pass like a second. But I warn you, once the thread has been pulled out, it cannot be pushed back in again. It will disappear like a puff of smoke. The ball is for you. But if you accept my gift you must tell no one, or on that very day you shall die. Now, say, do you want it?"

10 Peter seized the gift from her joyfully. It was just what he wanted. He examined the silver ball. It was light and solid, made of a single piece. The only flaw in it was the tiny hole from which the bright thread hung. He put the ball in his pocket and ran home. There, making sure that his mother was out, he examined it again. The thread seemed to be creeping very slowly out of the ball, so slowly that it was scarcely noticeable to the naked eye. He longed to give it a quick tug, but dared not do so. Not yet.

11 The following day at school, Peter sat daydreaming about what he would do with his magic thread. The teacher scolded him for not concentrating on his work. If only, he thought, it was time to go home. Then he felt the silver ball in his pocket. If he pulled out a tiny bit of thread, the day would be over. Very carefully he took hold of it and tugged. Suddenly the teacher was telling everyone to pack up their books and to leave the classroom in an orderly fashion. Peter was overjoyed. He ran all the way home. How easy life would be now! All his troubles were over. From that day forth he began to pull the thread, just a little, every day.

12 One day, however, it occurred to him that it was stupid to pull the thread just a little each day. If he gave it a harder tug, school would be over altogether. Then he could start learning

a trade and marry Liese. So that night he gave the thread a hard tug, and in the morning he awoke to find himself apprenticed to a carpenter in town. He loved his new life, clambering about on roofs and scaffolding, lifting and hammering great beams into place that still smelled of the forest. But sometimes, when payday seemed too far off, he gave the thread a little tug and suddenly the week was drawing to a close and it was Friday night and he had money in his pocket.

13   Liese had also come to town and was living with her aunt, who taught her housekeeping. Peter began to grow impatient for the day when they would be married. It was hard to live so near and yet so far from her. He asked her when they could be married.

14   "In another year," she said. "Then I will have learned how to be a capable wife."

15   Peter fingered the silver ball in his pocket.

16   "Well, the time will pass quickly enough," he said, knowingly.

17   That night Peter could not sleep. He tossed and turned restlessly. He took the magic ball from under his pillow. For a moment he hesitated; then his impatience got the better of him, and he tugged at the golden thread. In the morning he awoke to find that the year was over and that Liese had at last agreed to marry him. Now Peter felt truly happy.

18   But before their wedding could take place, Peter received an official-looking letter. He opened it in trepidation and read that he was expected to report at the army barracks the following week for two years' military service. He showed the letter to Liese in despair.

19   "Well," she said, "there is nothing for it, we shall just have to wait. But the time will pass quickly, you'll see. There are so many things to do in preparation for our life together."

20   Peter smiled bravely, knowing that two years would seem a lifetime to him.

21   Once Peter had settled into life at the barracks, however, he began to feel that it wasn't so bad after all. He quite enjoyed being with all the other young men, and their duties were not very arduous at first. He remembered the old woman's warning to use the thread wisely and for a while refrained from pulling it. But in time he grew restless again. Army life bored him with its routine duties and harsh discipline. He began pulling the thread to make the week go faster so that it would be Sunday again, or to speed up the time until he was due for leave. And so the two years passed almost as if they had been a dream.

22   Back home, Peter determined not to pull the thread again until it was absolutely necessary. After all, this was the best time of his life, as everyone told him. He did not want it to be over too quickly. He did, however, give the thread one or two very small tugs, just to speed along the day of his marriage. He longed to tell Liese his secret, but he knew that if he did he would die.

23   On the day of his wedding, everyone, including Peter, was happy. He could hardly wait to show Liese the house he had built for her. At the wedding feast he glanced over at his mother. He noticed for the first time how gray her hair had grown recently. She seemed to be aging so quickly. Peter felt a pang of guilt that he had pulled the thread so often. Henceforward he would be much more sparing with it and only use it when it was strictly necessary.

24   A few months later Liese announced that she was going to have a child. Peter was overjoyed and could hardly wait. When the child was born, he felt that he could never want

for anything again. But whenever the child was ill or cried through the sleepless night, he gave the thread a little tug, just so that the baby might be well and happy again.

25   Times were hard. Business was bad and a government had come to power that squeezed the people dry with taxes and would tolerate no opposition. Anyone who became known as a troublemaker was thrown into prison without trial and rumor was enough to condemn a man. Peter had always been known as one who spoke his mind, and very soon he was arrested and cast into jail. Luckily he had his magic ball with him and he tugged very hard at the thread. The prison walls dissolved before him and his enemies were scattered in the huge explosion that burst forth like thunder. It was the war that had been threatening, but it was over as quickly as a summer storm, leaving behind it an exhausted peace. Peter found himself back home with his family. But now he was a middle-aged man.

26   For a time things went well and Peter lived in relative contentment. One day he looked at his magic ball and saw to his surprise that the thread had turned from gold to silver. He looked in the mirror. His hair was starting to turn gray and his face was lined where before there had not been a wrinkle to be seen. He suddenly felt afraid and determined to use the thread even more carefully than before. Liese bore him more children and he seemed happy as the head of his growing household. His stately manner often made people think of him as some sort of benevolent ruler. He had an air of authority as if he held the fate of others in his hands. He kept his magic ball in a well-hidden place, safe from the curious eyes of his children, knowing that if anyone were to discover it, it would be fatal.

27   As the number of his children grew, so his house became more overcrowded. He would have to extend it, but for that he needed money. He had other worries too. His mother was looking older and more tired every day. It was of no use to pull the magic thread because that would only hasten her approaching death. All too soon she died, and as Peter stood at her graveside, he wondered how it was that life passed so quickly, even without pulling the magic thread.

28   One night as he lay in bed, kept awake by his worries, he thought how much easier life would be if all his children were grown up and launched upon their careers in life. He gave the thread a mighty tug, and the following day he awoke to find that his children had all left home for jobs in different parts of the country, and that he and his wife were alone. His hair was almost white now and often his back and limbs ached as he climbed the ladder or lifted a heavy beam into place. Liese too was getting old and she was often ill. He couldn't bear to see her suffer, so that more and more he resorted to pulling at the magic thread. But as soon as one trouble was solved, another seemed to grow in its place. Perhaps life would be easier if he retired, Peter thought. Then he would no longer have to clamber about on drafty, half-completed buildings and he could look after Liese when she was ill. The trouble was that he didn't have enough money to live on. He picked up his magic ball and looked at it. To his dismay he saw that the thread was no longer silver but gray and lusterless. He decided to go for a walk in the forest to think things over.

29   It was a long time since he had been in that part of the forest. The small saplings had all grown into tall fir trees, and it was hard to find the path he had once known. Eventually he

came to a bench in a clearing. He sat down to rest and fell into a light doze. He was woken by someone calling his name, "Peter! Peter!"

30   He looked up and saw the old woman he had met so many years ago when she had given him the magic silver ball with its golden thread. She looked just as she had on that day, not a day older. She smiled at him.

31   "So, Peter, have you had a good life?" she asked.

32   "I'm not sure," Peter said. "Your magic ball is a wonderful thing. I have never had to suffer or wait for anything in my life. And yet it has all passed so quickly. I feel that I have had no time to take in what has happened to me, neither the good things nor the bad. Now there is so little time left. I dare not pull the thread again for it will only bring me to my death. I do not think your gift has brought me luck."

33   "How ungrateful you are!" the old woman said. "In what way would you have wished things to be different?"

34   "Perhaps if you had given me a different ball, one where I could have pushed the thread back in as well as pulling it out. Then I could have relived the things that went badly."

35   The old woman laughed. "You ask a great deal! Do you think that God allows us to live our lives twice over? But I can grant you one final wish, you foolish, demanding man."

36   "What is that?" Peter asked.

37   "Choose," the old woman said. Peter thought hard.

38   At length he said, "I should like to live my life again as if for the first time, but without your magic ball. Then I will experience the bad things as well as the good without cutting them short, and at least my life will not pass as swiftly and meaninglessly as a daydream."

39   "So be it," said the old woman. "Give me back my ball."

40   She stretched out her hand and Peter placed the silver ball in it. Then he sat back and closed his eyes with exhaustion.

41   When he awoke he was in his own bed. His youthful mother was bending over him, shaking him gently.

42   "Wake up, Peter. You will be late for school. You were sleeping like the dead!"

43   He looked up at her in surprise and relief.

44   "I've had a terrible dream, Mother. I dreamed that I was old and sick and that my life had passed like the blinking of an eye with nothing to show for it. Not even any memories."

45   His mother laughed and shook her head.

46   "That will never happen," she said. "Memories are the one thing we all have, even when we are old. Now hurry and get dressed. Liese is waiting for you and you will be late for school."

47   As Peter walked to school with Liese, he noticed what a bright summer morning it was, the kind of morning when it felt good to be alive. Soon he would see his friends and classmates, and even the prospect of lessons didn't seem so bad. In fact he could hardly wait.

VOCABULARY

1. What is a *widow*? (para. 1)_____

2. Find a word in paragraph 5 that means "long for or wish for." _____

3. The word *flaw*, in paragraph 10, means:
   a. piece of string.
   b. light.
   c. blemish or defect.

4. *He gave the thread a hard tug.* (para. 12) What is a synonym (a word that means the same thing) for *tug*? _____

READING COMPREHENSION

1. How was the silver ball of thread "magic"? _____
   _____

2. Why did Peter initially want time to pass quickly? _____
   _____
   _____

3. Why did Peter keep pulling the thread more and more? Why didn't he just put it away?
   _____
   _____

4. When did Peter first realize that he was missing some of the good things in life by pulling the thread? (*Hint*: Look at the wedding scene.) _____
   _____
   _____

5. Write a short character description of Peter. What type of person is he? What is he like at the beginning of the story? How does he change? Write about three or four sentences.
   _____
   _____
   _____
   _____
   _____
   _____

6. What is the moral of "The Magic Thread"?_____
   _____
   _____

DISCUSSION

1. How does the story end? Was it all a dream? Did the old woman really give him a silver ball?

2. When does time seem to move quickly? When does it move slowly? Does it seem to move more quickly as you get older? Why do you think this is?

3. Many young children wish time would pass quickly ("Oh, when I only finish my schooling") and many older people wish they could turn back time ("If I could only be young again"). What does this short story teach all of us?

Writing Tips

Opinion Essay Review

This is a review of all the opinion essay writing tips.

Before you begin your opinion essay, you should make an **essay plan**. Make sure that your essay is well-structured. Your completed essay should have the following elements:

1. *Introduction:* Your introduction should get the attention of the reader. If you simply list the reasons for your opinion in the introduction, you take the punch out of your essay. Try to introduce your topic in a creative and interesting way. Making a controversial statement is one way to get the reader's attention. You could also begin your essay with a short anecdote, or you could give background information about your subject.

Your introduction should contain an **opinion statement** that expresses your point of view.

2. *Body:* A good **topic sentence** introduces the subject of each paragraph in the body of the essay. Each paragraph should contain **supporting facts or examples**. The body paragraphs should provide supporting reasons for your main opinion. Guide the reader through your ideas with transitional words or phrases.

3. *Conclusion:* The conclusion should give no new information. Instead, remind the reader of your main opinion and main supporting points. You could end your conclusion with a final suggestion or prediction.

Correct Your Errors: Before you hand in your essays, carefully reread them. Check them for your "typical" errors. Record your spelling mistakes and your most common grammatical problems in a copybook or list, and refer to those errors. Try to stop repeating the same old mistakes!

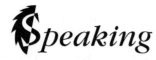Speaking

Oral Presentation Tips

There are a few points to remember when you make an oral presentation.

Structure Your Presentation: Your oral presentation should be clearly structured, with an introduction, your main points, and a conclusion that brings your presentation to a satisfactory closing.

Don't Read: When you come to class, be prepared to speak to the audience. Do not read your presentation, as it is very boring for the audience.

- **Use cue cards**. Prepare your assignment in advance. First, you should make an outline. Then, on your cue cards, write down main words for your introduction, your arguments, and your conclusion.
- **Do not write down every word of your text on the cue cards**. You only refer to your cue cards to remind you of your points. If your entire text is written on the cards, you will need to hunt for information, which will distract your audience. You should not have any breaks in the flow of your presentation.

For example, if the first point in your argument is this:

> Hockey players are now able to get away with grabbing, hooking (when the end of the stick is used to trip the player) and nasty checking (when an elbow or stick gets involved in the ramming of someone against the boards). This violence has meant that the games are no longer as interesting as they were in the past. Almost every week, one of the better players gets injured and has to sit out the game. This means that the elite players can't demonstrate their skill on the ice.

then your cue card will look like this:

```
1st point
Hockey players      - grabbing
                    - hooking
                    - nasty checking
Games less interesting
Weekly, better players get hurt
Can't demonstrate skill
```

REHEARSE: Rehearse your presentation! Your teacher will not be impressed if you must frequently pause to think of something to say.

QUESTIONS: If you are required to ask questions during an oral presentation, study the typical question forms. Memorize some common question auxiliaries. You should be able to ask questions in the following tenses, and questions should have the following structure:

	Question Word(s)	Auxiliary	Subject	Verb
Present tense	What	do	you	want?
	When	does	that nurse	work?
be	Who	is	she?	
Past tense	Where	did	that event	happen?
	Why	did	you	leave?
be	Why	was	he	late?
Future tense	When	will	we	meet again?
	Where	are	you	going to live?

Good luck!

Be / Pronouns

This grammar section looks at the verb *be*. This verb is seemingly simple to use and conjugate, yet it isn't always easily translatable. For example, while French speakers "have hunger," English speakers "are hungry." Pay particular attention to ways in which the English use of *be* differs from your language's use of *be*.

This section also provides you with a basic review of pronoun forms. Pronouns are simply words that substitute for nouns. Some English pronoun forms will require getting used to. For example, the possessive pronoun forms *his* and *her* often get misused by French and Spanish speakers. Carefully try these exercises to improve your use of pronoun forms.

Like all grammar sections in this book, there is a short Vocabulary Boost at the start of the section. These exercises review general vocabulary. In this section, the Vocabulary Boost focuses on home and office tools.

The section ends with a communication activity that reinforces the "tools" vocabulary. This activity also gives you a chance to practice forming questions with the verb *be*.

VOCABULARY BOOST	Home and Office Tools

These are common tools found in both the home and the office.

nail	a thin, sharp piece of metal that is pounded into objects to fasten them together.
saw	a tool with a long metal blade. The blade has many sharp "teeth" and it is used for cutting through wood, etc.
magnifying glass	a hand-held device containing a convex glass. When you look through the glass, the size of objects appears enlarged.
nut	a small block of metal that has a hole in it, with grooves inside the hole

bolt	a small metal object with a thread of metal that winds down it. This has a flat end, unlike a screw, which has a pointed end. A bolt fits into a nut.
glue	sticky substance used for bonding paper objects together
tack	a metal object with a flat, round head and a short, pointed end. This is mainly used to fasten paper to a soft wood or cork board.
pin	a long, very thin piece of metal with a pointed end and a tiny, rounded head. This is mainly used to hold pieces of cloth together.
paper clip	a long piece of wire twisted into oblong shapes. This is used to fasten pieces of paper together without puncturing the paper.
staple	a small, U-shaped piece of metal used to fasten papers together
stapler	a hand-held device containing many staples. This device forces a staple through paper and then bends the end of the staple so that the paper is fastened together.

EXERCISE 1

Write the name of the object directly under each picture.

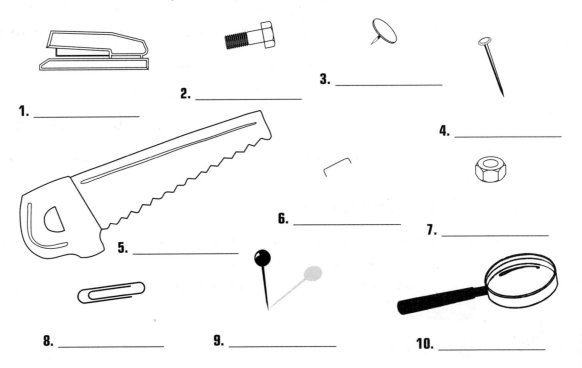

1. _____

2. _____

3. _____

4. _____

5. _____

6. _____

7. _____

8. _____

9. _____

10. _____

Be

The verb *be* is used when we want to identify:

age	He is 40 years old. (Never use *has* to depict age!)
hunger and thirst	Ellen is thirsty and I am hungry.
size and shape	Fred is 175 cm tall.

temperature   It is very cold and rainy outside. It is never warm at this time of year.
condition, mood   Mark is sick. He is unhappy about it.

Do not use *be* to express agreement.   Incorrect: *I am agree.*
                                          Correct: *I agree.*

CLASS EXERCISE

With a partner, fill in the blanks below. Write the proper form of the verb *be* next to each of the following pronouns.

> When you add *not* to the verb *be*, you sometimes have more than one way to make the contraction. Remember, you can only make one contraction at a time in contractions with *not*. Either contract the subject and the verb, or contract the verb and *not*.

	Subject Pronoun	*Be*	Contraction	Contraction with *not*
1.	I	_____	_____	*I'm not* _____
2.	You	_____	*You're*	_____
3.	He	_____	_____	*He's not* OR *He isn't* _____
4.	She	*is*	_____	_____
5.	It	_____	*It's*	_____
6.	We	_____	_____	*We're not* OR *We aren't* _____
7.	They	*are*	_____	_____

Subject Pronouns

Subject pronouns replace the subject in a sentence.

> *Diego is busy.* **He** *is writing a report.*

> *He* is a subject pronoun, and replaces "Diego."

EXERCISE 2

A *noun* is a person, place or thing.

The *subject* tells you who or what the sentence is about, and the subject is usually at the beginning of the sentence.

The *verb* is the action word.

Circle the subject and underline the verb. Then write the subject pronoun in the space provided and make the verb negative.

Example: (Mr. Brando) is very friendly.   *He isn't OR He is not* _____

1. Gene and Marie are great dancers.   _____

2. The book is beside the fireplace.   _____

3. Wolves are monogamous.   _____

4. The pencils are in my pencil-case.   _____

5. Betty is too busy these days.   _____

EXERCISE 3

Write the correct form of the verb *be* in the space provided.

Example: The boys ____*are*____ in bed.

1. The tin cans _____ in the recycling box.

2. My twin sisters _____ both sick today.

3. The doctor _____ in her office every Saturday.

4. My neighbours _____ very friendly.

5. Mr. Heath's fence _____ old and broken.

6. I _____ very excited about my promotion.

7. You _____ a great student.

8. My stepsister and I _____ very good buddies.

Be: Question Form

Verb *be*: When making a question, change the word order so that *be* appears *before* the subject.

Ellen (**is**) thirsty.   (**Is**) Ellen thirsty?

                              Why **is** Ellen thirsty?

EXERCISE 4

Write a yes/no question for each of the following sentences and change the subject into a subject pronoun.

Example: The music is too loud. _Is **it** too loud?_

1. The children are asleep. _____

2. My grandmother is 67 years old. _____

3. Ken and Rita are very annoying. _____

4. That plate is very dirty. _____

5.. Karen and I are late. _____

There is / There are

There is means "il y a" in French or "hay" in Spanish. Note the following:

There **is** [one thing].   There **are** [two or more things].

EXERCISE 5

Put *there is* or *there are* in the space provided.

Example: ___*There are*___ a dozen eggs in the carton.

1. _____ many boys in the club.

2. _____ one tomato left.

3. _____ two books on the shelf.

4. _____ a can of beans on the kitchen counter.

5. _____ a blue box in the closet.

Write five sentences describing what is in your schoolbag. Use "there is" or "there are."

_____

_____

_____

_____

_____

This / That / These / Those

This and *these* are used to refer to people and things that are physically close to the speaker. *That* and *those* are used to refer to things that are physically distant from the speaker.

Near: *This* [one thing]   *These* [many things]
Far: *That* [one thing]   *Those* [many things]

EXERCISE 6

Write *this*, *that*, *these* or *those* in the space provided.

1. Look at _____ shoes that I'm wearing.

2. What is _____ thing in the sky over there?

3. What are _____ red dots on my hands?

4. What is _____ man doing over there, across the parking lot?

5. Look at _____ new purse that I am carrying. Isn't it nice?

6. Look out the window. _____ people are marching in the parking lot.

Object Pronouns

Sentences have subjects (the actor) and objects (the thing affected by the action). Pronouns can replace the object of a sentence. The words in italics are object pronouns:

Example: Clara gave *me* some advice. She didn't give *him* any advice.

I	*me*	it	*it*
you	*you*	we	*us*
he	*him*	they	*them*
she	*her*		

EXERCISE 7

Replace the words in italics with an object pronoun.

Example: I will return the *video cassette*.   _____*it*_____

1. Please give that disk to *Audrey*.   _____

2. When will you see *the Swains* next?   _____

3. There is mail for *you and me*.   _____

4. Marnie wants to visit *her parents*.   _____

5. Alfred has a gift for *his father*.   _____

6. Aldo wants to speak to (*I*).   _____

7. Natalia always makes *the bed*.   _____

8. Please put *those dishes* away.   _____

Possessive Adjectives

Possessive adjectives describe a noun and appear before the noun that they describe. These adjectives indicate possession.

Remember:

When something belongs to a female, always use *her* "thing."

When something belongs to a male, always use *his* "thing."

The possessive adjectives are:

I	*my*	it	*its*
you	*your*	we	*our*
he	*his*	they	*their*
she	*her*		

EXERCISE 8

PART 1: Draw a line from the subject to the possessive adjective. Notice that possessive adjectives relate to *the person who possesses*, not to the object that is possessed. The possessive adjectives are in italics.

Example: Kelly visited *her* parents with *her* brother.

1. Joey canceled *his* date with *his* new girlfriend.

2. Maria took *her* dog, Toby, to the vet to get *his* shots.

3. Anna and Ted don't think that *their* new television is very good.

4. You should finish *your* supper before you go outside.

5. Cali is leaving *her* husband and moving into *her* new house. Her husband is staying in *their* old house.

PART 2: Put *their, they're* or *there* in the spaces.

their	possessive adjective
they're	they are (contraction)
there	at that place; not here

Note: *There* is also used at the beginning of a sentence to indicate that something does or does not exist, e.g., *There are no eggs left.*

6. The boys have to clean _____ room today. _____ is too much junk on the floor and on the beds. _____ grandparents are coming to visit and _____ going to sleep in the boys' room. The boys love _____ grandparents and the boys always say that _____ glad to see _____ grandparents. In fact, the boys say that _____ are about one thousand reasons to love _____ grandparents.

EXERCISE 9

Fill in the blanks with the correct possessive adjective. When deciding what adjective to use, ask yourself the question, "Who owns it?" For *his* and *her*: if the owner is male, use *his*; if the owner is female, use *her*.

Example: I have two cats. Those are ___my___ cats.

1. You have some pens. Those are _____ pens.

2. That dog belongs to me! That is _____ dog.

3. Pedro is Alicia's son. He is _____ son. (Remember that Pedro "belongs" to a female. Therefore use the "female" possessive adjective.)

4. Bob has a house. That is _____ house.

5. Steve is Anne's brother. Steve is _____ brother.

6. Sid and Nancy have a daughter. The daughter is _____ child.

7. You have two tickets. Those are _____ tickets.

8. Anna is Dan's mother. Anna is _____ mother.

9. Rachel and Sue are Ed's daughters. They are _____ daughters.

10. Mary and I own a boat. That is _____ boat.

11. Alice is Ed and Rebecca's mother. Alice is _____ mother.

12. Kelly is Tom's wife. She is _____ wife.

Pronouns Review Chart

	Subject	Object	Possessive Adjective	Possessive Pronoun	Reflexive
Singular	I	me	my	mine	myself
	you	you	your	yours	yourself
	he	him	his	his	himself
	she	her	her	hers	herself
	it	it	its		itself
Plural	we	us	our	ours	ourselves
	you	you	your	yours	yourselves
	they	them	their	theirs	themselves

CLASS EXERCISE ▪ REVIEW

PART 1: Change the italicized word to the correct pronoun.

Example: I saw ___*Jeff*___ yesterday.   ___*him*___

1. I saw *Melinda* yesterday. _____

2. Give the receipt to *my stepfather*. _____

3. Don't speak to *I* about it any more. _____

4. Please give *those students* another chance. _____

5. Rebecca is *Gregory's* sister. _____

6. The children gave *Eddy* a biscuit. _____

7. Is that *Simon's* car? _____

8. He often helps *Jason and me*. _____

9. This house is *my and Bill's* house. _____

10. Mr. Firth is *Anna's* father. _____

PART 2: Each sentence contains an error with *be*. Circle the error and write the correct word in the space provided.

Example: Mr. Bell (is'nt) here. _____*isn't* OR *is not*_____

11. The kids are'nt in the living room. _____

12. I'm sorry, but I am agree with Jack. _____

13. Why you are so tired? _____

14. Why is Carol is so unhappy? _____

15. We're aren't scared of ghosts. _____

COMMUNICATE　　　　**What Is It?**

This game provides you with the chance to practice asking questions. You will also need to remember the vocabulary that you learned at the beginning of this section.

The teacher will place a set of items in some bags, or write the names of the items on pieces of paper. Students form groups of five or six. One student from each group knows the name of the item. The other students must form yes/no questions to discover what the item is.

For example, if the item is a metal paper clip, the students can ask yes/no questions.

Questioner	Student holding item
Is it round?	No
Is it made of plastic?	No
Is it made of metal?	Yes
Do you use it to hold paper together?	Yes

The Simple Present Tense

The simple present tense is the first verb tense most students learn, but it is also the most complicated. When using this tense, you must remember to pronounce and write the final *s* on verbs that refer to third-person singular subjects. What further complicates this tense is the importance of adding the auxiliaries *do* or *does* when forming some questions or negatives. If you have ever found yourself forgetting the *s* on verbs, or omitting the *do* or *does*, then study this section with particular care.

Sometimes students have a tendency to repeat the subject of a sentence. For example, in the following sentence there is a "double subject": *The book, it is really terrific*. Practice eliminating double subjects in Exercise 12.

The Vocabulary Boost concentrates on health terms. You will need to use your dictionary to do the vocabulary exercise. This section ends with a communication activity that provides you with an occasion to practice using the simple present tense.

VOCABULARY BOOST   Medical Terms

EXERCISE 1

Write the letter of the correct definition beside the word in column A.

A. Term		B. Definition
1. cyst	k	a. to lose consciousness
2. swallow	e	b. to expand due to internal pressure
3. rash	f	c. a crust of hardened blood over a wound
4. ache	i	d. sutures used to close a wound

5. faint   _a_   e. action where the throat muscles contract, forcing objects into the stomach

6. scab   _c_   f. red spots on the skin, sometimes caused by allergies

7. swell   _b_   g. a mark remaining after injured tissue has healed

8. lice   _h_   h. insects that nest in human hair

9. dizzy   _l_   i. to feel deep pain

10. choke   _j_   j. to have an obstruction in the windpipe

k. a fluid-filled lump under the skin

l. having a spinning sensation in the head

Simple Present

Use this tense (also called General Present) to refer to an action that is a habit or a fact. Add *s* or *es* to third-person singular verbs.

> Blue whales **live** in the ocean. (fact)
>
> Elise **visits** the doctor twice a year. (habit)

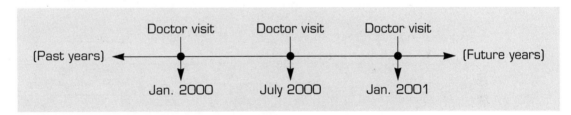

Key words: always / often / usually / sometimes / seldom / rarely / never / every day, week, etc.

Question Form: Add *do* or *does* before the subject.

> **Do** blue whales live in the ocean?   **Does** Elise visit the doctor twice a year?

Negative Form: Add *do* or *does* AND *not* after the subject.

> Birds **do not** live in water.   Elise **does not** visit the doctor twice a year.

CLASS EXERCISE

Try this exercise with a partner or in a small group. You can refer to the "simple present" section preceding this exercise.

1. Look carefully at the following sentences. Underline the subject in each sentence. The verb is in italics.

    a. <u>My uncle</u> *owns* many cars. fact

    b. <u>The factory</u> *hires* older workers. Fact

    c. <u>My sister</u> *lives* in Mexico. Fact

    d. <u>The team</u> *has* fourteen players. Fact

Why is the simple present tense used in these sentences? (*Hint*: Do these verbs indicate facts or habits?)

Facts

Why do these verbs end in *s*? *it is third - person singular*

Change the subject in each of the above sentences into the plural form. Make any necessary changes to the verb. The first one is done for you.

a. *My uncles own many cars.*
b. *The factories hire older workers.*
c. *My sisters live in Mexico*
d. *The members of the team have fourteen players*

2. Underline the subject in each of the following sentences. The verb is in italics.
a. My sons always *do* their homework before supper.
b. The little dogs across the street always *chase* me.
c. We usually *obey* the rules.
d. I never *eat* in restaurants.
e. You sometimes *work* too hard.

Why is the simple present tense used in these sentences? *habit*

When do verbs have no *s* or *es* ending? *Third-person plural*

EXERCISE 2

Put the verb in parentheses in the simple present. After each sentence, write *F* for fact or *H* for habit.

Example: John always (visit) _____*visits*_____ his mother on Saturdays. ___*H*___

1. Sylvia Lewinsky (have) ___*has*___ brown hair. ___*F*___

2. The envelope (need) ___*needs*___ to be sealed. ___*F*___

3. My aunt rarely (stay) ___*stays*___ with us. ___*H*___

4. My grandparents always (stay) ___*stays*___ with us. ___*H*___

5. The stamps (cost) ___*cost*___ about fifty cents. ___*F*___

6. Your book (cost) ___*costs*___ about twenty dollars. ___*F*___

7. My brother always (eat) _eats_ all of the ice cream.   H

8. Mr. Sinclair (sell) _sells_ second-hand furniture.   F

9. Sometimes Mr. Sinclair (give) _gives_ me a piece of furniture.   H

10. My brother and I (share) _share_ an apartment but he (pay) _pays_ more rent than I do because he (have) _has_ a better job than I do.   F

EXERCISE 3

Write the base form of each of the following italicized verbs.

1. That worker *fixes* radios.   _fix_

2. Martin *wishes* he knew how to speak Spanish.   _wish_

3. Ms. Legault *teaches* French in that school.   _teach_

4. The boy *misses* his mother when he is at school.   _miss_

5. Anne's hair *frizzes* when she walks in the rain.   _frizz_

6. Alan *does* the chores on Saturdays.   _do_

For each of these verbs, *es* must be added to the third-person singular form, instead of just *s*. These verbs end with these letters: *x, sh, ch, s, z* or *o*.

Write a rule about when to add *es* to verbs.

Add ES to verb ending in x, sh, ch, S, z or o

EXERCISE 4

Look at the simple present tense, third-person singular form of the following verbs.

Verb ends in vowel-y		_Verb ends in consonant-y_	
play	→ *plays*	study	→ *studies*
stay	*stays*	marry	*marries*
portray	*portrays*	try	*tries*

There is a difference in spelling when verbs end in vowel-*y* and when they end in consonant-*y*. Write the rules:

a. When verbs end in vowel-*y*, _we don't change the y add s_

b. When verbs end in consonant-*y*, _change (y) to i and add es_

EXERCISE 5

Write the third-person singular form of the following verbs.

      Example: carry   _carries_

1. kiss   _kisses_
2. speak   _speaks_
3. fly   _flies_
4. wish   _wishes_
5. desire   _desires_
6. play   _plays_
7. miss   _misses_
8. answer   _answers_

9. wash   _washes_
10. rely   _relies_
11. make   _makes_
12. watch   _watches_
13. hurry   _hurries_
14. spray   _sprays_
15. have   _has_
16. do   _does_

EXERCISE 6

Each verb is in italics. Underline the subject for each verb. Put an *s*, where necessary, on verbs that follow third-person singular subjects. Only the verb *to be* is already conjugated correctly. There are sixteen verbs to conjugate, not including the example.

Warning: Never put an *s* on verbs that follow *to*. *To eat, to sleep,* etc. are infinitives, and infinitives never change form.

1. My uncle *own* a bicycle shop. He often *ask* me to visit him. Sometimes I *come* to help him at the store. Every weekend, on Saturday or Sunday, my sister and I *try* to make a trip to Bicycle World. My sister *ride* her 12-speed bike and I *take* my 5-speed. My sister always *wants* the latest, newest type of bike. I *am* happy with my old bike.

2. The Wilsons *are* very nice people. Mrs. Wilson always *offers* to help her neighbours. When a new person *enter* the district, Mrs. Wilson *greet* that person. Mr. Wilson *cuts* our lawn every Sunday because our lawnmower is broken. He *say* that he *like* to do it for the exercise. My mother even *offer* to pay him for the gas for his lawnmower, but he *refuse* to accept any money. The Wilsons *have* a lot of friends because they *treat* everybody so well.

3. That flashlight *need* a new battery. One battery *cost* about six dollars. That flashlight *require* special, large batteries. My father *fix* small items, and he *need* a good flashlight for his work.

EXERCISE 7

Circle any verb errors in the following sentences, and write the verb(s) correctly in the space provided. The verbs are in italics. If the sentence is correct, write *C* in the space.

Example: The stapler *need* more staples. _____*needs*_____

1. The pencil *have* a broken lead. _____has_____

2. Wendy and Monica always *fights* over guys. _____fight_____

3. The car door *need* to be repaired. _____needs_____

4. My brothers always *share* their CDs. _____C_____

5. That anthropologist *visit* many exotic countries. _____visits_____

6. Those leather boots *costs* eighty dollars a pair. _____cost_____

7. My grandmother, who *live* near us, *has* a very large yard. _____lives, C_____

8. My brother, who I rarely *sees*, *work* in the United States. _____see, works_____

9. Mr. Winston *wear* very interesting pants. _____wears_____

10. The study *look* at the habits of chimpanzees. _____looks_____

Simple Present Tense: Negative Form

With the verb *be*, just put *not* after the verb.

    Carol is friendly.   Carol **is not** friendly. *(or **isn't**)*

With all other verbs, place *do* or *does* and *not* between the subject and the verb.

    Carol and I watch a lot of TV.   We **do not watch** a lot of TV. *(or **don't**)*
    Ms. Arnold listens carefully.   She **does not listen** carefully. *(or **doesn't**)*

EXERCISE 8

Combine the words in parentheses using the simple present tense.

Example: (I / want / not) coffee. _____*I don't want coffee.*_____

1. (Kiko / need / not) a new computer. Kiko doesn't need a new computer

2. (The desks / be / not) in the storage room. The desks aren't in the storage room

3. (Nurses / wear / not) blue hats. Nurses don't wear blue hats

4. (All snakes / be / not) poisonous. All snakes aren't poisonous

5. (William / study / not) regularly. William doesn't study regularly

6. (Those children / eat / not) liver. Those children don't eat liver

EXERCISE 9

Underline the verb and make it negative. Use the contracted negative form.

Example: The doctor <u>has</u> a nice bedside manner.   *doesn't have*

1. Carlos is a very shy person.   *isn't*

2. Tomatoes are very tasty.   *aren't*

3. The children have the measles.   *don't have*

4. Those horses run every day.   *don't run*

5. Ronald remembers every detail about his childhood.   *doesn't remember*

6. June has thirty-one days.   *doesn't have*

7. Marilyn owns three horses.   *doesn't own*

8. The students need new books.   *don't need*

Simple Present Tense: Question Form

Remember that when the verb is a form of *be*, you just move *be* before the subject to make the question.

> Karen is tired.   ***Is*** *Karen tired?*

With all other verbs, add the auxiliary *do* or *does* to create questions. When you add *does* to the sentence, the *s* is no longer needed on the verb.

subject	*verb*		*auxiliary*	*subject*	*verb*
Rebeka	runs every morning.		***Does***	*Rebeka*	***run*** *every morning?*
The Mikos	live near us.		***Do***	*the Mikos*	***live*** *near us?*

EXERCISE 10

Circle the subject in each sentence. Then write *do*, *does* or a form of the verb *be* in the space provided.

Example: ___*Does*___ (Jerry) like spaghetti?   ___*Is*___ (he) hungry?

1. ___Do___   the books need new covers?

2. ___Does___   that little boy have any parents?

3. ___Do___   you believe in magic?

4. ___are___   we alone?

5. ___Does___   Eric need stitches?

6. ___Does___ your watch have the correct time?

7. ___Do___ I know you?

8. ___Does___ your mother know where you are?

Make negative questions. To do this, just add *not* to the auxiliary.

Example: ___Don't___ you like me?   ___Isn't___ she sweet?

9. ___Don't___ you know what time it is?

10. ___Doesn't___ your sister have a boyfriend?

11. ___Isn't___ that man handsome?

12. ___Don't___ we have enough time to discuss this?

EXERCISE 11

Circle the subject in each sentence. Create questions for which the answer is yes or no. Change the subject to a subject pronoun.

		Auxiliary	**Subject**	**Verb**	
Example:	(Jeff) hates dogs.	*Does*	*he*	*hate*	*dogs?*
1.	Kate needs more money.	Does	she	need	more money?
2.	The twins hate school.	Do	they	hate	school?
3.	Aldo lies to people.	Does	he	lie	to people?
4.	The printer needs more paper.	Does	it	need	more paper?
5.	The children have piano lessons.	Do	they	have	piano lessons?
6.	Jughead eats too much food.	Does	he	eat	too much food?
7.	The movie lasts for two hours.	Does	it	last	for two hours?
8.	Those trains need to be fixed.	Do	they ~~Those trains~~	need to be	fixed?

The next four sentences contain the verb *be*. *Be* acts as an auxiliary, therefore move *be* before the subject to make your question. Remember to change the subject to a subject pronoun.

		Aux. (be)	**Subject**	
Example:	The boy is tall.	*Is*	*he*	*tall?*
9.	The piano is very heavy.	is	it	very heavy?
10.	The boxes are in the basement.	are	they	in the basement?
11.	You are very wise.	are	you	very wise?
12.	Ms. Mukerjee is pregnant.	Is	she Ms. Mukerjee	pregnant?

Double Subjects

When the subject of a sentence is mentioned, it is repetitive and unnecessary to repeat the subject in its pronoun form.

Incorrect: *Jim, he has a large bruise on his leg.*
            (*Jim* is the subject. *He* is a repetition of the subject.)

Correct: *Jim has a large bruise on his leg.*

EXERCISE 12

In the following paragraphs, delete any double subjects.

1. This cat, ~~he~~ is very annoying. I don't really like animals, but this cat, ~~he~~ was lent to me. My friend moved to Haiti and my ~~friend~~, she left this cat here. The cat's name is Toby. Toby, ~~he~~ is really a rascal. He puts his toys in my shoes. I always return Toby's toys to his bed, but ~~Toby~~, he brings them back.

2. The toys, ~~they~~ are small things. Toby has a soft little mouse. The ~~mouse~~, it squeaks when you step on it. Whenever I step on the mouse, I scream. Almost every day that mouse, ~~it~~ appears in my shoe!

CLASS EXERCISE ▪ REVIEW

PART 1: Write sentences in the simple present tense using the words in parentheses. Change the subject to a subject pronoun. Do this on a separate piece of paper.

Example: (Andy / love / chocolate) _____ *He loves chocolate.* _____

1. (Susan / eat / Mexican food / every Friday) _She eats Mexican food every Frid_

2. (The exam / have / forty questions) _The exam has forty questions_

3. (The doctors / meet / in that hotel) _The doctors meet in that hotel_

4. (Toyotas / be / quite expensive) _Toyotas are quite expensive_

5. (That man / talk / on the phone / every day) _That man talks on the phone every d_

6. (The car / need / not / new tires) _The car doesn't need new tires._

7. (The tires / cost / not / a lot of money) _That tires doesn't cost a lot of money_

8. (Horses / be / not / taller than elephants) _Horses aren't taller than elephant_

PART 2: Make yes/no questions out of the following sentences. Change the subject to a subject pronoun.

Example: Monica has three children. _____ *Does she have three children?* _____

9. John hates broccoli. <u>Does he hate brocoli?</u>

10. The children are very tired. <u>Are they very tired?</u>

11. Those jeans need to be washed. <u>Do those jeans need to be washed?</u>

12. The earth travels around the sun. <u>Does the earth travel around the sun?</u>

13. The books are on the bookshelf. <u>Are the books on the bookself?</u>

14. Nurses sometimes wear uniforms. <u>Do Nurses sometimes wear uniforms?</u>

15. Freddy wears a mask every evening. <u>Does freddy wear a mask every evening?</u>

COMMUNICATE	Blank

In this game, you can practice forming simple questions using *do* or *does*. A student comes to the front of the class and is given a verb, such as "shave." The student must answer his or her classmates' questions with *yes, no* or *sometimes*. In each question, the student substitutes the verb with the word *blank*. For example, Marco has the word "shave." A classmate asks, "Do you *blank* every day?" Marco must answer with *yes, no* or *sometimes*. Another student then asks a question. As soon as someone is certain about the mystery verb, that person can make a guess.

Each student in the class should ask a question. It is simplest if you start at the beginning of a row and move towards the back, with one student after another asking a question. The one who guesses correctly comes to the front of the class. (This game could also be done with teams of students. Each team could work independently, and students would have more opportunity to speak.)

For example: (The word is "shave.")

Student A:	Do you *blank* alone?	Yes.
Student B:	Do you *blank* outside?	No.
Student C:	Do you *blank* indoors?	Yes.
Student D:	Do you *blank* in the kitchen?	No.
Student E:	Do you *blank* with a tool?	Yes.
Student F:	Do you *blank* when you are tired?	Sometimes.

The student who guesses "shave" must come to the front of the class. The following verbs can be used, or more verbs could be added to this list.

bathe	knock	mow the lawn	kiss	fly
sleep	cook	sew	wake up	drive
shower	read	eat	dance	type
sing	laugh	cut your hair	sweep	hug
snore	argue	type	write	wash the dishes
swim	play the piano	ski	shovel snow	do homework

The Present Tenses

You have practiced using the simple present tense. There is another tense in English that is used to discuss the present time. However, the present progressive differs from the simple present in that it refers to events that are in progress now. For example, at this moment *I am writing this sentence.* I would not say *At this moment I write this sentence.* Sometimes students forget to add *be* before the verb (*I writing*), but it is important to form this tense correctly.

There are some verbs that cannot be used in the progressive form. There is a list of these "non-progressive verbs" after exercise 4. You should remember that these verbs are non-progressive in all tenses. This section also contains a short exercise that will help you remember when to put apostrophes in words.

The chapter begins with a Vocabulary Boost that explores common gestures. Halfway through this section there is a communication activity that gives you an opportunity to practice using these "gesture" verbs. The final communication activity gives you an opportunity to speak using the present tenses.

VOCABULARY BOOST ▶ Gestures

Most of these short words describe actions that are instinctive. Some of these actions are done specifically to send a message.

bow	bend forward from the waist to express appreciation
wink	close and open one eye rapidly
blink	close and open both eyes rapidly
scratch	scrape or rub a surface with claws or fingernails
clap	hit the hands together to express approval
tear	pull a piece of paper or material until it splits

laugh	show happiness with an explosive sound
whistle	make a clear sound by blowing through a small space between the lips
whisper	speak without making the vocal cords vibrate
whimper	make a low complaining sound
snore	breathe heavily when asleep, causing a rasping sound
snicker	make a noise of suppressed laughter
cough	force air from the lungs with a loud noise, usually to expel mucus
sneer	raise one side of the upper lip, combined with a look of indifference or contempt
frown	turn down the corners of the mouth in an expression of unhappiness
sneeze	force air from the nose with a loud noise

EXERCISE 1

Fill in the blanks with one of the terms from the "gestures" list. Because these gestures are regular verbs, you must add *s* to the ones that have a third-person singular subject. If there is a "to" before the verb, never add *s* to it. Use each gesture once only.

1. After Wayne Chu finishes conducting the orchestra, he always turns and smiles when the audience members ___clap___ to show their approval. Mr. Chu then ___bows___ deeply to express his appreciation.

2. Mrs. Graham is very frustrated. She cannot sleep well at night. Her husband always ___snores___ and the noise keeps her awake.

3. I have a bad cold and I need to ___sneeze___ . Could you give me a Kleenex?

4. You should always cover your mouth when you ___cough___ . Otherwise the germs could spread and infect other people.

5. I have a mosquito bite on my back. I really need to ___scratch___ it because it is so itchy.

6. My dog is very obedient. When I want him to come, I just have to ___whistle___ loudly.

7. When I watch a funny movie with Jim Carrey in it, I always ___laugh___ and ___snickers___ .

8. My baby cousin doesn't need toys. He is happy with a piece of newspaper. He ___tears___ the piece of newspaper and listens carefully to the sound that it makes.

9. Why do you always look so unhappy? Why do you always ___frown___ ? Your mouth could freeze in that unhappy expression!

10. When my dog is hungry, he makes a very annoying sound. He stands outside my
bedroom door and he ___whimpers___.

Present Progressive

Use this tense to refer to an activity that is occurring *right now*.

*Listen! The children **are laughing**.*

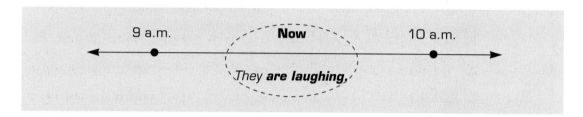

This tense can also describe an activity in progress during a current, limited period of
time.

*These days Mia **is writing her thesis**.*

Key words: now, at this moment, presently, nowadays, these days

Question Form: Move *be* before the subject.　　***Are** the children laughing?*

Negative Form: Add *not* after *be*.　　*The children **are not** laughing.*

CLASS EXERCISE

PART 1: Look around the classroom and make four sentences about what is happening
right now.

1. _____

2. _____

3. _____

4. _____

PART 2: Look carefully at the following verbs in their *ing* form. Notice that the last letter of the verb is doubled in Group 2.

<table>
<tr><th colspan="2" align="center">Group 1</th><th colspan="2" align="center">Group 2</th></tr>
<tr><td>Base form</td><td>"ing" form</td><td>Base form</td><td>"ing" form</td></tr>
<tr><td>a. wait</td><td>*waiting*</td><td>run</td><td>*ru**nn**ing*</td></tr>
<tr><td>b. rain</td><td>*raining*</td><td>stop</td><td>*sto**pp**ing*</td></tr>
<tr><td>c. wish</td><td>*wishing*</td><td>sit</td><td>*si**tt**ing*</td></tr>
<tr><td>d. stand</td><td>*standing*</td><td>grin</td><td>*gri**nn**ing*</td></tr>
</table>

1. In Group 1, the base-form verbs *a* and *b* have how many vowels?   A, T

Rule 1: When one-syllable verbs contain two vowels, do not double the last letter!

2. In Group 1, the base-form verbs *c* and *d* end in how many consonants?   2

Rule 2: When verbs end in two consonants, do not double the last letter!

3. In Group 2, the base-form verbs have how many vowels?   one

The base-form verbs end in how many consonants?   one

When should the last letter of verbs be doubled?

Rule 3: ___doubled the last___

Note: Never double the last letter of verbs ending in *w* or *x*. Snow ——►Snowing

4. Look at these verbs:

write   *writing*   smile   *smiling*

What happens when verbs end in the letter *e*? Write your own rule.

Rule 4: ___delete e and add ing___

EXERCISE 2

Write the following verbs in their *ing* form. If necessary, refer to the preceding class exercise for rules.

Example: hope ___*hoping*___

1. smile   smiling
2. jog   jogging
3. laugh   laughing
4. study   studying
5. scratch   scratching
6 snap   snapping
7 cry   crying
8 try   trying

9. run   running
10. plan   planning
11. write   writing
12. star   staring   starring
13. sit   sitting

6. snap   _snapping_   **14.** blink   _blinking_

7. cry   _crying_   **15.** clap   _clapping_

8. try   _trying_   **16.** marry   _marrying_

EXERCISE 3

Read the description. Write what the person is doing, using one of the following verbs. Look up any unfamiliar terms in the dictionary.

whisper	scratch	sneeze	cough	wash
eat	bow	snore	wink	watch

Example: Alfred is sitting at the table. A bowl of soup is in front of him. He is picking up the spoon. What is he doing?   _He is eating soup._

1. Celine has a hose in her hand. She has a large brush. She is standing in front of her car. What is she doing? _she is cleaning her car_

2. Allie and Mandy are sitting on the couch. The remote is in Allie's hands. They are laughing, and staring at the TV. What are they doing? _They are watching T.V_

3. He is lying on his bed and he is sleeping. He is breathing deeply. As he breathes, he makes a noise. What is he doing? _he is snoring_

4. Steve is speaking to his girlfriend and trying to fool his father. Steve is telling his father a little lie. Steve wants his girlfriend to know that it is a joke, but he wants her to play along with him. What is he doing with one eye?

he is winking

5. The performance of _Othello_ is over and the actors are at the front of the stage. They are facing the audience. The audience is clapping loudly. What are the actors doing to express their appreciation? _They are bowing_

6. Jake has a mosquito bite on his foot. Jake is using his fingers to do something to the bite. What is Jake doing? _he is scratching his hand_

7. Rebecca has a secret. She wants to tell this secret to her friend, but she doesn't want her brother to hear the secret. Rebecca cups her hands near her mouth and gets close to her friend's ear. What is Rebecca doing? _She is whispering_

8. Diego is allergic to cats. He is visiting his cousin. His cousin has a cat, and the cat is sitting on Diego's lap. Now Diego's nose is twitching. What is Diego doing?

he is sneezing

Present Progressive Tense: Question and Negative Forms

Question Form: *be* acts as an auxiliary and goes before the subject.

Rick (is) climbing a ladder.   Why (is) Rick climbing a ladder?

Negative Form: Place *not* after the verb *be*.

Alf is studying for his test.   Alf **isn't** studying for his test.

EXERCISE 4

Make a statement, a question and a negative sentence out of the words in parentheses.
Use the present progressive tense.

Example: (Carol / bite her lip / now)   *She's biting her lip now.*
                                                                    Is she biting her lip now?
                                                                    She isn't biting her lip now.

1. (Ms. Olf / speak / to the assembly)

Statement _Ms. Olf's speaking to the assembly_

Question _Is she speaking ( )?_

Negative _She isn't speaking to the assembly?_

2. (that lady / wink / at Richard)

Statement _That lady is winking at Richard._

Question _Is that lady winking at Richard?_

Negative _That lady isn't winking at Richard?_

3. (Listen! / somebody / knock / on the door)
Note: *Everybody, Somebody, Anybody* and *Nobody* are considered third-person
singular; therefore, use *is*.

Statement _Listen! Somebody is knock on the door_

Question _Is somebody knocking on the door?_

Negative _Somebody isn't knocking on the door?_

4. (the dogs / sleep / right now)

Statement _The dogs are sleeping right now._

Question _Are the dogs sleeping right now?_

Negative _The dogs aren't sleeping ( )_

Non-Progressive Verbs

Sometimes, even though we are talking about this moment, we cannot use progressive verb forms. The following verbs are generally not used in the progressive tense.

Perception Verbs:	Preference Verbs:	State Verbs: *no action*		Possession Verbs:
see	like	know	mean	own
smell	hate	suppose	believe	have (meaning
look (meaning	care	realize	forgive	"own")
"appear")	fear	understand	forget	possess
appear	appreciate	remember	doubt	belong
sound	wish	recognize	refuse	
hear	need	imagine	trust	
taste	love	owe		
seem	prefer	think (meaning "in my		
feel	want	opinion")		
	envy			
	desire			

Some of these verbs can be used in the progressive tense when they indicate that an action is in progress.

I am looking at you.   *That dinner looks good.*
I am having a baby.   *I have three houses.*

Comparing the Simple Present and the Present Progressive

EXERCISE 5

Combine the words in parentheses to make a simple present or present progressive sentence. If the action is a fact or a habit, use the simple present tense. If the action is happening now, use the present progressive (*ing*) tense. After each sentence, write:

H   if the action is a habit.
F   if it is a fact.
N   if the action is happening now.

Example: Look! (My cat / sleep).   *Look! My cat is sleeping*   N

1. (My mother / own) a hotel. _My mother own a hotel_   F

2. Listen! (The dog / bark). _Listen! The dog is barking_   N

3. (The doctor / work) at this moment. _The doctor is working at this moment_   N

4. (Ms. Ramirez / work) in a bank. _Ms. Ramirez works in a bank_   F

5. (He / always make) dinner. _He always makes dinner_   H

6. (The movie / begin) now. _The movie is begining now_   N

7. Shhh! (I / try) to watch the movie! _Shhh! I am trying to watch_ N
the movie

8. (We / go) out every week. _We go out every week_   H

9. (My sister / always come) with me. _My sister always comes_ H
with me

10. (Jerry / listen) to my tape now. _Jerry is listening to_   N
my tape now

COMMUNICATE	Charades

This game gives you an opportunity to practice using the present progressive tense, and it reinforces "gestures" vocabulary.

Form teams with about five students on each team. Students are not allowed to look in their books. The teacher writes down a gesture and shows it to one student. That student must then act out the gesture. The team must say what the student is doing. The other teams can guess only if the initial team is unable to guess the gesture within thirty seconds.

For example: Alex picks out a paper with the word "snicker" on it. Alex acts out this action. Alex's team must say "He is snickering." The team has thirty seconds to guess the action. If Alex notices that his team is having problems remembering the word "snicker," then Alex could cup his hand near his ear to indicate "sounds like" and Alex could then act out a word that sounds like *snicker*, such as *kicker*. Alex's teammates are not allowed to refresh their memories by looking up the meanings of gestures in their books.

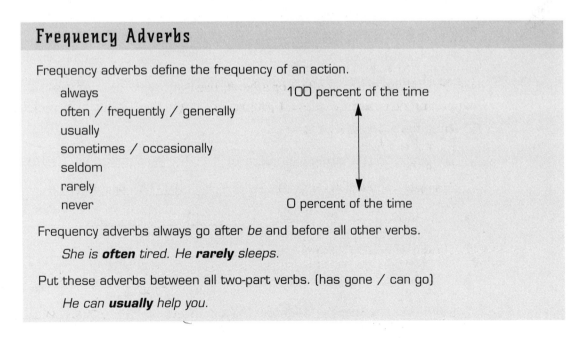

Frequency Adverbs

Frequency adverbs define the frequency of an action.

always	100 percent of the time
often / frequently / generally	
usually	
sometimes / occasionally	
seldom	
rarely	
never	0 percent of the time

Frequency adverbs always go after *be* and before all other verbs.

   *She is **often** tired. He **rarely** sleeps.*

Put these adverbs between all two-part verbs. (has gone / can go)

   *He can **usually** help you.*

EXERCISE 6

Put a slash (/) in the sentence indicating where the frequency adverb should be placed.

    Example: Alan | takes the bus home from work. (sometimes)

1.   Julie is in a good mood. (usually) *usually*
2.   The teacher is absent. (seldom) *seldom*
3.   Claire knows the answer. (often) *often*
4.   Julie's sister, Ellen, can tell what Julie is thinking. (often) *often* *often*
5.   Francisco is a good student. (generally) *generally*
6.   Sam plays hockey on the weekends. (usually) *usually*
7.   Randy is in day care. (rarely) *rarely*
8.   Carolyn likes to travel. (generally) *generally*

Questions: Place the adverb after the subject, e.g. Does she sometimes complain about it?

9.   Do you feel homesick? (occasionally) *occasionally*
10.   Is your mother in a bad mood? (sometimes) *often*
11.   Does Dick complain about the food? (often) *often*
12.   Does your cat sleep in your bed? (always) *always*

EXERCISE 7

Complete the sentences using the simple present or the present progressive. Use the present progressive (*be —ing*) when the action is in progress now, or for this temporary period of time.

1.   I (know) __know__ Jake. He (work, sometimes) __sometimes works__ with me. My boss (hire) __hires__ Jake every summer when the restaurant gets very busy. I (think) __think__ that Jake (work) __is working__ right now.

2.   This coffee (smell) __smells__ good. I (like) __like__ strong coffee, but my boyfriend (drink, not) __doesn't drink__ it. He (believe) __believes__ that caffeine is unhealthy. Now he (relax) __is relaxing__ in front of the TV set. He (watch) __is watching__ a football game now. Now I (try) __am trying__ to convince him to go for a walk.

3.   My sister always (complain) __complains__ about her boss. She (like, not) __doesn't like__ him at all. She (think) __thinks__ that her boss is too picky. Listen to her! Right now she (complain) __is complaining__ again.

she/his were fussy

Question Words

Question word	Refers to:	Question	Answer
who	a person	*Who is there?*	*Martin.*
where	a place	*Where do you live?*	*Spain.*
what	a thing	*What is that?*	*A bug.*
when	time	*When do you finish work?*	*5 p.m.*
why	a reason	*Why is Ted late?*	*He is sick.*
how	in what way	*How do you fix this?*	*With tape.*
how long	duration	*How long does the movie last?*	*Two hours.*
how far	distance	*How far is Laval from here?*	*10 km.*
how often	repetition of habit	*How often do you visit him?*	*Every month.*
how many	quantity	*How many candles are there?*	*Ten of them.*
how much	quantity	*How much money do you have?*	*Forty dollars.*

EXERCISE 8

The answers to the questions are in **bold**. Write the question in the space provided.

Example: Evan keeps his money **in his wallet.**   *Where does Evan keep his money?*

1. Franz has **a dog.** _what does Franz have?_

2. Monica lives **in San Diego.** _where does Monica live?_

3. He wants **coffee.** _what does he want?_

4. Sam starts work at **6 a.m.** _when does Same ~he~ start work?_

5. Ella lives with **Fred.** _who does Ella live with?_

6. He is crying **because he hurt himself.** _why is he crying?_

7. The course lasts **for three hours.** _How long does the course last?_

8. She is **cleaning the bathroom.** _what is she doing?_

9. The paper is **in the cupboard.** _where is the paper?_

10. Many people visit us **in the spring.** _when do many people visit us?_

Who / What Questions

When *what* and *who* ask about the object of a question, an auxiliary is necessary.

My car needs **new tires.**   *What **does** your car need?*
Hugh phones **Diane** every day.   *Who **does** Hugh phone every day?*

However, when *what* and *who* ask about the subject of a question, no auxiliary is needed.

My car needs new tires.   *What needs new tires?*
Hugh phones Diane every day.   *Who phones Diane every day?*

EXERCISE 9

PART 1: Write questions for each underlined answer. The answer is the subject.

    Example: <u>Ms. Ardon</u> is a great mechanic.   *Who is a great mechanic?*

1. <u>That child</u> needs new shoes.   *Who needs new shoes?*
2. <u>The stapler</u> needs more staples.   *What needs more staples?*
3. <u>Andrew</u> is crying.   *Who is crying?*
4. <u>His mother</u> is holding him.   *Who is holding him?*
5. <u>The cupboard door</u> has no handle.   *What has no handle?*

PART 2: Write questions for each underlined answer. Determine whether the answer is the subject or the object of the question. Begin each question with *Who* or *What*.

    Example: The boy has <u>marbles</u> in his pocket. *What does the boy have in his pocket?*

6. The doctor has <u>a stethoscope</u>.   *What does the doctor have?*
7. <u>That house</u> has a large garage.   *What has a large garage?*
8. That house has <u>a large garage</u>.   *What does that house have?*
9. Felix is allergic <u>to cats</u>.   *What is Felix allergic to?*
10. <u>Felix</u> is allergic to cats.   *Who is allergic to cats?*

Apostrophes

Use apostrophes to:

1. join a subject and verb together.   **We're** late. **There's** nothing to eat.
2. join an auxiliary with *not*.   I **can't** come. They **aren't** very friendly.
3. indicate possession.   That is **Simon's** car. **Ross's** computer is new.

Never use an apostrophe before the *s* at the end of a verb.   Incorrect: *She make's*
    Correct: *She makes*

EXERCISE 10

Add apostrophes, when necessary.

1. Jim's brother, Eddy, works for Pizza Villa, but Eddy's taking a vacation right now.
2. The Dereks don't live near us, but the Smiths' home is across the street.
3. Mr. Dereks's son, Eric, loves animals, but he doesn't have any because his dad's allergic.

4. Eric often asks to walk our dog and Im *[I'm]* happy when he does it.

5. Its always nice when someone else walks the dog. Youre *[You're]* going to think Im *[I'm]* lazy, but Im *[I'm]* not.

EXERCISE 11

Underline and correct the present-tense errors in the following sentences.

Example: Mark <u>is</u> often <u>complaining</u>.   *complains*

1. Lydia is very athletic and she <u>is exercising</u> every second day.   *exercises*

2. Mike and Lydia <u>eats</u> dinner together every Friday night.   *eat*

3. Mike <u>isn't exercising</u> often.   *doesn't exercise*

4. Helen, who <u>work's</u> with me, <u>is</u> very <u>ill</u> right now.   *works,*

5. Why <u>is</u> Clara <u>is</u> sitting all alone over there?   *why is Clara sitting*

6. <u>Do</u> she is lonely?   *is she lonely?*

7. Sorry, but Mary <u>don't</u> like to eat meat.   *doesn't like*

8. <u>Do</u> anybody want more coffee?   *Does*

9. Sammy <u>do not</u> want more sauce.   *doesn't*

10. The children <u>are'nt</u> listening to me now.   *aren't*

CLASS EXERCISE ▪ REVIEW

PART 1: Combine the words in parentheses to make a sentence. The sentence may be in the simple present or in the present progressive tense. Change the subject to a subject pronoun.

Example: (My aunt / often / write) to me.   *She often writes to me.*

1. (The stapler / need / not) more staples.   *it doesn't need more staples*

2. (The babysitter / do) his homework now.   *she is doing her homework now*

3. (Mark / spend / always) too much money.   *Mark always spends too much money*

4. (Alf / study) for his exam right now.   *Alf is studying for his exam right now*

5. (These shoes / usually / fit / not) very well.   *they don't usually fit very well.*

PART 2: Make questions. The answers to the questions are in italics.

   Example: She wants *ice cream*.   <u>*What does she want?*</u>

6.   Sam is whispering *because I asked him to*.

<u>why is Sam whispering to me?</u>

7.   Karen usually does her homework *after school*.

<u>when does Karen usually do her homework?</u>

8.   The pictures are *in the photo album*.

<u>where are the pictures?</u>

9.   Those hockey players usually travel *during the night*.

<u>when do those hockey players travel?</u>

10.   The dishes have *spots* on them.

_____

COMMUNICATE   >   Interview a Student

Together with a partner, come up with questions based on the following list. (Use proper question form.) Then take turns interviewing each other. This activity could be done in a language lab. After the interview, you could write a paragraph about your partner's habits.

Use frequency adverbs in your questions and answers.

   Example: *Q.*   Do you often play sports?
              A.   No, I rarely play sports.

Question topics:

1. sleep in past 11 a.m.
2. write letters
3. drive drunk
4. go to movies
5. lie
6. use a computer

7–10. Create your own questions.

Do you often sleep?

4 The Simple Past Tense: Regular Verbs

The simple past tense in English is relatively straightforward. Each verb has one past form (with the exception of the verb *be*) and this past form stays the same for all subjects. For example, the verb *watch* becomes *watched* in the past tense, and does not change even with a third-person singular subject. Only the verb *be* has two past forms (*was* and *were*).

In this section you will practice using the past forms of *be* and of regular verbs. Regular verbs are all verbs that end in *ed*. This section also contains a "tense shift" exercise. Students sometimes forget to be consistent when writing a story, and a text that begins with past tense verbs suddenly shifts into the present tense, creating confusion for the reader.

This section begins with a Vocabulary Boost about emotions. There is a communication activity at the end of the chapter that gives you the opportunity to use the past tense and to use some of the vocabulary that you learned in earlier sections of this book.

VOCABULARY BOOST ⟩ Emotions

EXERCISE 1

Some emotions are positive. For example, we feel good when we are excited about something. Of course, some emotions have the opposite effect; no one enjoys feeling stressed. Look at the emotions below and sort them into positive and negative emotions. Write down the definition of any word that you don't understand directly beside it.

شاوبار دنتاح / مؤوته

bored /   annoyed   relieved   lonely   stressed

ارسال   thrilled قلول اضطا   disappointed   ashamed   ecstatic   excited
محرور ارامن   pleased   proud   embarrassed   disgusted

<table>
<tr><th colspan="2">Positive Emotions</th><th colspan="2">Negative Emotions</th></tr>
<tr><td colspan="2">excited</td><td colspan="2">stressed: anxious</td></tr>
<tr><td colspan="2">thrilled</td><td colspan="2">bored</td></tr>
<tr><td colspan="2">pleased</td><td colspan="2">annoyed</td></tr>
<tr><td colspan="2">proud</td><td colspan="2">disappointed</td></tr>
<tr><td colspan="2">relieved</td><td colspan="2">ashamed</td></tr>
<tr><td colspan="2"></td><td colspan="2">lonely</td></tr>
<tr><td colspan="2">ecstatic</td><td colspan="2">disgusted</td></tr>
<tr><td colspan="2"></td><td colspan="2">embarrassed</td></tr>
</table>

Simple Past

The simple past tense relates an event in the past to an understood or stated past time.

*We **visited** Mexico last March.*

Key words: last week, last month, last year, yesterday, when I was young, once upon a time, long ago (any word or phrase that refers to a past time when the action occurred)

Be

The past forms of the verb *be* are:

I / he / she / it	**was**
You / we / they	**were**

EXERCISE 2

Write the correct past form of the verb *be* in the space provided.

Example: Carol and I   <u> were </u>   busy last weekend.

1. My sister ___was___ late for class yesterday.

2. Alice and Raymond ___were___ angry with each other this morning.

3. The papers ___were___ on the table yesterday evening!

4. Pedro's homework ___was___ not competed last week.

5. The animals, which ___were___ in the cage yesterday, are no longer there.

6. Many people ___were___ at the baseball game last Friday night.

7. I ___was___ lazy and my husband ___was___ very active last Saturday.

8. My sisters ___were___ in Toronto last month.

9. Kevin's birthday party ___was___ last Saturday.

10. You ___were___ very rude to me yesterday!

EXERCISE 3

Note the differences between *there was* and *there were*:

> *There* **was** (one thing).   *There* **were** (two or more things).

Put *was* or *were* in the space provided.

1. There ___were___ some groceries in the cart when I looked ten minutes ago.

2. There ___were___ almost no people at the game last night.

3. There ___was___ one cookie left in the cookie jar this morning.

4. There ___was___ not any information in that Web site when I looked yesterday.

5. Alex took his computer to the store last month because there ___were___ several problems with the hard drive. There ___was___ also a major problem with the video card. Now his computer runs perfectly.

Be (Past Tense): Question and Negative Forms

Question Form: When making a question, change the word order so that the verb *be* appears before the subject.

> They (were) late.   (Were) they late?
>   Why **were** they late?
> There was a fire yesterday.   **Was** there a fire yesterday?

Negative Form: When making the verb negative, simply put *not* after the verb *be*.

> They **were not** late.   Sara **was not** tired.

EXERCISE 4

Turn the following sentences into questions. The answer to the question is in italics.

    Example: Susan was very sick *last weekend.* _____*When was Susan sick?*_____

1. Claire was *in the office* yesterday. _Where was Claire yesterday?_

2. The files were on my desk *last week.* _When were the files on my desk?_

3. There were many jobs available *last year.* _When were there many jobs available?_

4. Henry's sister was busy last Friday *because she had to finish the "Hilton" report.*
Why was Henry's sister busy last Friday?

5. Those girls were born *in Vancouver.* _Where were those girls born?_

Spelling of Regular (ed) Past Tense Verbs

1. Double the *last* letter of one-syllable verbs that end in a consonant-vowel-consonant combination.

    stop   *sto**pp**ed*   jog   *jo**gg**ed*

2. When verbs end in consonant-y, change the *y* to *i* and add *ed.*

    fry   *fr**ied***   apply   *appl**ied***

    When verbs end in vowel-y, usually keep the *y.*

    play   *played*   Exception: pay   *paid*

EXERCISE 5

Write the *ed* form of these regular verbs.

    Example: shop   _shopped_

1. part _parted_   **6.** rain _rained_   **11.** remain _remained_

2. stay _stayed_   **7.** fail _failed_   **12.** study _studied_

3. rely _relied_   **8.** snap _snapped_   **13.** plan _planned_

4. marry _married_   **9.** hope _hoped_   **14.** die _died_

5. share _shared_   **10.** fry _fried_   **15.** rob _robbed_

EXERCISE 6

Fill in the blanks with the simple past verbs.

1. When I (*be*) _was_ a child, I (*visit*) _visited_ my aunt's house every
summer. She (*live*) _lived_ in a tiny house on the edge of town. A

company (*destroy*) __destroyed__ my aunt's house in 1984. That street is now a supermarket. My aunt (*die*) __died__ in 1992.

2. My aunt (*own*) __owned__ many different types of clothing. Her closet (*contain*) __contained__ dresses from the 1930s and 1940s. Some of the dresses (*be*) __were__ almost new. One dress that I (*love*) __loved__ to look at (*be*) __was__ pale yellow, and there (*be*) __were__ small white daisies on it.

3. As a child I often (*touch*) __touched__ those dresses and I (*want*) __wanted__ to try them on. My aunt (*explain*) __explained__ to me that when I (*stop*) __stopped__ growing, at about age 15, I could try some of the dresses on.

4. When I (*turn*) __turned__ 15, my aunt (*shop*) __shopped__ for a present for me. Then she remembered what I really wanted. She came to my house holding a gift-wrapped box. She (*tap*) __tapped__ the box with her finger and told me that I would love my present. When I (*open*) __opened__ the box, I was very happy because the yellow dress (*be*) __was__ in the box.

Pronunciation of *ed*

When verbs end in *k, sh, ch, x* or *s*, the final *ed* is pronounced as *t*.
When verbs end in *t* or *d*, the final *ed* is pronounced as a separate syllable.

EXERCISE 7

Pronounce the following verbs, and decide if they are pronounced as one or two syllables. If the *ed* sounds like *t*, put a *t* in the space.

1. hated	2	**7.** hoped	1 t	**13.** raked	1 t
2. coughed	1 t	**8.** counted	2	**14.** pasted	2
3. rented	2	**9.** twisted	2	**15.** wished	1 t
4. needed	2	**10.** bowed	1	**16.** pointed	2
5. marched	1 t	**11.** smiled	1	**17.** cared	1
6. sounded	2	**12.** landed	2	**18.** added	2

Past Tense: Question and Negative Forms

Question: With all past tense verbs except *be*, add the auxiliary *did* to create questions. When you add *did* to the sentence, you no longer need to keep the verb in the past tense. ***Did*** **makes the question a past tense question**.

	auxiliary
Victor married Siri in 1971.	When ***did*** Victor ***marry*** Siri?
Negative:	Victor ***did not marry*** Siri in 1970.

EXERCISE 8

Make a contraction in each of the following phrases.

Example: You are not.   _____*You aren't.*_____

1. I was not.   _____wasn't_____   **4.** We were not.   _____weren't_____

2. The dogs were not.   _____weren't_____   **5.** Ann was not.   _____wasn't_____

3. She did not talk.   _____didn't talk_____   **6.** I do not like it.   _____don't like_____

EXERCISE 9

Make questions or negative sentences from the words in parentheses. Use the past tense.

Example:
[She / have / a lot of time yesterday?]   *Did she have a lot of time yesterday?*
[She / have / not / a lot of time yesterday.]   *She didn't have a lot of time yesterday.*

1. (Bill / see / Lia last night?) Did Bill see Lia last night? ✓

2. (He / see / not / her.) He didn't see her ✓

3. (Lia / be / home last night?) Was Lia home last night? ✗

4. (She / be / not / home.) She wasn't home. ✓

5. (Lia / know / where Bill was?) Did Lia know where Bill was? ✓

6. (She / know / not / where he was) She didn't know where he was. ✓

EXERCISE 10

Make questions from the following sentences. The answer is in italics. Remember that when *who* or *what* ask about the subject of a question, no *did* is required.

Example:

Yesterday Becky opened the shop *at 6 a.m.*   *When did Becky open the shop?*

1. Marco called *Alicia* yesterday.   ~~who~~ *or whom* did Marco call yesterday?

2. *Marco* called Alicia yesterday.   who called Alicia yesterday? *✗*

3. *Frank* baked muffins last weekend.   who baked muffins last weekend?

4. Frank baked *muffins* last weekend.   what did Frank bake last weekend?

5. The party was *three blocks* from here.   How far was the party from here? *✗*

6. That ring belonged to *my late aunt.*   whom did that ring belong to?
   who did that ring belong to?

Tense Shifts

If you start to tell a story, do not shift tenses unless the time frame really does change.

Jerry **left** *his apartment and Kramer* **enters** *moments later.*

(The tense incorrectly shifts from the past to the present.)

EXERCISE 11

In the following exercise, correct any tense shifts. In the past tense, use *would* instead of *will.*

1. I watched a funny rerun of a TV show yesterday. In the show, Elaine and Kramer walked into Jerry's apartment, as usual, and Kramer ~~opens~~ *opened* the fridge. He took out a bag of muffins and ~~offer~~ *offered* one to Elaine.

2. They wondered what they ~~will~~ *would* do if Jerry came in. Then, when they ~~finish~~ finish*ed* the last muffin, Jerry walked in the door. Jerry went to the fridge and looked for his muffins. The muffins ~~are~~ *were* not in the fridge. Jerry turned, and looked at his friends. They look*ed* very guilty, but they didn't say anything. Then Elaine and Kramer grabbed their coats and left.

CLASS EXERCISE • REVIEW

Do this class exercise on a separate piece of paper.

PART 1: Combine the words to make a past tense sentence or question. Change the subject to a subject pronoun.

Example: Harry / shave / last night?   *Did he shave last night?*

1. The newspaper / not / arrive / last Monday.   It didn't arrive last Monday

2. The children / watch / not / any TV last night.   They didn't watch any TV last night

3. You / watch / TV last night? _Did you watch TV last night?_

4. What / you / do / last night? _what did you do last night?_

5. Joe / walk / not / to work yesterday. _Joe didn't walk to work yesterday_

PART 2: Make questions. The answers are in italics.

Example: Martin visited his sister *yesterday.* _When did Martin visit his sister?_

6. The mail was late *yesterday.* _when was the mail late?_

7. Last month Fred borrowed a *rake.* _what did Fred borrow last month?_

8. Barney asked *Fred* for the rake. _who did Barney ask for the rake?_

9. Fred returned it *two weeks later.* _when did Fred return it?_

10. *The lawnmower* was very expensive. _what was very expensive?_

PART 3: Circle the past tense error and correct it in the space provided.

Example: Why (you were) late? _Why were you late?_

11. The boys shoped for socks yesterday. _shopped_

12. Why Melanie ignored us last night? _why did Melanie ignore us last night?_

13. That bar did'nt open last Friday. _didn't open_

14. Why Arthur was so angry yesterday? _why was Arthur so angry ___?_

15. I studyied for three hours last night. _studied_

COMMUNICATE ▶ Interview

Interview a partner in the language lab or classroom. You could also do this activity at home, and interview a family member. Ask your partner about the following topics. After the interview you could make a short oral presentation explaining the most interesting information that you discovered during the interview.

Ask questions about the following subjects or invent your own subjects. If your partner is not comfortable talking about a certain topic (such as "medical history"), you could skip that topic and go to another. You will need your dictionary so that you can look up any unfamiliar terms. Make sure that you use correct question forms.

- best year of his/her life
- worst job
- biggest mistake
- medical history
- most embarrassing moment
- best memory
- favorite hobby or activity
- greatest achievement
- first job
- most thrilling moment
- worst injury
- recurring dream or nightmare

5 The Simple Past Tense: Irregular Verbs

In the previous section you looked at regular verbs. However, a great number of English verbs are irregular, that is, the verb changes spelling in the past tense. If you have trouble remembering how to write past tense verb forms, then you must memorize the past form of the most common verbs.

This section provides you with an opportunity to review question and negative forms of the present and past tenses. The Vocabulary Boost contains pet-related vocabulary. There is a communication activity at the end of this section that reinforces the past tense.

VOCABULARY BOOST **Animal Kingdom**

EXERCISE 1

PART 1: Match the adult animal with its infant.

dot	**1.** human	kitten
calf	**2.** horse	puppy
kitten	**3.** cow	duckling
puppy	**4.** cat	child
piglet	**5.** dog	kid
kid	**6.** pig	calf
duckling	**7.** goat	piglet
	8. duck	colt

PART 2: Match each animal to its *significant* body part. If any words are unfamiliar, consult your dictionary. Although some animals have more than one of the body parts listed, match each animal to only one body part.

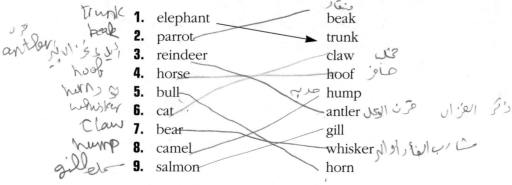

(handwritten margin notes): trunk, beak, antler, hoof, horn, whisker, claw, hump, gill

1. elephant — beak
2. parrot — trunk
3. reindeer — claw حلب
4. horse — hoof صنو
5. bull — hump حدب
6. cat — antler قرن الايل
7. bear — gill
8. camel — whisker
9. salmon — horn

(Arabic annotations): ذكر العزال قرن الايل / شباريب الفأر والقط

Does your country have a "national" animal? What is it?   **Camel**

Irregular Past Tense Verbs

EXERCISE 2

Do you know the past tense form of these irregular verbs? Put the past form in the spaces provided. Do as many as you can. If you need help, check the irregular verb list in the appendix; look at the middle, "simple past" column.

#	verb	past	#	verb	past	#	verb	past
1.	be	was, were	16.	drive	drove	31.	lend	lent
2.	become	became	17.	eat	ate	32.	lose	lost
3.	begin	began	18.	fall	fell	33.	make	made
4.	bite	bit	19.	feel	felt	34.	meet	met
5.	break	broke	20.	fight	fought	35.	pay	paid
6.	bring	brought	21.	find	found	36.	read	read
7.	buy	bought	22.	get	got	37.	ride	rode
8.	catch	caught	23.	give	gave	38.	sing	sang
9.	choose	chose	24.	go	went	39.	sleep	slept
10.	cost	cost	25.	grow	grew	40.	speak	spoke
11.	cut	cut	26.	have	had	41.	take	took
12.	dig	dug	27.	hear	heard	42.	teach	taught
13.	do	did	28.	hold	held	43.	tell	told
14.	draw	drew	29.	know	knew	44.	think	thought
15.	drink	drank	30.	leave	left	45.	win	won

EXERCISE 3

In the following sentences, underline the verb(s) and change it/them to the past tense.

	Now	**In the 1980s**
Example:	Sam <u>keeps</u> his valuables under his mattress	*kept*
1.	Mr. Riffo <u>teaches</u> students how to speak Spanish.	taught
2.	I <u>think</u> that I <u>know</u> you.	thought, knew
3.	Patrick <u>writes</u>, but <u>doesn't speak</u>, Spanish.	wrote, didn't speak
4.	I always <u>tell</u> the truth.	told
5.	Clair <u>doesn't</u> understand her mother's point of view.	didn't understand
6.	Lise <u>spends</u> a lot of time at the club.	spent
7.	I <u>choose</u> to speak English at home.	chose
8.	Karen <u>pays</u> for her own flying lessons.	paid

NEVER use the past verb form after:

1. *to* in infinitive forms. Incorrect: *The children needed to spoke with us.*
   Correct: *The children needed **to speak** with us.*

2. *did. Did* makes a sentence past tense, and the following verb must be in the base form. Incorrect: *Mother didn't told us why you were late.*
   Correct: *Mother **didn't tell** us why you were late.*

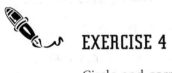

EXERCISE 4

Circle and correct the past tense errors. If the sentence is correct, write *C* in the space provided.

1. Moe didn't <u>realized</u> that the movie was over. didn't realize

2. Why you pretended to recognize me? why did you pretend___?

3. My mother taught me to <u>ate</u> slowly. to eat

4. Why didn't you finish your coffee? C

5. I really <u>thougth</u> that I knew the answer. thought

6. There <u>was</u> forty people at the show. were

7. Bernie didn't <u>knew</u> what to say last night. didn't know

8. Where she <u>went</u> on her last trip? Where did she go___?

Tense Review: Past and Present

CLASS EXERCISE

Fill in the blanks using the correct tense of the verb. Then rewrite the sentence as a question, and as a negative statement. Finally, write down what verb tense was used and why.

Example: Chelsea (be) ___is___ from England.

Question: *Is Chelsea from England?*

Negative: *Chelsea isn't from England.*

Verb tense? *Simple Present, because the action is a fact.*

1. Leo (speak) ___speaks___ four languages.

    Question: _Does leo speak four languages?_

    Negative: _leo doesn't speak four languages_

    Verb tense? _Simple Present, because the action is a fact_

2. Cecelia (be) ___was___ very tired yesterday.

    Question: Why _was cecelia very tired yesterday_

    Negative: _cecelia wasn't very tired yesterday_

    Verb tense? _Simple Past, because the action is in the past_

3. Lauren often (fight) ___fights___ with her sister.

    Question: Why _often does Lauren fight with her sister?_

    Negative: _Lauren often doesn't fight with her sister._

    Verb tense? _Simple present, because the action is a fact_

4. John (drink) ___drank___ too much coffee yesterday.

    Question: Why _did John drink too much coffee yesterday?_

    Negative: _John didn't drink ___

    Verb tense? _Simple past, the action in the past_

5. Rachel (write) _is writing_ a letter right now.

    Question: _Is Rachel writing a letter right now_

    Negative: _Rachel isn't writing ___

    Verb tense? _Present progressive, because the action is happened right now._

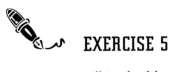

EXERCISE 5

Fill in the blank using the correct <u>present</u> or past tense of the verb.

1. Isn't that sweet? That little girl (pet) _is petting_ that poodle. (She, know) _Does she know_ that poodle?

2. My uncle (believe) _believes_ in ghosts. He (think) _thinks_ that our house is haunted. Right now, he (try) _is trying_ to find the ghost.

3. Last weekend, my friend (lend) _lent_ me ten dollars. I (pay) _paid_ her back yesterday. I (give) _gave_ her the money when we (be) _were_ in math class yesterday afternoon. Now she (think) _thinks_ that I still (owe) _owe_ her ten dollars. Why (I, borrow) _did I borrow_ ten dollars last weekend? Never borrow money from a friend.

4. Why (you, cry) _are you crying_ right now? (You, need) _Do you need_ a Kleenex? Look! Your sister (get) _is getting_ you a Kleenex right now. Try to stay calm.

EXERCISE 6

Make questions from the following sentences. The answer is in bold.

1. She is **seventeen** years old. _____*How old is she?*_____

2. Siri has **three children**. _How many children does she have?_

3. Raoul is thinking about **his father**. _Who is Raoul thinking about?_

4. The boy asked for **food**. _What did the boy ask for?_

5. William did **very well** on the test. _How did William do on the test?_

6. The theater is **four kilometers** from here. _How far is the theater from here?_

7. That word means "**really**." _What does that word mean?_

8. Mark gave the money to **Jenna**. _Who did Mark give the money to?_

9. **Jenna** made the mess. _Who made the mess?_

10. Alex went to the movie **yesterday**. _When did Alex go to the movie?_

Short Answers

You can answer questions with short answers.

Do you take cream with your coffee? **Yes, I do.** OR **No, I don't.**

(It is not necessary to repeat the question; just repeat the auxiliary.)

EXERCISE 7

Write short answers for the following questions. Use pronouns in your answers.

		Affirmative	**Negative**
1.	Do you like coffee?	*Yes, I do.*	*No, I don't.*
2.	Does your brother live nearby?	yes, he does	No, he doesn't
3.	Did Mr. Axel phone Jane?	yes, he did	No, he didn't
4.	Is the room warm enough for you?	yes, it is	No, it isn't
5.	Are your children with their father?	yes, they are	No, they aren't
6.	Do you want some spinach?	yes, I do	No, I don't
7.	Did the bell ring?	yes, it did	No, it didn't
8.	Was Moira sick yesterday?	yes, she was	No, she wasn't
9.	Does the course last for three hours?	yes, it does	No, it doesn't
10.	Is the wine cold?	yes, it is	No, it isn't

Embedded Questions

When a question is part of a larger sentence (when it is **embedded**), no longer use the special question word order.

Question	**Embedded Question**
*What **do** you want for your birthday?*	*He wonders **what you want for your birthday**.*

Use *if* or *whether* if there is no question word.

| ***Did** you finish your salad?* | *He wonders **if you finished your salad**.* |

EXERCISE 8

Make a new sentence from these questions.

Example: What does "harness" mean?   I wonder   *what "harness" means.*

Since you do not need to follow the regular question word order, in embedded questions you can drop the auxiliary *do, does* or *did*.

1. What is Steve doing?   I want to know _what steve is doing?_
2. Where does Ian live?   She wonders _where Ian lives_
3. Why are the guests late?   I would like to know _why the guests are late_
4. Does Ted smoke?   Can you tell me if _Ted someks_
5. What is that boy doing?   She wonders _what that boy is doing?_
6. When did she leave?   Can you tell me _when she left_
7. Is Kim watching TV?   I would like to know if _Kim is watching T.V_
8. What do the children want?   She wants to know _what the children want_

EXERCISE 9: PRONUNCIATION REVIEW

Are the following words pronounced as one or two syllables? Put *1* or *2* in the blanks.

1. kisses _____2_____   6. tries _____1_____   11. hopes _____1_____
2. guarded _____2_____   7. pleases _____2_____   12. folded _____2_____
3. adds _____1_____   8. crosses _____2_____   13. reaches _____2_____
4. wasn't _____2_____   9. weren't _____1_____   14. thanked _____1_____
5. wasted _____2_____   10. helped _____1_____   15. prompted _____2_____

EXERCISE 10

PART 1: Combine the words in parentheses using the present or past tenses.

1. (Alf / go) to Acapulco every winter. _Alf goes_
2. (Those snakes / be / not) poisonous. _Those snakes aren't_
3. Last March (they / go) to Europe. _Last March they went_
4. (That magic card / cost) $10. _That magic card costs $10_
5. Yesterday (we / buy) new shoes. _we bought_
6. (Mark / come / not) home yesterday. _Mark didn't come_
7. (The dogs / eat not) yesterday. _The dogs didn't eat_

PART 2: Circle and correct any present or past tense errors in the following sentences. The verb is in italics.

8. Marnie *didn't liked* her Christmas present. _didn't like_

9. Look! The survey *prove* that most people *hate* spinach. _proves_

10. Why Gary *plays* piano every evening? why _does Gary play --?_

11. Where Becky *ate* lunch yesterday? where _did Becky eat --?_

12. Ryan *thought* that we *ate* too much yesterday. _thought_

13. My team *have* too many people in it. _has_

14. Carol *work's* with juvenile delinquents. _works_

15. Last night my sister *didn't liked* the pizza. _didn't like_

CLASS EXERCISE ▪ REVIEW

Change the verbs in parentheses into the correct tense. The verb may be in one of the present or past tenses. If this is used as a quiz, there are twenty spaces in this exercise.

1. The study (prove) _proved_ that chimpanzees can use sign language. Mark (want) _wants_ the government to continue to fund his work.

2. Last year Louise (drive) _drove_ an old Chevy. Now she (own) _owns_ a Honda. Her husband (has, not) _doesn't have_ a car because he (know, not) _doesn't know_ how to drive.

3. Right now the mice (eat) _is eating_ some cheese. Where (be) _is_ the cats?

4. Look out the window. It (rain) _is raining_ cats and dogs.

5. Jo: (You, do) _Did you do_ your homework last night?

   Tim: No, I (do, not) _didn't do_ my homework last night.

6. Sue: When (Ron, leave) _did Ron leave_ for work yesterday?

   Rita: Ron (go, not) _didn't go_ to work yesterday. He (feel) _felt_ sick yesterday, but today he (be) _was_ fine.

7. My mother (know, not) _doesn't know_ how to use the Internet. (You, know) _Do you know_ how to use it?

8. Three weeks ago I (see) _____saw_____ a concert at the arena. There (be) _____were_____ too many people at that concert.

9. Elliot (buy) _____bought_____ some bagels last weekend. Now the bagels are stale.

| COMMUNICATE | Tell the Truth |

The game Tell the Truth provides you with the opportunity to practice question formation and correct use of the present and past tenses. In groups of three, brainstorm about interesting or life-changing incidents that have happened to each of you. One story that is the most interesting is then chosen. In front of the class, each one of you must pretend that the story is true for you, even though it is really true for only one of you. The other two must answer classmates' questions with lies.

If you can't think of an interesting event in your life, ask yourself the following questions. Have you ever:

- won an award?
- been on a good sports team?
- met a famous person?
- been lost?
- been badly hurt?
- lost something valuable?
- been in the hospital?
- done something silly when you were very young?

- seen a crime?
- won a trophy?
- visited a foreign country?
- saved someone?
- been in a car accident or a bike accident?
- done something silly to your brother or sister?
- won a prize?

Remember, you need just one interesting statement per group of three students. For example:

> Bob, Pedro and Pierre decide to use Bob's story about winning a tennis trophy. All three students begin by announcing to the class, "I won a tennis trophy a while ago." The class proceeds to question the three students in an attempt to find out who really won the tennis trophy. A student in the class asks the three boys when they won the trophy. Pedro and Pierre lie about the event and the circumstances, but Bob tells the truth. For example, Pedro says that he won the trophy when he was 15. Pierre says he won last summer. Bob tells the truth: he won it when he was 16 years old. After about ten minutes the class votes for the student that they believe is telling the truth.

6 Spelling and Word Choice

Spelling correctly in another language can be difficult. Even native speakers make spelling errors. However, correct spelling is important if you want to present yourself as professionally as possible.

Most of us have certain bad spelling habits. For example, many students misspell the word *with* by writing *whit*. The best way to break a bad spelling habit is to keep a list of your spelling errors. Then, after you write a text, always reread your text and consult your list to check that your habitual errors have not reoccurred. It is also very important to have a dictionary handy when you do a writing assignment.

If you are proficient on the computer, then you know that most computer programs have a spell-check function. Be careful, however: spell-checks can find some misspelled words, but not words that sound alike but differ in meaning. For example, a spell-check would not find the mistakes in this sentence: *Your to young to drive to there house alone* (**You're too** young to drive to **their** house alone).

Because this section already focuses on the proper choice of word, there is no Vocabulary Boost.

Spelling

Adding a Prefix or a Suffix

When you add a prefix (*un, pre, il, ir,* etc.) to a word, keep the last letter of the prefix and the first letter of the base word.

    ir + regular = i<u>rr</u>egular   (two *r*s)

The same rule applies to the addition of a suffix. If you add *ly* to a word that ends in *l,* then your new word will have double *l.*

    final + ly   = fina<u>ll</u>y   (two *l*s)

EXERCISE 1

The following words are incorrectly spelled. Write each word correctly.

Example: actualy _____*actually*_____

1. mispelled _____

2. hopefuly _____

3. finaly _____

4. ilegal _____

5. nicelly _____

6. unecessary _____

7. generaly _____

8. surelly _____

9. realy _____

10. iliterate _____

Spelling Rule

i before *e* except after *c*, or when sounding like "ay" as in *neighbor* and *weigh*

EXERCISE 2

This exercise contains words that have an "ie" spelling problem, as well as words that are commonly misspelled. Which word is correctly spelled? Put *A, B* or *C* in the space provided.

1. A. receive   B. recieve   C. receeve   _____

2. A. writting   B. writing   C. writeing   _____

3. A. buisness   B. busines   C. business   _____

4. A. believe   B. beleive   C. believ   _____

5. A. suceed   B. succede   C. succeed   _____

6. A. reciept   B. receipt   C. reseipt   _____

7. A. human   B. humin   C. humain   _____

8. A. exemple   B. example   C. exempel   _____

9. A. an other   B. anoter   C. another   _____

10. A. whit   B. with   C. wiht   _____

11. A. compagny   B. companie   C. company   _____

12. A. responsible   B. responsuble   C. responsable   _____

EXERCISE 3

These sentences each have one spelling mistake. Circle the spelling error in each sentence and write the word correctly in the space provided.

> ### *Witch* vs. *Which*
>
> A *Witch* is a person who practices a pre-Christian religion.
> *Which* indicates one choice among several: *Which cake do you want?*

1. When you smoke, you give a bad exemple to your children. _____

2. I'm not shure what the answer is. _____

3. Please do the work whit me. _____

4. I would like to order an other coffee please. _____

5. Can you tell me wich flavor of gum you prefer? _____

6. Monica is writting a letter to her boyfriend again! _____

7. Witch day of the week do you have off? _____

8. I realy want to help you do the work. _____

9. The buisness is going very well. _____

Word Choice

CLASS EXERCISE

Alone or with a partner, write sentences using the following words.

1. Use *then* when you continue a story and *than* when you compare two things. Write sentences using the following:

Than _____

Then _____

2. A *desert* is a hot, sandy place. You eat *dessert* after a meal. Write sentences using the following:

Dessert _____

Desert _____

3. Write sentences using each of the following words:

Wear _____

Where _____

We're _____

4. Write sentences using each of the following words.

They're _____

Their _____

There _____

5. Students often mistake "he has" for "there is." Write down the translation for these phrases, then write two sentences.

He has _____

There is _____

EXERCISE 4

Choose the correct words from the lists provided.

1. *(still / steal / steel)*

Which word means "to rob"? _____

Which word means "not moving" or "continuing to exist"? _____

Which word means "a hard alloy of iron and carbon"? _____

Put one of these words in each space below.

Does your father _____ work for that company that produces

_____? I heard that the company treats its employees very badly. In

fact, didn't the owner _____ some money from the employee pension

fund? I'm surprised that your dad _____ works there.

2. *(lose / loose / lost)*

Which word is a present-tense verb? _____

Which word is a past-tense verb? _____

Which word is an adjective meaning *not tight*? _____

Put one of these words in each space below.

I didn't _____ my new belt; I gave it to my friend because it isn't tight

enough. It is too _____ for me. I don't know why you thought that

I _____ my shoes. I never _____ things.

3. *(their / there / they're)*

Which word is a possessive pronoun? _____

Which word means *they are*? _____

Which word means *not here*? _____

Put one of these words in each space below.

_____ are many people in this country who can't find work. I have two unemployed uncles. _____ trying very hard to find jobs, but _____ are no jobs available. Both uncles have lost _____ cars, and now they may lose _____ homes because they can no longer pay the mortgages.

4. *(to, too, two)*

Which word means *also* or *excessive*? _____

Which word means *between one and three*? _____

Which word follows verbs of movement such as *go, run, move*, etc? _____

Put one of these words in each space below.

There are _____ reasons for me to stay at my job. There are perhaps several reasons that I should leave, _____. If I go _____ another workplace, I may find myself with the same types of problems. It's really _____ difficult to make a decision now.

5. *(his / is / has / as)*

Put one of these words in each space below.

_____ that Don's desk? I need to leave this package on _____ desk. _____ he in _____ office or _____ he at _____ home? Also, Don _____ my report. _____ soon _____ he arrives, could someone let me know? _____ anyone listening to me?

6. *(your / you're)*

Put one of these words in each space below.

Is that _____ pen? I need to sign that letter. If _____ not using that pen right now, could I borrow it please?

Learn vs. Teach

The person discovering information *learns*. The person giving the information *teaches*.

EXERCISE 5

Circle and correct the errors in the following sentences. If the sentence is correct, write *C* in the space provided.

1. My mother learned me how to make cookies.   _____

2. I want to learn how to speak Russian because I might go there one day.   _____

3. The engineering students must learn how to read blueprints.   _____

4. Please learn me how to sew!   _____

5. My father often teaches me how to repair the car.   _____

6. I learned myself how to type.   _____

Some and Any

Generally use *some* in affirmative sentences and *any* in negative sentences. (This rule also applies to *something, somewhere, someone,* and *anything, anywhere, anyone.*)

> There is **something** in my soup.

> No, there isn't **anything** in your soup.

Any can also mean "it doesn't matter which."

> Borrow **any** book that you like.

EXERCISE 6

1. Use *some* or *any*.

Anne: Would you like _____ coffee?

Joe: Yes, I'd love _____ coffee.

Anne: Would you like _____ cream and sugar?

Joe: Well, I'd like _____ cream, but I don't want _____ sugar.

2. Use *some, any, something* or *anything*.

Anne: And would you like _____ else to eat?

Joe: No thanks. I don't want _____ else. Excuse me, but do you know where I could change _____ traveller's checks?

Anne: Oh, you can change them at _____ bank.

3. Use *someone* or *anyone*.

Joe: Is there a bank near here?

Anne: I don't know. You'll have to ask _____ else.

Joe: But you don't understand. I don't know _____ in this town!

Watch, Look and Listen

We *look* at something that is immobile; for example, we look at a picture or a house. Follow *look* with the preposition *at*.

Look at me! **Look at** this picture!

We *watch* something that is moving; for example, we watch a movie or people who pass by.

Did you **watch** TV last night?

We *listen* to something that makes noise. Although in French it is correct to say "We listen to TV," in English we *watch* TV; we *listen* to the radio. Always follow *listen* with the preposition *to*.

Listen to the teacher.

EXERCISE 7

Each of the following sentences contains a word-choice error. There may also be a missing preposition (*to, at*). Correct the error in the space provided. If the sentence is correct, write *C* in the space.

1. Mr. Dahti listened to a movie last night. He thought the visual   _____
   effects were great.

2. My friends and I listen the radio every Saturday morning.   _____

3. I like to look to paintings by Vincent Van Gogh.   _____

4. What TV show do you listen most often?   _____

5. Please concentrate and listen the professor. He is very interesting.   _____

6. Why are you watching the ceiling? What is so interesting?   _____

7. The people in the audience listened to the beautiful music.   _____

8. When I speak, I would like you to listen me!   _____

Make vs. Do

Do usually means "to perform or accomplish."

Do: *your homework / an exercise / a good job / your best / the taxes*
the housework (the dishes / the ironing / the cleaning)

We do not *do* the beds; we *make* them.

Generally, *make* means "to construct, manufacture or create."

Make: *a cake / a sculpture / meals / plans / a mess / an effort*

We also use *make* with the following:

Make: *a mistake / money / an appointment / a reservation / a telephone call*

EXERCISE 8

Fill in the blanks with *make* or *do*. Use the correct verb tense!

Eric got up early yesterday. It was a very busy day. First, he (**1**) __made__ the bed. Then

he (**2**) _____ breakfast for his children. Next he had to (**3**) _____

the cleaning. He (**4**) _____ the laundry, and then he decided to (**5**)

_____ a phone call to Dan.

At noon, Eric (**6**) _____ lunch, and then he called the doctor. He

(**7**) _____ an appointment for 4 p.m. instead of 3 p.m., because he had

to (**8**) _____ his math homework. He (**9**) _____ three pages.

After he finished his homework, Eric (**10**) _____ his taxes, because

the deadline was coming. Most of Eric's friends don't (**11**) _____ their

own taxes; they pay a tax specialist to (**12**) _____ them. What do you

(**13**) _____ for a living?

Say vs. Tell

Use *say:*	in direct quotations	*Don* **said**, *"I am going to bed."*
	in indirect quotations	*Don* **said** *that he was going to bed.*
		(*that* is optional)
Use *tell:*	When you give a message to somebody. *Tell* is generally followed by a name or a pronoun.	
	Don **told me** *that he was going to bed. Did he* **tell you** *that too?*	
	Also use *tell* with these expressions: *tell a lie / the truth / a secret.*	

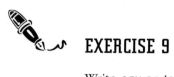

EXERCISE 9

Write *say* or *tell* in the spaces provided. Use the proper verb tense.

1. Last night Martin _____ that he was going to bed, but he really _____ a lie.

2. His parents _____ him to turn out his lights and go to sleep.

3. They _____ that Martin had been grumpy all day and they _____ Martin that he needed a good night's sleep.

4. Martin _____ his parents that he would obey them, but instead he grabbed a book and a flashlight and he read under the covers.

5. In the morning, Martin's parents _____ that he looked very tired.

6. Martin _____ his parents that he couldn't sleep.

7. When Martin's mother _____ that she knew he had been reading during the night, Martin then _____ the truth to his parents.

EXERCISE 10

Identify the *say/tell* errors. Write the correction in the space provided.

1. She said me that she can't come to the movie with us. _____

2. Eric told that he had to work late. _____

3. Carolyn always tells to me that she likes pizza. _____

4. What did you just tell? _____

5. Alan told that he must finish his report. _____

CLASS EXERCISE ▪ REVIEW

PART 1: Circle the letter of the correctly spelled word.

1. a. for example   b. for exemple

2. a. wich   b. which

3. a. whit   b. with

4. a. humain   b. human

5. a. shure   b. sure

6. a. really   b. realy

PART 2: Put *some* or *any* in the spaces provided.

7. Please don't ask me _____ more questions.

8. I would like _____ cheese on my spaghetti.

9. I don't want _____ chilies.

10. My sister doesn't eat _____thing with salt in it.

11. Mary really doesn't want _____ pity.

PART 3: Put *learn* or *teach* in the space provided. Use the correct tense of the verb.

12. Every Saturday, my mother _____ me how to use the computer.

13. My sister wants to _____ how to type. Maybe I will show her how to do it.

14. Jerry _____ his dog how to do many tricks last summer.

15. I always _____ a lot of interesting things from my grandmother.

PART 4: Put *say* or *tell* in the space provided. Use the correct tense of the verb.

16. What did Jennifer just _____ you?

17. Mr. James always _____ that he has nine lives.

18. What did you just _____ ?

19. You should never _____ a lie.

PART 5: Circle and correct the spelling error. There is one error in each sentence.

20. The day is just beginning and their aren't any more donuts left. _____

21. I think that man is steeling some money from the cash register. _____

22. I tought that I finished that project a week ago! _____

23. Becky always gets more food then I do. It isn't fair. _____

24. Can someone tell me wich person ate the last donut? _____

25. Look! Angela is winning an other race! _____

COMMUNICATE   Spelling Contest

The class will be divided into teams of about five students each. The teacher will ask each group in turn to spell a difficult word. The teacher may also give the group a sentence with an error in it and ask the group to identify the error. Each team must discuss the proper spelling. However, no student is allowed to look in the dictionary.

Review of Sections 1 to 6

CLASS EXERCISE A ▪ PRONOUNS

Change the italicized nouns in the following sentences into pronouns. (15 points)

Example: *Jeff* likes *soup*.   *He / it.*

1. *The children* gave a gift to *their mother*. _____

2. *Ms. Hornby* met *my brother and me* at the station. _____

3. *Sally* gave *her children* some chocolate. _____

4. *That house* is *my and Richard's* house. _____

5. The doctor drove *the boys* to the clinic. _____

6. Is that little girl *Mark's* sister? _____

7. Did *Donna* tell *Donna's* husband about the affair? _____

8. Why is Jimmy talking to *Jimmy's* mother? _____

9. Give the extra money to *my brother*. _____

10. Gregory is *Diane's* boyfriend. _____

CLASS EXERCISE B ▪ SIMPLE PRESENT TENSE

Make sentences out of the following sets of words. (20 points)

Example: Uday / like / not / coffee.   *Uday doesn't like coffee.*

1. The children / agree / not / with you. _____

2. My uncle / work / at that store.   _____

3. I / be / not / very hungry.   _____

4. Those roads / be / very dangerous.   _____

5. That nurse / have / a white uniform.   _____

Make questions out of the following sets of words.

6. The piano / be / very heavy?   _____

7. Your son / want / more cereal?   _____

8. You / have / a cat?   _____

9. Ron / agree / with us?   _____

10. Your mother / be / very wise?   _____

CLASS EXERCISE C ▪ THE PRESENT TENSES

Fill in the blanks with either the simple present or the present progressive tense. (20 points)

1. Right now, Simon (give) _____ a speech before a large group of people. There (be) _____ about two hundred people in the room. Simon usually (feel) _____ nervous when he (speak) _____ before a group, but at the moment he (be) _____ quite relaxed. He (breathe) _____ slowly. To help him relax, Simon (imagine) _____ that the people in the audience are just wearing their underwear.

2. Look! An airplane (fly) _____ very low. The plane (look) _____ like it might hit a building! What (the pilot / do) _____ ?

3. Martin (hate) _____ violent movies. He (think) _____ that the story of a movie is more important than the action. (You / agree) _____ with Martin? I (agree / not) _____ with him. I (enjoy) _____ action movies.

4. There (be) _____ many birds in that tree. Listen. The birds (sing) _____ . Every spring the birds (build) _____ nests in that tree. If you look carefully, you can see that a bird (build) _____ a nest right now. It (be) _____ a sparrow.

CLASS EXERCISE D ▪ TENSE REVIEW

Option: Do this exercise in teams.

For each of the following sentences, indicate what verb tense was used (simple present, present progressive or simple past) and explain why that tense was used. The verb is in italics. Then rewrite the sentence in question form and in negative form. (20 points)

> Example: They always *walk* to work.   Tense: ___simple present tense___
>
> Reason for this tense? ___Because the action is a habit.___
>
> Question form: ___Do they always walk to work?___
>
> Negative form: ___They don't always walk to work.___

1. Alli *lives* alone.   Tense: _____

Reason for this tense? _____

Question form: _____

Negative form: _____

2. David often *sees* Shiva.   Tense: _____

Reason for this tense? _____

Question form: _____

Negative form: _____

3. David *went* to the opera last Saturday.   Tense: _____

Reason for this tense? _____

Question form: _____

Negative form: _____

4. Right now Kyle *is writing* a note.   Tense: _____

Reason for this tense? _____

Question form: _____

Negative form: _____

5. Bob *voted* for the Green Party last year. Tense: _____

Reason for this tense? _____

Question form: _____

Negative form: _____

CLASS EXERCISE E ▪ TENSES: QUESTION FORMS

Choose the correct verb or set of verbs. Write the letter of the answer in the space provided. (10 points)

1. Where ... they usually ... supper? _____
   a) does / eat   b) do / eat   c) did / ate   d) (nothing) / eat

2. ... Willy and Alex ... to San Francisco together last July? _____
   a) Did / went   b) Do / went   c) Did / go   d) Does / went

3. ... the judge ... some more tea? _____
   a) Does / want   b) Do / wants   c) (nothing) / wants   d) Do / does want

4. ... the report ... ready now? _____
   a) Do / is   b) Does / is   c) Is / (nothing)   d) Is / is

5. Why ... Jane often ...... all of the work alone? _____
   a) does / do   b) do / does   c) (nothing) / does   d) does / (nothing)

6. ... your little sister ... a new doll last Christmas? _____
   a) Did / gets   b) Did / got   c) Do / got   d) Did / get

7. Last night, my mother ... that I was rude to her. _____
   a) thought   b) thougth   c) thinks   d) thinked

8. ... you ... to me right now? _____
   a) Do / are listening   b) Are / listening
   c) Are / are listening   d) (nothing) / are listening

9. ... the girls ... in bed now? _____
   a) Are / are   b) Do / are   c) Are / (nothing)   d) (nothing) / are

10. Why ... Mary ... on the test last Monday? _____
   a) did / cheated   b) do / cheated   c) did / cheats   d) did / cheat

CLASS EXERCISE F ▪ EMBEDDED QUESTIONS

Make the following questions into embedded questions. (10 points)

   Example: What are you doing.   I wonder _____ *what you are doing.* _____

1. When is the interview?   Can you tell me _____

2. What do you want?   I wonder _____

3. Does Jean like peas?   Do you know if _____

4. Are there any leftovers?   I want to know if _____

5. Why is she crying?   Can you tell me _____

6. What did Zeke say to her?   Do you know _____

7. When is the next bus?   Can you tell me _____

8. Why did Laura leave?   Do you know _____

9. Where is the bus station?   Do you know _____

10. Did he wash the dishes?   Do you know if _____

CLASS EXERCISE G ▪ SPELLING AND WORD CHOICE

PART 1: Write the misspelled word correctly in the space provided. (10 points)

1. though   _____   **6.** compagny   _____

2. finaly   _____   **7.** iregular   _____

3. shure   _____   **8.** whit   _____

4. writting   _____   **9.** humain   _____

5. exemple   _____   **10.** realy   _____

PART 2: Circle the correct word in the following sentences. (10 points)

11. This work is making me (loose / loss / lose) my mind.

12. Henry wants to (look at / see / watch / listen to) TV now.

13. Please (learn / teach) me how to speak French!

14. Gerald thinks that he is (to / too / two) fat.

15. The Schinkles keep (there / their / they're) new car in a private garage.

16. When (there / their / they're) is more jewellery in this case, I worry that someone will (still / steel / steal) some of it.

17. What is (your / you're) last name? I need to know because (your / you're) on my list.

18. Ask Jerry to (say / tell) us the correct answer.

Prepositions and Plurals

Prepositions are those tiny words like *in, on, for, from* and so on. What complicates the learning of prepositions is that there are no rules that apply to all prepositions. However, there are some rules that apply some of the time. This section begins with a Vocabulary Boost that looks at some directional prepositions. You can then attempt an exercise that focuses on *in, on* and *at*.

The majority of the section focuses on problems with plurals, the articles *a* and *the*, and count and non-count nouns. There is a communication activity at the end of this section that gives you an opportunity to speak using prepositions.

VOCABULARY BOOST	Prepositions

EXERCISE 1

Look at the following pictures. Put the correct preposition under the picture.

Choose one of the following prepositions:

under	above	on	beside
behind	between	inside	in front of

1. The man is _____ the square.   **2.** The man is _____ the square.

3. The man is _____ the square.

4. The man is _____ the squares.

5. The man is _____ the square.

6. The man is _____ the square.

7. The man is _____ the square.

8. The man is _____ the square.

EXERCISE 2

Fill in the blanks with the appropriate prepositions of time and place. You can use *in*, *on* or *at*. The following diagram indicates when you can use *in*, *on* and *at* most of the time.

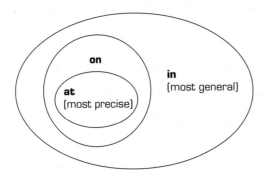

Place		**Time**	
in:	city, country	*in*:	year, month
on:	street	*on*:	day
at:	specific address	*at*:	time of day

1. Detective Spade was, _____ 5 a.m. in the morning, trying to find the address of Joe McBain. Spade knew that Joe lived _____ King Street, _____ number 213. Although Spade found King Street, there wasn't a number 213. Maybe Joe McBain was _____ another town or _____ another state. Maybe McBain was _____ another country. McBain was a murderer, and Spade had to find him.

2. Spade decided to call on an informer, Jimmy Green. Spade called Jimmy and arranged to meet _____ March, _____ the 23rd, _____ five o'clock in the morning. Spade would meet Jimmy _____ an all-night garage _____ Angel Street.

3. Spade waited _____ the garage for hours. Finally, _____ about 6 a.m., Spade recognized Jimmy passing by the window with his arm around Joe McBain. Spade hurried outside and grabbed Joe.

4. There was a trial _____ April. The trial ended _____ June 30. The trial took place _____ the old courthouse _____ Gibson Avenue.

Plurals

CLASS EXERCISE

PART 1: Look at the plural noun. Write the singular form of the noun in the space provided.

1. children   _____*child*_____   **6.** knives   _____

2. women   _____   **7.** lives   _____

3. men   _____   **8.** boys   _____

4. teeth   _____   **9.** cities   _____

5. feet   _____   **10.** parties   _____

PART 2

11. The nouns in numbers 1 to 5 are irregular plurals. Why are they called irregular?

_____

12. The nouns in numbers 6 and 7 change from the singular to the plural form. Write a rule about the change.

_____

13. The nouns in numbers 8 to 10 end in *y* in the singular form. When should the *y* change to *i*?

_____

If you have trouble answering the above questions, you can refer to the following box.

Plural Forms

	Singular	Plural
Most plural nouns simply have an *s* ending.	cat	cats
Add *es* to nouns ending in *s*, *ch*, *sh*, *x* or *z*.	fax	faxes
	church	churches
For most nouns ending in *f*, the *f* changes to *ves* in the plural form.	life	lives
	knife	knives
When nouns end in consonant-*y*, change the *y* to *ies* in the plural form.	company	companies
	body	bodies

Irregular Plurals

	Singular	Plural
Some nouns have irregular plural forms. These irregular forms do not need an additional s!	child	children
	man	men
	woman	women
	person	people
	mouse	mice
	foot	feet
	tooth	teeth
Many animal names do not change in the plural form.	fish	fish
	deer	deer
	sheep	sheep

EXERCISE 3

Write the plural form of the following nouns in the spaces provided.

1. woman _____
2. child _____
3. fish _____
4. kiss _____
5. lottery _____
6. box _____
7. bush _____
8. factory _____

9. leaf _____
10. person _____
11. boy _____
12. fly _____
13. hose _____
14. church _____
15. gentleman _____
16. dish _____

Non-Count Nouns

You can put a number before count nouns; count nouns are nouns that have a plural form.

*I know **three people** in this room.*   *There are **fifty cars** in the parking lot.*

If you can't put a number directly before a noun *(a noun is a person, place or thing)*, then it cannot be counted, and it has no plural form.

Count Nouns vs. Non-Count Nouns

Category nouns

These non-count nouns designate a category of objects.	The specific objects in each category can be counted, and are considered count nouns.
change	loonies, quarters, dimes, nickels, pennies
money	dollars
jewelry	necklaces, bracelets, rings
mail	letters, packages
homework	assignments, essays, projects
luggage	suitcases, boxes, trunks
equipment	helmets, bats, balls
furniture	sofas, chairs, tables
music	CDs, records, cassettes
clothing	shirts, skirts, pants
work	jobs, assignments

The following groups are also considered non-count nouns, and they have no plural forms.

Abstract nouns

advice, research, information, knowledge, violence, time (free time, extra time), evidence, experience, effort

Nature-related nouns

lightning, thunder, snow, hail, slush, sunshine, pollution, smoke, dust, dirt, grass, air, hair, electricity, radiation

Food nouns

water, milk, coffee, tea, meat, bread, cheese, ice, wine, rice, sugar, salt

CLASS EXERCISE

Make any of the italicized nouns plural, if necessary. If there is no plural form, write _**X**_ in the space.

Example: The *mail*__**X**__ is on the table. There are three *letter s* for you.

1.   I must write two *essay*____ this weekend. I have three science *assignment*____. I also have to do a lot of *research*____. I guess I have a lot of *homework*____.

2. Jan loves *pea____* and *carrot____*. In fact she loves all *vegetable____*. She doesn't like *bread____* or *cheese____*.

3. We need some *equipment____* for this office. We need some *desk____*, *table____* and *chair____*.

4. The man would like some *map____*. He also wants some *information____* about *camp-site____*.

5. I have three *problem____*. Please give me some *advice____*.

6. How many *time____* have I told you not to disturb me. I don't have any free *time____*!

EXERCISE 4

Read the following words. Write *C* beside words that can be counted; write *NC* beside words that cannot be counted and do not have a plural form. Write the plural form of the noun next to all count nouns.

1.	suitcase	*C suitcases*	**11.**	baseball	_____
2.	person	_____	**12.**	knowledge	_____
3.	music	_____	**13.**	stapler	_____
4.	office	_____	**14.**	clothing	_____
5.	homework	_____	**15.**	necklace	_____
6.	assignment	_____	**16.**	tooth	_____
7.	woman	_____	**17.**	equipment	_____
8.	desk	_____	**18.**	child	_____
9.	luggage	_____	**19.**	jewelry	_____
10.	advice	_____	**20.**	research	_____

Much vs. *Many*

With non-count nouns, use *much* or *a little*.

> How **much homework** do you have?   I just have **a little homework** tonight.

With count nouns, use *many* or *a few*.

> How **many suitcases** do you have?   I just have **a few bags**.

You can always replace *much* or *many* with the words *a lot of*.

EXERCISE 5

Write *much* or *many* in the spaces provided.

    Example: How   *much*   does that sofa cost? (*Money* is implied.)

1. I don't know _____ people in this room.

2. How _____ pages of homework do you have tonight?

3. I don't have _____ change. Can I borrow a quarter?

4. Those children don't have _____ clothing. I, on the other hand, have too _____ shirts. I should give away some clothing.

5. There isn't _____ information that I can give you. Call back later.

6. How _____ times have I told you that I'm very busy. I don't have _____ free time.

7. How _____ jewelry was stolen? Did you have _____ pieces of jewelry in that safe?

8. My late grandfather didn't have _____ different jobs in his life. Because there wasn't _____ work available, he remained a farmer throughout his life.

Articles

A / An

The article *a* (or *an*) means "one," therefore you cannot put *a* before a non-count noun. Put *a* or *an* before singular count nouns when you want to discuss general, rather than specific, items. Generally, put *an* before words beginning with a vowel.

Exceptions: Sometimes you must put *an* before the consonant *b*, when the *b* is silent. For example, the word "hour" is pronounced "our"; therefore you must write *an hour*. Sometimes you must put *a* before the vowel *u* when it sounds like "you," as in *a union*.

EXERCISE 6

Words beginning with a vowel or silent *b* take the article *an* instead of *a*. Some silent *b* words are *hour, honest, heir*. Write *A* or *An* before each of the following words.

    Example: *A*   horror film
                   An hour

1. _____ hospital	5. _____ holiday	9. _____ handkerchief
2. _____ heir	6. _____ history book	10. _____ helmet
3. _____ hero	7. _____ hourglass	
4. _____ hockey stick	8. _____ hill	

In the vast majority of words beginning with *h*, the *h* is pronounced.

EXERCISE 7

Put *A* or *AN* before the following count nouns. Put an *X* beside the non-count nouns. Remember that *a*, meaning "one," cannot be placed before a non-count noun.

    Example: __A__ doctor
                   __X__ advice

(*Advice* is a non-count noun; therefore, you cannot put an article meaning "one" before it.)

1. _____ opera	5. _____ old man	9. _____ dollar
2. _____ information	6. _____ letter	10. _____ homework
3. _____ hero	7. _____ mail	11. _____ university
4. _____ island	8. _____ underpass	12. _____ umbrella

The

The is placed before any nouns (count or non-count) and is used to indicate specific things. When we use *the*, the object is known to both the speaker and the listener.

    *I really need **a** new car. That Toyota is **the** car that I want to buy.*
            ↗   ↗
      general   specific

Do not put *the* before:

- languages. *English is easier to learn than Latin.*
- most country names. *I often visit Canada and the U.S., but I never visit England.*
- most city names. *I like Chicago and New York, but I prefer Montreal.*
- the nouns *life* and *death*. *His novels are about life and death.*

EXERCISE 8

Circle the errors in article usage in the following sentences. Write the correct article or noun form in the space provided. If the sentence is correct, write *C* in the space provided.

Example: I have (an) advice for you.   _____delete "an"_____

1. A children need to be disciplined.   _____

2. Henry is a best person for that job.   _____

3. The boys on my hockey team are really nice.   _____

4. I would like a honest answer to my question.   _____

5. The Vancouver is the best city in Canada.   _____

6. Many religions help people feel less afraid of the death. _____

7. Mr. Blair requires an information about the project.   _____

8. The French is a beautiful language.   _____

Adjectives: No Plural Form

Only nouns have a plural form. Adjectives always remain singular.

Incorrect: *Those are simples exercises.*   Correct: *Those are simple exercises.*

In some cases, adjectives can appear after *be* or after words like *appear, seem, look, feel*. These adjectives still keep the singular form.

*Those giraffes look **very intelligent**.*   *Those cars seem **expensive**.*

Sometimes nouns are used as adjectives. Like all adjectives, these adjectives remain singular.

*Those were **important life** lessons.*   *They are **earth-worm** breeders.*

EXERCISE 9

If the sentence is correct, write *C* in the space provided. If the sentence has an error in plural forms, correct it in the space provided.

Example: Many persons helped me.   _____people_____

1. There are some interesting fact about this case.   _____

2. Children are intelligents and they should be respected. _____

3. Those shoes are very practicals.   _____

4. That doctor gives her patients good advices.   _____

5. Kevin works in two differents places.   _____

6. There are many goods rules at that school.   _____

7. Sara doesn't have much informations about that show.   _____

8. We need some simples explanations about the meaning of life. _____

CLASS EXERCISE ▪ REVIEW

If the sentence is correct, write *C* in the space provided. If the sentence has an error related to plural form, correct it in the space provided.

Example: I enjoy simples stories.   _simple stories_

1. Abraham does his homeworks very carefully.   _____

2. Some of the new employee don't know how to use the
    cash machines.   _____

3. Childrens are not allowed on the new construction site.   _____

4. I met some wonderful old woman on my trip to Alaska.   _____

5. Carol has several others friends.   _____

6. Those children are very intelligents, but they are also very noisy.   _____

7. The company is planning to build a two-levels building.   _____

8. There are many differents songs on the CD.   _____

9. There are not many companys that are as good as this one.   _____

10. Gerry has many funny pieces of advices to give you.   _____

COMMUNICATE   **Where Is It?**

An object will be hidden in the classroom. The object could be a watch, a sock or any small object. One student must leave the classroom while the other students hide the object. When the student returns to the room, he or she must ask questions in order to find the object. The student cannot look for the object.

For example, Chris leaves the class. A sock is hidden under Jane's school bag. Chris comes in and asks questions that help narrow down the possible location of the object. Possible questions:

Is the object behind me? Is it on my left? Is it on somebody's body? Is it in somebody's desk? Is it under the garbage can?

8 Comparisons

We compare and contrast things in our lives constantly. For example, we may ask questions like "What is the best movie in town right now?" There are some common mistakes that second-language learners make. Notably, some students overdo their comparisons. The sentence "Your car is more newer than mine" is incorrect because *more* and the *er* on *new* mean the same thing. The sentence should read "Your car is newer than mine."

This grammar section begins with a "relationship" Vocabulary Boost. The section ends with a communication activity that concentrates on comparatives and superlatives.

VOCABULARY BOOST   **Relationships**

EXERCISE 1

Put the words in the correct spaces. Use your dictionary if necessary.

celibate	widow	single	engaged	hired
groom	only	unique	wedding	bride

1. When a woman's husband dies, the woman is called a ___widow___.

2. A man, on the day of his wedding, is called a ___groom___.

3. This means "not married." ___single___.

4. My sister never has sex because she is a nun in the Roman Catholic Church. She is ___celibate___.

5. Uncle Terry just got a new job with an aerospace company. He was ___hired___ yesterday.

6. My sister wants to get married next year. Her fiancé already proposed and now they are ___engaged___.

7. I have no brothers or sisters. I am an ___Unique___ child.

8. My sister is very unusual. She wears very colorful clothing, and she always listens intently to others. I think she is ___only___.

9. When my sister gets married, she wants to have a very big, expensive ___wedding___.

10. My sister is so unusual that she wants to wear a yellow wedding dress. She will be a very colorful ___bride___.

Adjectives

Adjectives give information about nouns. In English, adjectives generally appear before the nouns that they modify or after the verb *be*.

That giraffe is a *tall, intelligent* and *beautiful* **animal**.

↑

adjectives before the **noun**

EXERCISE 2

Put the adjective in parentheses in the proper space. Put __X__ in the unused space.

Example: (smart) Lucy is a very ___smart___ woman _X_ .

1. (big) He is a _____ liar _____ .

2. (dark) She has _____ eyes _____, and _____ pants _____.

3. (decent) Dariane is a _____ writer _____.

4. (fun) That amusement park is a _____ place _____ to visit.

Comparatives and Superlatives

An adjective describes a person, place or thing. When two things are compared, we use the following form:

Comparative: ◯ ←This ball is **bigger than** that ball. → ◯

Superlative: ◯ ◯ ◯ ◯ ← This ball is **the biggest** in the group.

For one-syllable adjectives, and two-syllable adjectives ending in *y*:

Compare two things:	*That building is **taller** than this one.*
One thing is better than all others:	*That is the **tallest** building that I have ever seen.*

Therefore, add *er* (comparative) or *est* (superlative). Do not use *more* or *most* with these short adjectives.

Incorrect: *She is more taller than I am.*

Correct: *She is taller than I am.*

Spelling: One-Syllable Adjectives and Adjectives That End in Y

Spelling of comparative and superlative forms:

		Comparative	**Superlative**
• For one-syllable adjectives, add *er* or *est*.	**short**	*shorter*	*shortest*
• If the adjective finishes in one vowel and one consonant, you should double the last letter.	**thin**	*thinner*	*thinnest*
• If the adjective ends in an *e*, just add *r* or *st*.	**cute**	*cuter*	*cutest*
• If the adjective ends in consonant-*y*, change the *y* to *i* and add *er* or *est*.	**happy**	*happier*	*happiest*

EXERCISE 3

Write the following adjectives in their comparative and superlative forms.

	Comparative Form	**Superlative Form**
Example: short	*shorter than*	*the shortest*
1. small	_____	_____
2. thin	_____	_____
3. green	_____	_____
4. sunny	_____	_____
5. blue	_____	_____
6. mad	_____	_____
7. easy	_____	_____
8. crazy	_____	_____

Spelling: Long Adjectives and Irregular Adjectives

To compare adjectives of two or more syllables, use the word *more*. For the superlative form, add *most* before the adjective.

Compare two things: *That book is **more interesting** than this one.*

One thing is better than all others: *That is the **most interesting** book that I have ever read.*

The following adjectives have irregular comparative and superlative forms.

	Comparative	**Superlative**
good	*better than*	*the best*
bad	*worse than*	*the worst*
little (meaning a small quantity of something)	*less than*	*the least*

CLASS EXERCISE

Write sentences comparing the following objects or people. There are many possible sentences for each set of words.

Example: diamond /plastic   *Diamonds are harder than plastic* OR *A diamond is more expensive than plastic.*

1. baby / adult   _____

2. man / woman   _____

3. elephant / mouse   _____

4. carrot / cake   _____

5. love / money   _____

6. boxing / tennis   _____

7. winter / summer   _____

8. blonde / brunette   _____

9. Honda Civic / Minivan _____

10. lemon / apple   _____

EXERCISE 4

Complete the sentences with the appropriate comparative or superlative. Remember to add *than* after the comparative form or *the* before the superlative form.

Example: He is (great) _____*the greatest*_____ boxer in the world.

1. A Mercedes is (expensive) _____ a Toyota. A Lada is (cheap) _____ a Toyota. What is (expensive) _____ type of car?

2. This banana is (tasty) _____ that one.

3. A hammer is (useful) _____ a rock.

4. I'm (thin) _____ my dad, but I'm (heavy) _____ my mother. My mom is (skinny) _____ person in the family.

5. My sister is (bad) _____ I am in school.

6. Your walls are (thin) _____ mine.

7. My stepbrother is (lazy) _____ anyone I know. Who is

(lazy) _____ person that you know?

8. Today it is (muggy) _____ yesterday was. Today is

(hot)_____ day I've ever seen.

EXERCISE 5

Complete these sentences with the correct comparative or superlative form of the adjectives.

Example: (small) A mouse is ____*smaller than*____ a horse.

1. (hot) My meal is _____ yours.

2. (difficult) I think biology is _____ history.

3. (careful) Annie is _____ her brother.

4. (good) That is _____ restaurant in Los Angeles!

5. (high) Mount Everest is _____ mountain in the world.

6. (easy) My job is _____ your job.

7. (bad) Many people think Hitler was one of _____ men in the world.

8. (spicy) Mexican food is _____ British food.

9. (childish) Sometimes adults are _____ children.

10. (little) He just ran a mile in _____ amount of time ever!

Adverbs

An adverb is any word (or group of words) that adds information about a verb.

*Ben speaks **well**.*
*Maria sings **beautifully**.*

Most adverbs end in *ly*. However, there are many exceptions. *Soon, late, early, often, hard* and *fast* are just a few examples where you do not add *ly*.

EXERCISE 6

In each sentence, circle the adverb. Underline the verb that the adverb modifies.

Example: Stephan (angrily) <u>slammed</u> the phone down.

1. Jodie desperately wants a vacation.

2. She cautiously asked her boss for time off.

3. He quietly refused her request.

4. She complained to her friends bitterly.

5. Her friends listened patiently.

6. The boss boldly looked at Anna.

7. Then he calmly told her to take some time off.

8. She politely thanked him.

EXERCISE 7

Make each adjective into an adverb. If the form doesn't change, put an X in the space provided.

Note that adjectives ending in consonant-*y* change to *ily* in the adverb form.

Example: happy   _____*happily*_____

1. easy   _____

2. clear   _____

3. hard   _____

4. sincere   _____

5. quiet   _____

6. silent   _____

7. often   _____

8. lazy   _____

9. smooth   _____

10. honest   _____

EXERCISE 8

Supply the proper form: adjective (describes a noun) or adverb (describes an action).

Example: Andrew speaks very (quick) _____*quickly*_____.

1. Please chew your food (slow)_____.

2. They are both (serious) _____ students.

3. Anna works very (serious) _____.

4. The banana is very (soft) _____.

5. Melanie speaks very (soft) _____.

6. She always does her work (careful) _____.

7. She is a very (careful) _____ student.

8. Come (quick) _____. We need your help.

9. He had to make a (quick) _____ decision.

As ...As

"As ... As" expresses equality.

> *Sharon is **as smart as** Doug.*
> *I can speak Spanish **as well as** you can.*

EXERCISE 9

The two items in each sentence are equal. Write the word in parentheses as an adjective or an adverb.

Example: Richard is (heavy) his brother. _____*as heavy as*_____

1. He came to the office (quick) he could. _____

2. I am (good) you are in math. _____

3. We go out (often) we can. _____

4. Vito is (old) I am. _____

5. Your homework is (easy) mine is. _____

6. Celine sings (beautiful) Barbra does. _____

7. Talia is (smart) Peter. _____

8. The boy ran home (fast) his legs could carry him. _____

9. She types (quick) I do. _____

10. He gets up (easy) a rooster. _____

EXERCISE 10

There is one error in each of the following sentences. Correct each error.

Example: She oftenly comes to my studio.   ___*often comes*___

1. Please try more harder to understand her.   _____

2. I can't believe you gave up so easy.   _____

3. Steve is worst in math than I am.   _____

4. Leather is more cheaper in Mexico.   _____

5. Bart is older then Lisa.   _____

6. This test is easyer than last week's test.   _____

7. The soup is more better if you add salt to it.   _____

8. Kevin is the tall as I am.   _____

9. Shelly sings very beautiful.   _____

10. Celia is best than I am in school.   _____

CLASS EXERCISE ▪ REVIEW

PART 1: Write the comparative or superlative forms of the following adjectives. *Do not use "as ... as."*

Example: Luigi is (short) _____*shorter*_____ than I am.

1. This job is (easy) _____ than my previous job.

2. Bill Gates is one of the (rich) _____ men in the world.

3. A ruby is (expensive) _____ than an emerald.

4. Where is the (good) _____ restaurant in Manhattan?

5. In general, cats are (lazy) _____ than dogs.

6. What is the (bad) _____ food that you have ever eaten?

7. Jerry is (bad) _____ at chess than I am.

8. Elaine is a (good) _____ baseball player than I am.

9. A meter is (long) _____ than a yardstick.

10. My sister is usually (happy) _____ than my brother is.

PART 2: Write "as ... as" with an adverb or an adjective in the space provided.

Example: Vicky sings (beautiful) _____*as beautifully as*_____ Catherine does.

11. George runs (quick) _____ Diego does.

12. A rabbit is (fast) _____ a cat.

13. A hammer is (useful) _____ a nail.

14. Calvin works (careful) _____ I do.

15. I am (careful) _____ you are.

16. Please speak (quiet) _____ you can.

17. A spider is (quiet) _____ a ladybug.

PART 3: There is one error in each of the following sentences. Correct the error.

Example: He is a best dancer than I am. _____*better*_____

18. That hot dog is worst than this one. _____

19. You are a more better football player than I am. _____

20. Kevin is the more incredible football player on our team! _____

21. Many people think that violent movies are more dangerous then sexually explicit movies. _____

22. Linda always speaks very slow. _____

23. Last Sunday was the happyest day of my life. _____

24. It is more easier to use a computer than a typewriter. _____

25. I think that *The Postman* is the worse movie in the world. _____

COMMUNICATE ▸ ## Snap Debates

This debate activity provides you with the opportunity to practice using comparative forms in an interesting way.

First, you should choose a partner. Then you and your partner should find another pair of students that you will debate against. Each group of four students must choose one of the following topics. Two students find arguments for the A side of the topic and the other two students find arguments for the B side of the topic.

Debate Topics:

A
It's better to live in Canada.
It's better to be tall.

B
It's better to live in the U.S.
It's better to be short.

Day care helps society.	Day care hurts society.
Cats are better pets.	Dogs are better pets.
Television is good for society.	Television is bad for society.
Money is better than love.	Love is better than money.
_____ is a great movie.	_____ is a terrible movie.
It's better to be the oldest child in a family.	It's better to be the youngest child in a family.
It's better to be an only child.	It's better to have brothers and sisters.
It's better to be a woman.	It's better to be a man.
Life is better now.	Life was better in the past.

In ten to fifteen minutes, each pair of students prepares five sentences. Do not let your opponents know what your arguments are. To make your sentences, you will practice using comparatives.

Sample argument:

    A. *Canada **is better** because there are **fewer guns**, and therefore the streets **are safer***.

    B. *The U.S. **is better** because the climate is **more diverse***.

(Bold words are comparatives.)

The team arguing side A presents all of their arguments and then their opponents state their arguments. The class votes on which side is most convincing.

(It takes about forty minutes for a class of twenty-five students to present their debates. The teams could also present their arguments in their small groups rather than doing it before the rest of the class.)

The Past Progressive Tense

The past progressive is formed with the past forms of the verb *be* (*was, were*) and a verb ending in *ing*. This tense is sometimes overused by second-language learners. For example, it is incorrect to say *Yesterday I was washing the dishes*. Unless you spent the entire day in front of the sink, such a sentence doesn't make much sense. It would be more appropriate in this case to use the simple past and say *Yesterday I washed the dishes*.

Keep in mind that some verbs are non-progressive, and the list in Grammar Section 3 of non-progressive verbs also applies to past progressive verbs. For example, you cannot say *I was knowing it* because *know* cannot be used in the progressive form.

This section's Vocabulary Boost takes a look at "physical and psychological characteristics." The section ends with a role-playing "communicate" activity.

VOCABULARY BOOST Physical and Psychological Characteristics

athletic	good in physical sports and games
gentle	mild, soft, delicate
handsome	good-looking in a strong or masculine way
rude	impolite
selfish	self-centered, egotistical
sensible	reasonable or showing good sense
sensitive	having strong emotional responses to events
shy	uncomfortable or timid around others

striking	physically remarkable or impressive
sympathetic	compassionate and sensitive towards others
witty	showing intelligent humor

EXERCISE 1

Insert one of the words from the previous list in each space.

1. Willy is very sweet with animals. He is not rough. He is _____.

2. Everyone thinks that Martin is very good-looking. He is _____.

3. Last year, my older sister saw *Titanic* seven times and cried each time. She is really too _____.

4. When Pepe gets his paycheck, he pays the rent and buys food before he spends money on luxuries. Pepe is very _____.

5. Arnie spits on the pavement, burps in public and makes unkind comments. He is very _____.

6. Diego loves playing sports. He plays soccer, baseball and hockey. He has well-developed muscles and looks very _____.

7. Chelsea gets very timid around new people. She is very _____.

8. Ms. Gale always listens to people. When people have problems, they go see her because she is so _____.

9. Jerry has a great sense of humor. His humor isn't slapstick; he doesn't make people laugh by throwing pies. Instead, he has very intelligent humor. He is very _____.

10. When my uncle won 2 million in the lottery, he refused to share the money with his own children. I hate to say it, but my uncle is extremely _____.

The Past Progressive

Use the past progressive to:

1. describe an action that was in progress when another action interrupted it.

   *Last Friday we **were eating** supper when the power went out.*

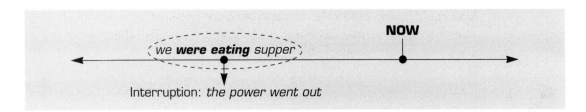

NOW

we **were eating** supper

Interruption: *the power went out*

2. describe an action that was in progress at a specific, indicated time.

Yesterday evening at 8 p.m. I ***was eating*** *supper.*

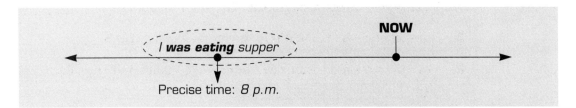

NOW

I ***was eating*** *supper*

Precise time: *8 p.m.*

3. describe two actions that were continuing at the same time.

Yesterday, while * *I* ***was setting*** *the table, my sister* ***was resting*** *on the sofa.*

Don't forget that some verbs, such as *understand*, are non-progressive.

EXERCISE 2

Fill in the blanks with the correct form of the past progressive.

Statement	Negative	Question
1. I was eating.	_____	Was I eating?
2. _____	He wasn't eating.	_____
3. She was eating.	_____	_____
4. _____	You weren't eating.	_____
5. _____	_____	Were we eating?
6. They were eating.	_____	_____

EXERCISE 3

Complete the following sentences using the past progressive tense.

1. This morning at 5 a.m. (I, sleep) _____.

2. Last Sunday, (Terry, work) _____ on the computer when there was a power failure.

_____
* Use the past progressive after *while*.

3. On Padma's sixth birthday, she saw a cobra while (she, walk)

_____ to school.

4. (We, talk) _____ on the phone yesterday when

suddenly the line went dead.

5. Do you remember what (you, do) _____ last Friday night at 11 p.m.?

EXERCISE 4

Read the pairs of sentences and then answer the question.

1. On Friday, at noon, Sumi was eating lunch.
On Friday, at noon, Judy ate lunch.

Who started eating before noon?   _____

2. At 7 a.m. this morning Diego was reading a book.
At 7 a.m. this morning Laura read a book.

Who started reading before 7 a.m.?   _____

3. Tricia entered the classroom when the teacher spoke.
Patty entered the classroom when the teacher was speaking.

Who interrupted the teacher.   _____

EXERCISE 5

Fill in the blanks with the simple past or past progressive tense.

Example: Last week I (go) _____*went*_____ to the dentist.

1. On March 1, at the time of the murder, I (babysit) _____

my sister's children in the park. I (see, not) _____ or

(hear) _____ a thing.

2. During my childhood, I (understand, not) _____

the value of education.

3. Yesterday evening, Evan (read) _____ a book in the

bathroom when I (yell) _____ that supper was ready.

4. The students (discuss) _____ the issue when Jean

suddenly (faint) _____.

5. In the past, my old teacher often (discuss) _____ that

issue.

6. I really had to complain to the landlord. Last night, while I (try)

_____ to sleep, my downstairs neighbor (play)

_____ his saxophone.

7. One day when I was about twelve years old, I (walk) _____

to school when suddenly a lightning bolt (strike) _____

a tree near me!

8. The police wanted us to explain what we (do) _____

at exactly 10 p.m. on Sunday, March 2.

EXERCISE 6

Look at the following sentences carefully. In each sentence, circle the auxiliary (helping verb) and underline the main verb. In the space provided, write the auxiliary and the main verb. *Note*: Sometimes the verb *be* has no main verb.

	Auxiliary	Main Verb
Example: When (do) you usually <u>eat</u> lunch?	*do*	*eat*
1. How long does the movie last?	_____	_____
2. Where did you live when you were young?	_____	_____
3. What is your best friend doing at this moment?	_____	_____
4. What are the best companies in Canada?	_____	_____
5. Why is that dog barking?	_____	_____
6. What were you doing last night at midnight?	_____	_____
7. When does that store usually open?	_____	_____
8. How far is the nearest convenience store?	_____	_____

EXERCISE 7

Create questions from the statements provided. Change the subject to a subject pronoun.

	Question word(s)	Auxiliary	Subject	Verb ...
Example: The dog sleeps a lot.	*Why*	*does*	*it*	*sleep ...*
1. Ian was playing baseball at noon.	*What*	_____	_____	_____
2. The judge is late.	*Why*	_____	_____	_____

3. The twins studied together. <u>_When_</u> _____ _____ _____

4. The office needs renovating. <u>_Why_</u> _____ _____ _____

5. The boss was tired yesterday. <u>_Why_</u> _____ _____ _____

6. Friday's meeting lasted for hours. <u>_How long_</u> _____ _____ _____

7. The company is twenty years old. <u>_How old_</u> _____ _____ _____

8. At 6 a.m. Rajiv was reading. <u>_What_</u> _____ _____ _____

EXERCISE 8

Put the verb in parentheses into the correct tense. Use any present or past tense.

Example: Right now Kelly (write) _____ _is writing_ _____ a letter.

1. Every day, Rebecca (wake) _____ up at 8 a.m. Right now she (talk) _____ on the phone.

2. Last night she (go) _____ to bed at 11 p.m. At 10 p.m., while she (watch) _____ TV, she (hear) _____ the siren of an ambulance.

3. What (you, do) _____ last Friday at midnight? (you, walk) _____ in the park at that time?

4. The children (go) _____ to the nearest school. They (walk) _____ to school every day. Yesterday, while they (walk) _____ to school, they (see) _____ a caterpillar on the road.

5. Pat (move) _____ to Mexico in 1995. She (buy) _____ a house near Colonel Sinatel in Mexico City. Why (she, move) _____ to Mexico? (She, get) _____ a job at the television station? (You, sometimes, phone) _____ Pat? I think that she (like) _____ Mexico City very much. She often (praise) _____ the city.

CLASS EXERCISE • REVIEW

Put the verb in either the simple past or the past progressive in the spaces provided.

Example: Last year Harry (meet) __*met*__ Sally while he (jog) __*was jogging.*__

1. In 1998, when Sara (be) _____ eighteen, she (go) _____ to England for a year. Sara (get) _____ a job at a large legal firm. She (work) _____ as a tea girl from March to October of that year. Every day, Sara (bring) _____ tea and biscuits to the lawyers on the second, third, fourth and fifth floors. She especially (like) _____ Mr. Edmund because he always (give) _____ her a tip.

2. One day, while Sara (push) _____ the tea trolley down the hallway, she (notice) _____ a strange, nervous man enter Mr. Edmund's office. While Sara (stand) _____ outside the office door, the man suddenly (approach) _____ her.

3. "(Mr. Edmund, speak) _____ to you yesterday?" the man asked.

4. "No," Sara replied. "I (speak, not) _____ to him yesterday. While I (serve) _____ tea on this floor, Mr. Edmund (be) _____ in a meeting with a client, and his door (have) _____ a 'Do Not Disturb' sign on it."

5. "Oh," said the man. "Then my father (tell, not) _____ you that I would be here today."

6. "No, he (say, not) _____ a word," Sara replied.

7. "My father (ask) _____ me to clean out his desk. It is in a terrible mess. But before I continue my chore, could I have a cup of tea, please?"

COMMUNICATE	Descriptions

Find eight interesting and difficult vocabulary words that describe a famous person. Four of the words should describe the person physically, and four words should describe the person's character. Classmates guess whom you are describing. If your classmates need more hints, they can ask you questions, but you can only answer "yes" or "no" to their questions. The person who guesses correctly must then present his or her eight words.

10 Modals

M odals are a special class of words. These words indicate things such as ability (*can*) and obligation (*must*). Modals differ from other verbs in the following way:

Modals have no distinct third-person singular form. (Exception: *have to*)

Compare: John **need<u>s</u>** money.   John **can have** money.

This section provides you with practice in forming and using modals. The "communicate" activity gives you a chance to be an advice columnist. You can read cases and discuss, with your partners, what the best solution would be for the letter-writers.

Modals

Function	Modal	Present Tense	Past Tense
Ability	*can*	She can speak Greek.	could speak
Polite requests	*may*	May I help you?	
	would	Would you like some tea?	
	could	Could you lend me $10?	
	can	Can I have some ice cream?	
Advice	*should*	Alice should see a doctor.	should have seen
Necessity	*must*	Bette must leave now.	had to leave
	*have to**	She has to go to the hospital.	had to go
Possibility	*could*	Daniel could help you.	could have helped
	might	Mary might do the job.	might have done
	may	Helen may help them.	may have helped

---

* Although *have to* is not a modal auxiliary, it is included on this list because it functions like a modal. *Have to* is the only item on the list that requires an *s* in the third-person singular form.

CLASS EXERCISE

Write sentences about yourself. Use modals in each sentence. The function of the modal is indicated in parentheses. Use a different modal in each sentence.

Example: (necessity) ___I have to floss my teeth every morning.___

1. (ability) _I can do my homework every day_

2. (possibility) _I could help my mother_

3. (possibility) _I may meet him tomorrow_

4. (possibility) _I might study for exam._

5. (advice) _I should study or I will not pass the exam_

6. (necessity) _I must see the doctor_

7. (necessity) _I have to visit my grandfather_

Ability: Can

EXERCISE 1

Look at the sentences and then answer the numbered questions.
- a. Can you speak Italian?
- b. I can't speak foreign languages.
- c. My little sister can read and she is only three.
- d. Sara cannot help you.
- e. Can you see better with your new glasses?

1. Which sentences contain negative forms of *can*? _can't_ _cannot_ What are the two negative forms of can? _b_ _d_

2. Sentences c and d have third-person singular subjects. Do you add *s* to the word *can* in these sentences? _NO_ Do you add *s* to the verb following *can* in these sentences? _No_

3. The first and last sentences are questions. Does the word *can* go before or after the subject in questions? _before the subject_
it goes

Past Ability: Could

The past form of *can* is *could*. (*Could* also means that something is possible.)

*When I was a child I **could** skip rope for hours, but now I can't.*

EXERCISE 2

Write a modal in the space provided. The function of the modal is stated.

Example: When Sam was young, he (past ability / ski) ___could ski___, but now he can't.

1. Arthur (past ability / run) ___Could run___ for miles, but now he can't.

2. Susan (present ability / speak) ___Can speak___ Spanish.

3. When I was a child, I (past ability / not / read) ___Could not read___ until I was eight years old.

4. Five years ago I (past ability / not / speak) ___could not speak___ English, but now I (present ability / speak) ___Can speak___ three languages.

5. My dog (past ability / chase) ___Could chase___ a stick, but now my dog (present ability / not / run) ___Can't run___ quickly any more.

Polite Requests

CLASS EXERCISE

The following telephone conversation is very impolite. Rewrite the dialogue to make it more polite.

1. Joe: Hello. What do you want?   How may I help you?

2. Siri: Get me Mark!   Can I speak to Mark

3. Joe: Mark is busy. What is your name?   Could give your name plea..

4. Siri: This is Siri. Who are you?   _____

5. Joe: Mark's new secretary.   _____

6. Siri: Tell Mark to phone me.   _____

7. Joe: What is your number.   Could you give me your number

8. Siri: 876-5545.   _____

9. Joe: OK. Bye.   _____

EXERCISE 3

Read the following dialogue and circle the word that is most appropriate.

1. Betty: (Would / May / Can) you like a piece of pie?

2. Hanna: Yes. (May / Would) I please see the menu again?

 Betty: Certainly.

3. Hanna: (Could / May) you show me the pecan pie?

4. Betty: We have no pecan pie left. (Could / May / Would) you like something else?

5. Hanna: OK. (May / Could) you bring me a piece of apple pie?

6. Betty: I'm sorry, we have no apple pie left. (Could / Would) I offer you a piece of pumpkin pie?

 Hanna: Is that the only pie left?

 Betty: Yes it is.

 permission
 possibility

7. Hanna: Another time, (could / may / can) you please let me know what you have before I look at the menu?

EXERCISE 4

Circle the modal-related error in each of the following sentences. Write the correct word in the space provided.

 Example: Yesterday I (can't) go.   _____couldn't_____

1. Marie can works with you on that project?   _work_

2. Can Marie can use a computer?   _Can Marie use_

3. Of course. Marie cans write very well on a computer. _can_

4. May you pass me the butter please?   _Could_

5. I could like another piece of cake please.   _I would_

permiss
futur

Advice and Necessity

When you think it is advisable that someone do something, use the word *should*.

When it is necessary that someone do something, use the words *must* or *have to*. These words mean that you have no choice but to do it. The meanings of these words change in the negative form.

Modal	Negative Form	Negative Meaning	Question Form
should go	shouldn't go	*No change in meaning.*	Should she go?
must eat	must not eat	*The action is forbidden.*	Must he eat?
have to leave	don't have to leave	*The person is not*	Do you have to leave?
has to leave	doesn't have to leave	*obliged to do something,*	Does she have to leave?
		but may if he or she	
		wishes.	

EXERCISE 5

Fill in the blanks with one of the following modals: *should, have to, must.*

Example: I think you ___*should*___ leave. It is getting late.

1. There is extra work tomorrow, but you (not) __do not have to__ come. It is not really necessary for you to be there. Jessica and I can do it.

2. The baby is asthmatic. It is extremely important to keep her room clean. You (not) __must not__ smoke in the baby's room. It is forbidden!

3. Mom is really tired tonight. You are being very noisy. Please take my advice. You __should__ try to be quieter.

4. You look tired. Why are you washing the dishes? You (not) __don't have to__ wash them now. We can wash them later.

5. Laura looks sick. She __should__ take a break, in my opinion. I like to give people advice.

Modals: Negative Forms

Examine the negative forms of the following modals. Notice that *have to* needs an auxiliary.

Statement	Negative	Negative contraction
He should work harder.	He **should not** work harder.	*(shouldn't)*
He can stay home.	He **cannot** stay home.	*(can't stay)*
Brian has to do it.	Brian **does not have to** do it.	*(doesn't have to)*

EXERCISE 6

Write the following modals in their contracted, negative forms.

Example: can ___*can't*___

1. would / not ___would'nt___
2. can / not ___can't___
3. have to / not ___don't have to___
4. should / not ___shouldn't___
5. could / not ___couldn't___
6. has to / not ___doesn't have to___

EXERCISE 7

Make the modals in the following sentences **negative**.

   Example: Eric <u>should</u> call me. | ___should not call (or shouldn't)___

1. Jason <u>has to</u> exercise more often.   ___doesn't have to___
2. The doctor <u>should</u> examine her.   ___shouldn't examine___
3. You <u>must</u> speak slowly.   ___mustn't speak___
4. That child <u>has to</u> go home now.   ___doesn't have to___
5. Selena <u>has</u> to visit her mother.   ___doesn't have to___
6. You <u>should</u> get some rest.   ___shouldn't get___
7. We <u>have to</u> work late.   ___don't have to___
8. Phil <u>can</u> do the job.   ___can't do___
9. When she was ten, Jamie <u>could</u> type.   ___couldn't type___
10. Ellen <u>can</u> help him.   ___can't help___

Modals: Question Forms

All modals act as auxiliaries. To form a question, move the modal before the subject.

Statement	**Question form**
I (can) hear you.	(Can) you hear me?
She should eat those.	**Should** she eat those?
Henry has to work late.	**Does** he **have to** work late?*

EXERCISE 8

Look at the following sentences carefully. In each sentence, circle the auxiliary (the helping verb) and underline the main verb. In the space provided, write the auxiliary and the main verb. *Note*: Sometimes the verb *be* has no main verb.

---

* *Have to* acts like all regular verbs, and requires the auxiliary *do, does* or *did* in the question form.

		Auxiliary	Main Verb
Example:	When (can) you <u>finish</u> the work?	*can*	*finish*
1.	Where did you live when you were young?	did	live
2.	What is your best friend doing at this moment?	is	doing
3.	When can you finish this course?	can	finish
4.	What should you do after class today?	should	do
5.	What can I have for lunch?	can	have
6.	Could you lend me some money?	could	lend

EXERCISE 9

Create questions from the statements provided. Change the subject to a subject pronoun.

		Question word(s)	Auxiliary	Subject	Verb ...
Example:	Fred should see a doctor.	*Why*	*should*	*he*	*see ...*
1.	John can run for hours.	*How long*	can	he	run ?
2.	The judge must work today.	*Why*	must	he	work today
3.	The office should close early.	*Why*	should	it	close ?
4.	He was tired yesterday.	*Why*	was	he	tired ?
5.	Friday's meeting lasted for hours.	*How long*	did	it	last ?
6.	She has to leave now.	*Why*	does	she	have to lea
7.	Mark can ski at Mont Tremblant.	*Where*	can	Mark	ski ?
8.	Terry is 20 years old.	*How old*	is	they	?
9.	Rajiv should retire.	*Why*	should	he	retire ?
10.	Laura can do that job.	*When*	can	Laura she	do that

EXERCISE 10

Make questions for the following answers. The specific answer to the question is in **bold**.

Example: <u>*Whom should she see?*</u>   She should see **a doctor**.

1. <u>Should Mario take a vacation ?</u>
Yes, Mario should take a vacation.

2. _when can Mario leave?_ ?
Mario can leave **tomorrow.**

3. _where should he go?_
He should go to **Mexico.**

4. _what_ _who does he have to bring with him?_
He has to bring **his children** with him.

5. _what should he buy?_
Well, he should buy **a sun hat.**

6. _Does he have to ask his boss about it?_
Yes, he has to ask his boss about it.

7. _what must he take with him?_
He must take **travellers checks** with him.

8. _Can he borrow my suitcase?_ _or your suitcase_
Yes, he can borrow my suitcase.

CLASS EXERCISE ▪ REVIEW

PART 1: Change the following sentences into yes/no questions.

    Example: Mark should go home. _Should Mark go home?_

1. Jeff has to eat now. _Does Jeff have to eat now?_

2. Nadia should phone her mother. _Should Nadia phone her mother?_

3. Helen can repair motors. _Can Helen repair motors?_

4. The children have to go to bed. _Do the children have to go to bed?_

5. We have to finish the job. _Do we have to finish the job?_

6. The boys can help us. _Can the boys help us?_

7. My sister has to buy another car. _Does my sister have to buy another car?_

8. Kelly would like more tea. _Would Kelly like more tea?_

9. The doctor should arrive soon. _Should the doctor arrive soon?_

10. Mr. Perrier has to leave. _Does Mr. Perrier have to leave?_

PART 2: Circle the error(s) and write the correction in the space provided.

    Example: (Do) you can go? _Can you go?_

11. The doctor should examined her soon. _should have examined_

12. Why Donald should come with us? _why should Donald come with us?_

13. Alice cans speak Japanese very well.   _Can_

14. Do you could lend me your car, please?   _Could you lend_

15. I could like another cup of coffee, please.   _would like_

COMMUNICATE	**Advice Letters**

Read the following letters. With a partner, or in teams of three, discuss what the letter-writer should do. After you have agreed on some good advice, write down the advice. Explain what the letter-writer should do and why. Write down your advice for each letter-writer on a separate sheet of paper.

1. My girlfriend is cheating on me. I saw her kissing another guy. When I confronted her about it, she said that I am overly possessive. She thinks it was no big deal that she was kissing someone else. She claims that she still wants to be my girlfriend. The problem is, I still love my girlfriend. I don't want to break up with her. What should I do?

Vince

2. My daughter is 19 years old and she lives with me. She is a total slob. She never cleans up after herself. She doesn't work and she doesn't go to school either. All she does is lay around the house watching soap operas. Now she wants me to give her the money to travel to Europe with her boyfriend. Should I give her the money? What should I do?

Lucy

3. I have a problem: my best friend is a shoplifter. When we are in a store, he always steals something. He even steals things that he doesn't need. When I tell him to stop, he acts like I'm a nerd. Luckily, he has never been caught, but I'm scared that he'll get in big trouble one day. Should I tell someone about it? Should I tell his parents?

Alan

4. I have a problem. My parents both work and they expect me to babysit my little brothers. I am studying in college and I have a lot of homework. I would like to have a social life. My parents say that since they are paying for my college, and since I am living at home, I should babysit for them when they need it. I understand their point, but I think that they are taking advantage of me. My life is taken up with studying and babysitting. My girlfriend even broke up with me because I always have to stay in and babysit. I am getting desperate!

Simon

5. I am a 16-year-old girl. I go to bars on weekends, but so do all of my friends. In fact, it is very easy to sneak into bars when you are underage in this city. I don't get drunk, and my friends and I take the subway or a taxi, so we don't drive when we are drunk. The problem is, my parents want me to stop going to bars, and they want me to stop seeing my friends. They think my friends are a bad influence on me. I am so mad that I even feel like running away. My parents are old-fashioned and they don't understand that teenagers these days all go to bars. What should I do?

Jessica

11 The Future Tenses

The future tenses are relatively simple to use. When you use *will*, there are no verbs to conjugate and no irregular verb lists to memorize. For example: *Next year I will go to Florida and my sister will meet me there.* Notice that no *s* is necessary on third-person singular verbs.

The future *be going to* sometimes confuses students. Often students write "gonna" because that is what they hear English people saying. However, "gonna" is not a word and should never be written.

Pay particular attention to the section containing future conditionals and future time markers, because there are cases where these future tense forms cannot be used in English even if they are used in other languages in the same situation. This section's Vocabulary Boost looks at some kitchen vocabulary.

VOCABULARY BOOST The Kitchen

EXERCISE 1

Match the vocabulary words in column A with the definitions in column B. Write the letter of the correct definition next to the vocabulary word.

A. Item		B. Definition or explanation of how it is used
1. *fork*	d	a. flat, round item used as a place to put food
2. *knife*	i	b. round item containing a screen filled with tiny holes
3. *spoon*	e	c. eating utensils
4. *plate*	a	d. a pronged item made of metal that is used for eating

5. *cutlery* ___c___

e. This item has a small scoop-shaped (rounded) end and is ideal for eating soup.

6. *oven* ___h___

f. When vegetables, such as carrots, are rubbed against this item, they are sliced into tiny fragments.

7. *stove* ___j___

g. This item is used to remove the outer layer of skin from potatoes, etc.

8. *grater* ___f___

h. a box-shaped item with heating elements at the top and bottom. It can be used for cooking or baking.

9. *peeler* ___g___

i. an object used for cutting

10. *strainer* ___b___

j. a flat surface containing, usually, four burners; used for cooking

Will

Use *will* to indicate that you are willing (or agreeing) to do something. *Will* is also used for future predictions.

I **will help** you, but Angela **will not** (or **won't**).

EXERCISE 2

Look at the following sentences and then answer the questions below.

   a. I will help you.
   b. Will you need my help?
   c. Lauren will help us too.
   d. Diego will not come because he is busy.
   e. When will Diego have some free time?
   f. Danny won't work tomorrow.
   g. Maybe Danny will be here on Friday.

1. Which sentences are questions? (Write the letters.)   _b, e_

2. Where does the word *will* appear in questions?   *put will* _before the subject_

3. Which sentences have a third-person singular subject?   _c, d, e, f, g_

4. Does *will* need an *s* after third-person singular subjects?   _No_

5. Which sentences contain the negative form of *will*?   _f, d_

6. What are the negative forms of *will*?   _won't, or will not_

7. Fill in the chart at the top of pg. 217:

Statement	Negative	Question
I will eat.	I won't eat.	Will I eat?
She will help.	She won't help	will she help?
he'll, he will do it	He won't do it.	will he do it?
or we'll we will stay	we won't stay	Will we stay?
You will rest.	you won't rest	will you rest?
They will go.	they won't go	will they go?

Be Going To

Use *be going to* to indicate that you plan to do something in the future. *Be going to*, like *will*, is also used for future predictions.

Fabiana **is going to visit** us, but her brother **isn't going to come** with her.

EXERCISE 3

Look at the following sentences and then answer the questions below.
- a. Alice is going to get married next June.
- b. Monica is going to be the flower-girl.
- c. My brother is going to take the photographs.
- d. I am not going to be there.
- e. Mr. Brandon is not going to buy Alice a present.
- f. The Smiths are going to pay for the wedding.
- g. They are not going to invite me.

1. Which sentences have a third-person singular subject?   a, b, c, e

2. What is the third-person singular form of *be going to*?   is going to

3. Which sentences have a plural subject?   f, g

4. How is *be going to* formed when the subject is plural?   are going to

5. What is the negative form of *be going to*?   is not going to
are not " "
am " " "

6. Complete the following chart.

Statement	Negative	Question
I am going to come.	I am not going to come	Am I going to come?
she's She is going to eat	She isn't going to eat.	Is she going to eat?
He is going to see it.	he isn't going to see it	Is he going to see it?
you're you are going to stay	you aren't going to stay	Are you going to stay?
we're we are going to help	We aren't going to help.	Are we going to help?
They are going to pay.	They aren't going to pay	Are they going to pay?

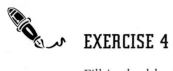

EXERCISE 4

Fill in the blanks with the future tenses. Use both *will* and *be going to*.

Example: Tam (visit) __is going to visit__ his mother next Friday.
            or Tam (visit) __will visit__ his mother next Friday.

1. Inka Corp. (hire, not) __is going to hire__ any new employees.

    or Inka Corp. (hire, not) __won't hire ~~will not~~__ any new employees.

2. What (you, do) __are you going to do__ during your next vacation?

    or What (you, do) __will you do__ during your next vacation?

3. Dylan (call) __is going to call__ me later.

    or Dylan (call) __will call__ me later.

4. Sara (be, not) __is not going to be__ home tomorrow.

    or Sara (be, not) __will not be__ home tomorrow.
    __won't be__

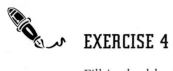

EXERCISE 5

Most of the time you can use either *will* or *be going to* in future sentences. However, there are some circumstances where one is preferable to the other. When you make a spontaneous decision to do something, use *will*. Also use *will* with "probably." If a decision is clearly planned in advance, use *be going to*.

Fill in the blanks with the future tense of the verb. Use either *will* or *be going to*, or indicate that both future tenses are possible.

Example: One day I (go) __will go OR am going to go__ to university.

1. The phone is ringing I (get) __will get__ it.

2. My project isn't finished. I (probably, finish) __will probably finish__ by Friday.

3. Vera said that she (visit) __is going to visit__ me tomorrow during the lunch hour.

4. One day I (be) __will be, am going to be__ rich.

5. What (you, do) __will you do, or are you going to do__ after you finish college?

6. The kettle is boiling. I (turn) __I will turn__ it off.

7. Where (they, go, probably) __will they probably go__ after work?

8. The electric company called. They (turn) __are going to turn__ off our power.

Short Answers

When you answer a question, you can use just the auxiliary. It is not necessary to repeat the verb in short answers.

Will you help me? _Yes, I will_ or _No, I won't._

EXERCISE 6

Answer the following questions with both "yes" and "no" short answers.

Example: Will you come home soon? Yes, I _____will_____ No, I _____won't_____

1. Are you working right now? Yes, I _am_ No, I _am not_

2. Is Ted going to pay you tomorrow? Yes, he _is_ No, he _isn't_

3. Did Jason finish his report last night? Yes, he _did_ No, he _didn't_

4. Will you lend me some money? Yes, I _will_ No, I _won't_

5. Would you like some ice cream? Yes, I _would_ No, I _wouldn't_

6. Does Becky have a computer? Yes, she _Does_ No, she _doesn't_

7. Are they going to eat lunch soon? Yes, they _are_ No, they _aren't_

8. Will mom help Tim finish his project? Yes, she _will_ No, she _won't_

9. Did you see a movie last weekend? Yes, we _did_ No, we _didn't_

10. Could you give me some chocolate? Yes, I _could_ No, I _couldn't_

Future Conditionals

Conditional sentences are sentences that impose a condition on the action. In future conditional sentences, it is very possible that the action will follow the condition. For example, *If Sid works hard, he will pass this course.* The result (passing) is very possible if the condition (studying) is met.

These sentences contain an *if* clause and a future clause. Notice the structure of these sentences. In the *if* clause, you must use the simple present tense.

If you need me, I will be there.

present tense
(the condition)

future tense
(the result)

CLASS EXERCISE

Write conditional sentences that contain an *if* section (the condition) and a *will* section (the result). Do this exercise on a separate sheet of paper.

Example: I want to pass my course.   *If you study, you will pass.*

1. Daniel's dog is hungry, but we have no dog food.

2. Mark is very tired. He works too much.

3. Karen doesn't see very well. She needs glasses.

4. Mr. Beal can't find his keys. He prefers to drive to work.

5. Tracy wants to learn how to play the piano and she needs a teacher.

EXERCISE 7

Complete the sentences. Use either the simple present tense or *will*.

Example: If I (have) ___*have*___ time later, I (visit) ___*will visit*___ you.

1. If you (ask) ___ask___ Ted, he (help) ___will help___.

2. Zachary (go) ___will go___ to the meeting if the boss (expect) ___expects___ him to.

3. If you (miss) ___miss___ class tomorrow, you (pass, not) ___will not pass___ the next test.

4. We (repair) ___will repair___ our roof if the bank (lend) ___lends___ us the money.

5. You (be) ___will be___ late if you (hurry, not) ___don't hurry___.

6. If you (tell, not) ___don't tell___ Jerry the truth, then I (tell) ___will tell___ him.

7. If the storm (hit) ___hits___ tonight, then I (go, not) ___will not go___ to the soccer game.

8. I (buy) ___will buy___ a new watch if I (have) ___have___ enough money.

9. Marcie (do) ___will do___ the work if you (be) ___are___ too busy.

10. I (be) ___will be___ very upset if John (remember, not) ___doesn't remember___ my birthday.

Future: Time Markers

In future sentences, use the present tense after the following time markers:
when, before, after, until, unless, as soon as, as long as.

 a. ***I'll call*** you when I ***get*** home.
 b. She ***will meet*** you as soon as she ***finishes*** work.
 c. We ***won't eat*** supper until Anne ***arrives***.

 EXERCISE 8

PART 1: Circle the time marker in each of the following future tense sentences. Write the verb that follows the time marker. Remember that verbs following time markers must be written in the simple present tense.

 Example: Alex will eat dinner (after) he (finish) _____*finishes*_____ work.

 1. I will visit as soon as I (finish) __*finish*__ work.

 2. When Mark (get) __*gets*__ his paycheck, he will buy some groceries.

 3. The boys will be home after they (finish) __*finish*__ their game.

 4. Calvin will arrive before the party (begin) __*begins*__.

 5. When I (be) __*am*__ older, I will buy a house.

PART 2: Circle the time marker in the following sentences. Correct any verb tense errors.

 Example: (When) you ~~will~~ call him, he will come.

 6. Jason will pay us as soon as he will get some money. *gets some money*

 7. I will call you when I ~~will~~ *have* have some time.

 8. As soon as you ~~will~~ *get* get home, you will see me.

 9. The lawyers will sit until the judge ~~will~~ enters the courtroom.

 10. When the doctor ~~will~~ arrives, Raymond will explain his symptoms.

 EXERCISE 9

Complete the following future tense sentences with the verbs in parentheses.

 Example: I (buy) __*will buy*__ a car when I (be) __*am*__ older.

 1. I (call, not) __*will not call*__ you after I (arrive) __*arrive*__ in
 Paris.   *won't*

2. Next week, when Monica (quit) _____quits_____ her job, everyone (be) _____will be_____ very happy.

3. Hugh (talk) _____will talk_____ to Ron about it as soon as Ron (get) _____gets_____ here.

4. Anne (do) _____will do_____ the work when she (get) _____gets_____ home.

5. Later, when I (have) _____have_____ some spare time, I (help) _____will help_____ Vince with his math homework.

6. We (take care) _____will take care_____ of the dog after the vet (leave) _____leaves_____ .

7. As soon as the weather (get) _____gets_____ warmer, Carrie (go) _____will going_____ swimming with us.

8. After Chelsea (apologize) _____apologizes_____ , I (complain, not) _____will not complain_____ about her again.

9. Tomorrow, when Richard (arrive) _____arrives_____ , Anne (tell) _____will tell_____ him about the party.

10. We (wash) _____will wash_____ the carpet when we (have) _____have_____ time on the weekend.

EXERCISE 10

Identify and correct the errors. If the sentence has no error, write *C* in the space provided.

    Example: What are you (gonna) do later?   _____going to_____

1. I will apply for a job when I will finish my schooling.   _____finish_____

2. Mario is gonna call you after work.   _____is going to call_____

3. Why Monica is going to university in another province?   _____is Monica going to_____

4. When I will get home later, I will phone my mother.   _____get_____

5. If you will not have any spare time, I will mow the lawn.   _____don't have_____

6. Jeff is gonna be a doctor one day.   _____is going to be_____

7. Why Simon will probably be late?   _____why will Simon probably be_____

8. We willn't eat dinner with Mr. Ray.   _____won't eat_____

9. If you practice, you will improve your writing. _____ C _____

10. When is dinner is going to be ready?

when is dinner going to be ready?

CLASS EXERCISE ▪ REVIEW

PART 1: Write the verb in the correct tense.

Example: Yves ____ *is going to study* ____ next week. OR ____ *will study* ____

1. (clean)

Jim _____ the bathroom tomorrow. OR _____

Jim _____ the bathroom now.

Jim _____ the bathroom yesterday.

Jim _____ the bathroom every week.

2. (work)

Where _____ those women usually _____ ?

Where _____ those women _____ last year?

Where _____ those women _____ next year? OR

Where _____ those women _____ next year?

PART 2: Circle and correct the future tense errors. Write the correction in the space provided.

Example: When (you will) move? _____ *will you* _____

3. Tomorrow the store is gonna open at 9 a.m. _____

4. Where will you work when you will finish this job? _____

5. If I will earn enough money, I will buy a new sofa. _____

6. What you will do tomorrow night? _____

7. Why is Ms. Rather is going to stay home tomorrow? _____

8. In the future, my brother is gonna move to Miami. _____

COMMUNICATE ▶ Interview

Interview a partner about his or her future plans. Find out information about the following topics:

- future job
- future travel plans
- future place to live
- future family plans

THE FUTURE TENSES 〉 223

12 The Present Perfect Tense

Second-language learning can be complicated when some languages have tenses that don't exist in other languages. For example, English has the present perfect tense, but this tense doesn't exist in French or Spanish.

When you listen to English people speak, you will notice that this tense is very common and is used in many circumstances.

The present perfect is formed with *have* or *has* and the past participle.

I
We
You
They
→ **have been** to China.

He
She
It
→ **has caused** many accidents.

This tense is used in two different ways:

1. when a past action continues up to the present time;

2. when a completed past action occurred at an unknown or unimportant past time.

CLASS EXERCISE

Read the following paragraphs. Circle all examples of the present perfect tense.

My family (has had) a difficult time since we moved to our new apartment. My sister has seen a mouse, and we have had several invasions of cockroaches. I can live with the occasional mouse, but I absolutely hate cockroaches. They get into the cupboards that contain cereal. I have even seen cockroaches inside our clean bowls.

My mother doesn't like to use pesticides in our kitchen, but because we have had such a serious pest problem, she has finally agreed to do something serious about it. In a Chinese herbal store, we found some cockroach chalk, and last week my father drew chalk lines around the kitchen floor. Luckily, most of the bugs have died. If the problem doesn't get completely under control, my father says that we will have to move again.

The Past Action Continues to the Present

This version of the present perfect is used with the prepositions *for* and *since*.

*Alicia **has lived in Mexico City** since 1989.*

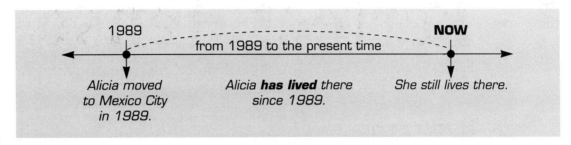

Key words: *never / ever / not ... yet / so far / up to now* (from past to present time)
since / for (period of time up to the present)

EXERCISE 1

Answer the following questions. For each sentence, explain what tense is used and why that tense is used. (For sentences 1 to 3, you can refer to the chart before this exercise.)

1. Alicia *moved* to Mexico City in 1989. Tense: _____ *simple past* _____

Why? *Action is over at a known time (1989).*

2. Alicia *has lived* in Mexico City since 1989. Tense: _Past Perafect_

Why? _Action is still from 1989 till now_

3. Alicia still *lives* in Mexico City. Tense: _Simple Present_

Why? _Now she is still   Fact_

4. Raymond *will move* to Winnipeg next July. Tense: _Simple futur_

Why? _Action is at a futur not now_

5. Right now Raymond *is sleeping*. Tense: _Present continue_

Why? _he start from awhile and still sleeping until now_

EXERCISE 2

Rewrite each sentence so that it begins with the words "Since last May." Make the appropriate changes to the verb tense.

Example: Louie knows Marley.   _Since last May, Louie has known Marley._

1. Louie lives with her.   _Since last May,_ Louie has lived with her
2. She is an accountant.   _Since last May,_ She has been an accountant
3. Louie is a musician.   _Since last May,_ Louie has been a musician
4. Marley is in love.   _Since last May,_ Marley has been in love
5. Marley has a cat.   _Since last May,_ Marley has had a cat
6. Louie owns a house.   _Since last May,_ Louie has owned a house

CLASS EXERCISE

Answer the following questions in complete sentences.

1. Where do you live?
2. How long have you lived there?
3. Where do you study?
4. How long have you studied there?
5. When did you get your shoes?
6. How long have you had your shoes?
7. Do you have a best friend? What is your best friend's name?
8. How long have you known your best friend?

EXERCISE 3

Circle the verb that should be used with the subject.

1. Dominique and Cassandra (have / has) been awake since 7 a.m.
2. There (is / are) many adult students in the college.
3. Everybody in the family (is / are) coming to the reunion. (Remember that *everybody, somebody, nobody* and *anybody* are considered third-person singular subjects.)
4. The reports (has / have) been on my desk since Monday.
5. Everyone in this room (have / has) to finish the exam.
6. Mr. Morito (has / have) worked here for many years.
7. The furniture (was / were) stored in the basement locker.
8. No one really (expect / expects) to win the lottery.
9. The information that she gave me (was / were) very interesting and relevant.
10. (Has / Have) anybody seen my car keys?

EXERCISE 4

Write the past tense and the past participle of each of the following verbs. For regular *ed* verbs, the past tense and the past participles are the same. For irregular verbs, you could refer to the irregular verb list in the appendix of this book.

Examples:

go _went_ _gone_   look _looked_ _looked_

1.	cry	cried	cried	**11.**	eat	ate	eaten
2.	sell	sold	sold	**12.**	sing	sang	sung
3.	tell	told	told	**13.**	think	thought	thought
4.	cost	cost	cost	**14.**	drink	drank	drunk
5.	know	knew	known	**15.**	buy	bought	bought
6.	write	wrote	written	**16.**	feel	felt	felt
7.	prove	proved	proved	**17.**	fall	fell	fallen
8.	come	came	come	**18.**	take	took	taken
9.	teach	taught	taught	**19.**	send	sent	sent
10.	hope	hoped	hoped	**20.**	lose	lost	lost

Since, For and Ago

Since refers to a specific time in the past when the action began.

For refers to the amount of time that the action lasts.

> *For* can be used in other tenses.

Compare: *Clark worked at IBM for three years just after the Vietnam war.*
Lois has worked at IBM for three years.
Next summer, Suki will visit me for three weeks.

Ago refers to a time in the past when a completed action occurred.

EXERCISE 5

Fill in the blanks with *since, for* or *ago*.

1. Do not call him. He left two days ___ago___.

2. The pizza has been ready ___for___ twenty minutes.

3. I turned off the stove half an hour ___ago___.

4. Joe has been working there ___for___ ages.

5. I have lived in that house ___since___ I was a little kid.

6. A long time ___ago___ an evil giant climbed down the beanstalk.

7. She has been ill ever ___since___ she had her tonsils out.

8. My uncle has had a cold ___for___ at least two weeks.

Present Perfect Tense: Question and Negative Forms

In the present perfect tense, *have* or *has* is the auxiliary. To make a question, simply put the auxiliary before the subject.

Question Form: Place the auxiliary *have* or *has* before the subject.

We (have) known him for ten years.   (Have) we **known** him for ten years?

How long **have** we **known** him?

Negative Form: Place *not* after the auxiliary *have*.

She has been to China.   She **has not been** to China.

EXERCISE 6

PART 1: Circle the auxiliary. Then, in the space provided, write down the auxiliary and the verb.

	Auxiliary	Verb
Example: How long (has) Rosie been an actress?	*has*	*been*
1. When will the children get home?	will	get
2. What are they doing now?	are	doing
3. Have they left yet?	have	left
4. Do you agree with me?	Do	agree
5. How long have you been here?	have	been

PART 2: Make yes/no questions out of the following sentences.

Example: Casey has been here for ten minutes.   *Has Casey been here for ten minutes?*

6. Mark likes beer.   Does Mark like beer?

7. He has had a car for three weeks.   Has he had a car for three week

8. Jane has lived here since July.   Has Jane lived here since Ju

9. He will get the job.   Will he get the job?

10. We have been here for hours.   Have we been here for hours

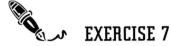

EXERCISE 7

Practice using the present perfect tense. Fill in the blanks using the present perfect tense only. Key words that indicate when the present perfect is used are in bold.

Dear Frank,

How (you, be) _have you been_ **lately**? I (miss) _have missed_ you so much **since you went away**. (You, finish) _Have you finished_ your tour **yet**? Nothing (be) _has been_ the same here **since you left**.

For six months I (be) _have been_ alone. I know that you like to work as a musician, but **since you left,** it (be) _has been_ difficult to live without you. I (try) _have tried_ to keep busy **for the last few months**. The children (grow) _have grown_ **since you left.** Our daughter often asks when you will come home, but I (find, not) _haven't found_ an answer **yet**.

So far, you (tour) _have toured_ throughout Europe. Do you still plan to go to Australia? I know that you (be, not) _have not been_ away **for long**, but we need you.

Love, Marta

EXERCISE 8

Fill in the blanks with the simple past or present perfect tense.

1. We (enter) _entered_ this class half an hour ago. We (be) _have been_ in this class for half an hour. We (be) _have been_ in our seats since 12:30.

2. Zena and Frank (get) _got_ engaged three weeks ago. They (be) _have been_ engaged for three weeks. They (be) _have been_ engaged since the party.

3. Vinnie (come) _came_ to Canada from Italy three months ago. Vinnie (be) _has been_ in Canada for a few months. (You, ever, be) _have you ever been_ to Italy?

4. Sam and Vicky (meet) _met_ many years ago. They (know) _have known_ each other for over twenty years. (You, meet, ever) _Have you ever met_ Sam and Vicky?

EXERCISE 9

Proofread and correct the errors in the following sentences. Each sentence has one error.

1. Yesterday I <u>have seen</u> the movie *Dracula*. *saw*

2. That is truly the best show that I have ever <u>saw</u>. *seen*

3. Eddy and Geena have fought over money since many years. *C*

4. Sara <u>is</u> the sweetest child that I ever seen. *was* *have*

5. Willy h̶a̶s̶ graduated from university last June.

6. Dominique <u>is</u> a secretary for ten years. *has been*

7. I h<u>ave seen</u> Karen's new baby two weeks ago. *saw*

8. We <u>are</u> in this class since 9:15 a.m. *have been*

9. The Levines <u>live</u> in Montreal for many years. *have lived*

10. The Levines ha̶v̶e̶ moved to Montreal in 1990.

CLASS EXERCISE

Use either the present perfect or the simple past tense in the following sentences. Key words or phrases are in bold in number 1.

1. Pierre (work) _____ with me **for almost ten years**. We (share) _____ an office **since last March**. I (meet) _____ Pierre in a staff meeting about **ten years ago**. **When the meeting was over,** I (invite) _____ Pierre for a coffee. We (be) _____ friends **ever since.**

2. In my life, I (never, be) _____ outside this city. I was born here, and I (live) _____ here my entire life. Pierre was born in Switzerland. He (be) _____ in Canada since 1984. In 1984 he (arrive) _____ in Vancouver, and then a few years later he (move) _____ here. He (go) _____ to Switzerland last March to visit his family.

3. At first, Pierre (like, not) _____ this city. Ten years ago Pierre (think) _____ that this was an unfriendly place. Now that he (be) _____ here for ten years, he (learn) _____ to love this place.

The Action is Over but the Time is Unknown

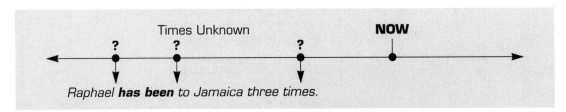

Raphael **has visited** many places. He **has been** to Jamaica three times.

Key words: *already / once / twice / three times / many times* ... (before now)

EXERCISE 10

Combine the words to make a sentence. You must use the present perfect tense, because each group of words is about a "repeated past action, time unknown."

Example: Ian / live / in many cities.   ___Ian has lived in many cities.___

1. We / see / over five hundred movies. _____

2. Jerry / travel / to many countries. _____

3. Tacho / lose / his key three times. _____

4. Over the years I / have / many bosses. _____

5. Eva / marry John / four times. _____

EXERCISE 11

Fill in the blanks with the simple past or present perfect tense.

1. Paolo (live) _____ with **many** women. He (live) _____ with Anne **in 1997**.

2. Daniel is a big drinker. He (try) _____ to quit drinking several times. At the moment he doesn't drink. He (be) _____ on the wagon for about three weeks.

3. We (work) _____ in every store on Fifth Avenue. Jason and I (work) _____ at Auclair's last March.

4. Ms. Griffin (meet) _____ several famous people. She (meet) _____ Courtney Love at a party last March.

5. Mr. and Mrs. Cantin (be) _____ to New York twice. (You, think, ever) _____ about visiting New York?

Compare the Present Perfect and Simple Past

Present Perfect
Time unknown
once, twice, many times
? ? ?

Last May

NOW

Present Perfect: *since, for*

Simple Past
Time is known
*ago, last week,
yesterday, etc.*

Ben moved to Halifax last May.   Past tense, because past time is known.

Ben has lived in Halifax since then.   Present perfect, because action began in the past and continues to the present time.

Suzi has seen Ben several times.   Present perfect, because past times are unknown.

CLASS EXERCISE ▪ REVIEW

Circle the letter of the best answer.

1. Paul (be) to California at least ten times.
a. has been   b. was   c. went   d. goes

2. Paul (go) to California last April.
a. has been   b. has gone   c. went   d. goes

3. The children (play) football right now.
a. played   b. were playing c. play   d. are playing

4. My favorite doctor works here. She (work) at this hospital for ten years.
a. has work   b. works   c. is working   d. has worked

5. Ms. Nesbit usually (expect) us to work late.
a. is expecting b. expect   c. expects   d. expected

6. We (take) the dogs for a walk two hours ago.
a. were taking   b. took   c. have taken   d. take

7. Mike (walk, not) to work yesterday.
   a. didn't walked   b. walked not   c. didn't walk   d. hasn't walked

8. (Sam, go) to Mexico every year?
   a. Sam goes   b. Do Sam go   c. Does Sam go   d. Did Sam goes

9. Eva (write) a letter right now.
   a. is writting   b. writes   c. is writing   d. has wrote

10. Peter and Mary (see) *Titanic* at least five times.
   a. has seen   b. saw   c. see   d. have seen

COMMUNICATE	Scavenger Hunt

Form teams of three to four students. Each team must race to complete this activity. The first team to correctly complete the activity wins.

On a separate piece of paper each team must write down the names of classmates (other than members of your team) who have done the following activities. Beside each number write the name of the person and when the incident happened. If no one in the class has done an activity, then write "No one has done this" on your sheet of paper.

Make sure that you ask questions properly. First you ask "Have you ever ..." questions, and if a student answers in the affirmative, then you can get more details and ask "When did you do it?" In other words, your initial question is in the present perfect, and your second ("when") question is in the past tense.

Find someone who has:

1. traveled outside this country.

2.. bought a lottery ticket.

3. dyed his or her hair.

4. been in a car accident.

5. been to a live music concert.

6. met a famous person.

7. owned a red car.

8. sung in public.

9. won money.

10. done a dangerous sport.

Review of Sections 7 to 12

CLASS EXERCISE A ▪ COMPARATIVES

Write the comparative and superlative forms of the following adjectives. (20 points)

		Comparative Form	Superlative Form
Example:	nice	*nicer than*	*the nicest*
1.	serious		
2.	good		
3.	interesting		
4.	thin		
5.	sweet		
6.	lazy		
7.	confusing		
8.	bad		
9.	funny		
10.	careful		

CLASS EXERCISE B ▪ PLURALS

Put the noun in parentheses in the singular or plural form. (15 points)

1. Many (year) __*years*__ ago, a small (boy) __*boy*__ named Peter discovered that he had a secret power. He could read the (mind) _____ of other (person)

_____. When a (person) _____ sat near Peter, he could discover a lot of (information) _____ about that person simply by observing.

2. For example, one day Peter sat in a doctor's office across from a woman named Mary. Peter knew, simply by looking at Mary, that she was thinking about her three (sweet) _____ (child) _____. Mary was worried about her youngest child. Mary's youngest daughter, Kate, was seven (year) _____ old, but she couldn't read yet.

3. Peter surprised Mary by giving her some (advice) _____. Peter told Mary that every (person) _____ is different. He then explained that Mary's youngest child was going to learn to read at her own pace. Each (human) _____ develops differently, Peter said.

4. Mary stared at Peter, shocked. "Do you know any of my (kid) _____?" Mary asked.

5. "No," replied Peter, "but I know that they are (intelligent) _____ children. I know that I am young, and I know that I do not have much (experience) _____ in life, but I can sense many (thing) _____ about other (person) _____."

CLASS EXERCISE C ▪ PRESENT AND PAST TENSES

Fill in the blanks with the correct verb tense. Use one of the present or past tenses. (15 points)

1. Last August, my family (take) _____ a trip to Scotland to visit my aunt. We (go) _____ over the Atlantic Ocean in an airplane. While we (fly) _____ over Iceland, the plane hit some turbulence.

2. We (eat) _____ lunch when suddenly the plane (drop) _____ quickly. In a split second, my lunch tray (fly) _____ up in the air and then it (fall) _____ back down. The food (go) _____ everywhere. There (be) _____ many pieces of food all over my clothing.

3. While I (try) _____ to wipe food off of my clothes, I (hear) _____ people screaming.

4. Luckily, no one (be) _____ hurt. We (be) _____ all very scared, though. Now I (be) _____ afraid of flying. My

father always (say) _____ that flying is safer than driving on a highway.

CLASS EXERCISE D • MODALS

Choose the correct modal. Write the letter of the correct answer in the space provided. (10 points)

1. Many people ..... late on a regular basis.   _____
    a. have to work   b. has to work   c. must to work   d. can to work

2. ..... Wanda and Alex ..... their mother as soon as possible?   _____
    a. Do / could visit   b. Could / visits   c. Could / visit   d. Can / to visit

3. The judge ..... some more tea.   _____
    a. would to like   b. would like   c. would likes   d. would liked

4. ..... the report ..... ready now?   _____
    a. Do / have to be   b. Does / has to be
    c. Does / have to be   d. Has / to be

5. Why ..... Cecelia ..... all of the work alone?   _____
    a. does / should do   b. should / do
    c. should / does   d. (nothing) / should do

6. ..... your little sister ..... books yet?   _____
    a. Can / can read   b. Does / can read
    c. Can / reads   d. Can / read

7. The customer at table three ..... for his coffee. I will pay for it.   _____
    a. have not to pay   b. don't have to pay
    c. doesn't have to pay   d. don't has to pay

8. ..... you ..... us finish the project?   _____
    a. May / help   b. Could / helps
    c. Could / may help   d. Could / help

9. Zachary ..... peanuts because he has a life-threatening peanut allergy.   _____
(Choose between *must* and *have to*.)
    a. must not eat   b. must not eats
    c. doesn't have to eat   d. don't has to eat

10. Mary ..... yet. Her mother called and said that she could stay here and   _____
finish the game. (Choose between *must* and *have to*.)
    a. must not leave   b. must not leaves
    c. doesn't have to leave   d. don't has to leave

CLASS EXERCISE E ▪ PRESENT, PAST AND FUTURE TENSES

Write the verb in the correct tense. You may use any past, present or future tenses.
(15 points)

1. Henry thinks that he (have) _____ children in the future.

2. In eight years, when Jay (turn) _____ 25, he (go) _____ to work at his father's company.

3. (Tavo, do) _____ the dishes last night? I (wash, not) _____ them yesterday.

4. What (you, watch) _____ on TV right now? (It, be) _____ interesting?

5. Marcia (come / not) _____ with us to next Friday's meeting.

6. Kelsy promises that next week she (finish) _____ the project after she (meet) _____ with the suppliers.

7. Where (you, eat, usually) _____ on Friday mornings?

8. Listen. The baby (cry) _____. (We, have) _____ any baby food?

9. Last night my sister (teach) _____ me how to parallel park.

10. Kiri (visit) _____ her mother next week. OR Kiri (visit) _____ her mother next week. (Use both future tenses.)

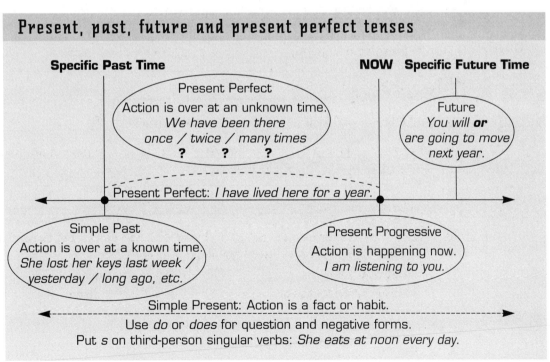

Present, past, future and present perfect tenses

Specific Past Time | NOW   Specific Future Time

Present Perfect
Action is over at an unknown time.
*We have been there
once / twice / many times*
?   ?   ?

Future
*You will **or**
are going to move
next year.*

Present Perfect: *I have lived here for a year.*

Simple Past
Action is over at a known time.
*She lost her keys last week /
yesterday / long ago, etc.*

Present Progressive
Action is happening now.
I am listening to you.

Simple Present: Action is a fact or habit.
Use *do* or *does* for question and negative forms.
Put *s* on third-person singular verbs: *She eats at noon every day.*

CLASS EXERCISE F ▪ ALL TENSE REVIEW

For each of the following sentences, indicate what verb tense was used and explain why that tense was used. The verb is in italics. *Option:* Do this exercise in teams. (20 points)

Example: The stores always *close* at 9 p.m.   Tense: ___*Simple Present*___

Why?   *Because the action is a fact.*

Question form: *Do the stores always close at 9 p.m.?*

Negative form: *The stores don't always close at 9 p.m.*

1. Shiva *works* at Cisco's Fabrics.   Tense: _____

Why? _____

Question form: _____

Negative form: _____

2. Shiva *has been* at the company since August.   Tense: _____

Why? _____

Question form: _____

Negative form: _____

3. Shiva *has made* many friends at this company.   Tense: _____

Why? _____

Question form: _____

Negative form: _____

4. Shiva *met* her fiancé last August.   Tense: _____

Why? _____

Question form: _____

Negative form: _____

5. Today she *is working* in the showroom.   Tense: _____

Why? _____

Question form: _____

Negative form: _____

Appendix 1

Writing Error Codes

Verb Problems

SV   (Subject–Verb agreement)   He (like) spagetti ⟶ *likes*

                              The studies (needs) to be completed. ⟶ *need*

VT   (Verb Tense)   Alan (is) here since May. ⟶ *has been*

                              When I was young, I (was believing) in God.
                              ⟶ *believed*

◯   (Missing word)   Where he lives? ⟶ *Where **does** he live?*

T. Sh.   (Tense Shift)   On Sunday we baked some bread and (eat) it. ⟶ *ate*

Word Problems

WF   (Word Form)   I am (interesting) in that project. ⟶ *interested*

                              She wanted to (found) the answer. ⟶ *find* (Infinitive)

                              She gave the box to (they) ⟶ *them*

WC   (Word Choice)   He is (listening to) TV. ⟶ *watching*

PL   (Plurals)   They were (drugs) dealers. ⟶ *drug dealers.* (No s
                              on adjectives)

                              One of the (book) fell off the desk. ⟶ *books*

P. Sh.   (Pronoun Shift)   Religious leaders speak to (his) followers. ⟶ *their*

SP   (Spelling)   Mark (tought) he had more money. ⟶ *thought*

DS   (Double Subject)   The movie that I saw (it's) the greatest. ⟶ *is*

Sentence Problems

FR   (Fragment)   I slept. (Because) I was tired. ⟶ *I slept because I
                              was tired.*

RO   (Run-on)   Carol was busy, I called her. ⟶ *Carol was busy so
                              I called her.*

WO   (Word Order)   He is enough old to know better. ⟶ *He is old
                              enough to know better.*

Appendix 2

Irregular Verb List

Base Form	Simple Past	Past Participle	Base Form	Simple Past	Past Participle
arise	arose	arisen	draw	drew	drawn
be	was, were	been	drink	drank	drunk
bear	bore	borne	drive	drove	driven
beat	beat	beaten	eat	ate	eaten
become	became	become	fall	fell	fallen
begin	began	begun	feed	fed	fed
bend	bent	bent	feel	felt	felt
bet	bet	bet	fight	fought	fought
bind	bound	bound	find	found	found
bite	bit	bitten	fly	flew	flown
bleed	bled	bled	forbid	forbade	forbidden
blow	blew	blown	forget	forgot	forgotten
break	broke	broken	forgive	forgave	forgiven
bring	brought	brought	forsake	forsook	forsaken
build	built	built	freeze	froze	frozen
burst	burst	burst	get	got	got, gotten
buy	bought	bought	give	gave	given
catch	caught	caught	go	went	gone
choose	chose	chosen	grind	ground	ground
cling	clung	clung	grow	grew	grown
come	came	come	hang	hung	hung
cost	cost	cost	have	had	had
creep	crept	crept	hear	heard	heard
cut	cut	cut	hide	hid	hidden
dig	dug	dug	hit	hit	hit
do	did	done	hold	held	held

Base Form	Simple Past	Past Participle	Base Form	Simple Past	Past Participle
hurt	hurt	hurt	sink	sank	sunk
keep	kept	kept	sit	sat	sat
know	knew	known	sleep	slept	slept
lay	laid	laid	slide	slid	slid
lead	led	led	speak	spoke	spoken
leave	left	left	speed	sped	sped
lend	lent	lent	spend	spent	spent
let	let	let	spin	spun	spun
lie	lay	lain	split	split	split
light	lit	lit	spread	spread	spread
lose	lost	lost	spring	sprang	sprung
make	made	made	stand	stood	stood
mean	meant	meant	steal	stole	stolen
meet	met	met	stick	stuck	stuck
pay	paid	paid	sting	stung	stung
prove	proved	proved/proven	stink	stank	stunk
put	put	put	strike	struck	struck
quit	quit	quit	swear	swore	sworn
read	read	read	sweep	swept	swept
rid	rid	rid	swim	swam	swum
ride	rode	ridden	swing	swung	swung
ring	rang	rung	take	took	taken
rise	rose	risen	teach	taught	taught
run	ran	run	tear	tore	torn
say	said	said	tell	told	told
see	saw	seen	think	thought	thought
sell	sold	sold	throw	threw	thrown
send	sent	sent	thrust	thrust	thrust
set	set	set	understand	understood	understood
shake	shook	shaken	upset	upset	upset
shine	shone	shone	wake	woke	woken
shoot	shot	shot	wear	wore	worn
show	showed	shown	weep	wept	wept
shrink	shrank	shrunk	win	won	won
shut	shut	shut	write	wrote	written
sing	sang	sung	withdraw	withdrew	withdrawn

Credits

"Weighty Considerations" by S.D.D. first appeared in the Dec. 29, 1997, issue of *Macleans* and is reprinted with permission of the publisher.

"I Am Not Free to Enjoy Food" by Dorothy Nixon is reprinted with permission of the author.

"What's Your Emotional IQ?" by Daniel Goleman reprinted with permission from the September 1996 *Reader's Digest*. From *Emotional Intelligence* by Daniel Goleman. Copyright © 1995 by Daniel Goleman. Used by permission of Bantam Books, a division of Bantam Doubleday Dell Publishing Group, Inc.

"Moonshine, Brightly" by Joe Fiorito is reprinted with permission of the publisher. Originally published in *Comfort Me With Apples*, Nuage Editions, 1994.

"Witches" by Monique Polak is reprinted with permission of the author. Monique Polak is a Montreal-based freelance writer who teaches english literature and humanities at Marianapolis College.

"My Brother" by Rick Klaus Thies is reprinted with permission of the author. He is also the author of *Recycled Words*.

"Rosa Parks" by Kai Friese is from *Rosa Parks: The Movement Organizes* by Kai Friese. ©1990 by Silver Burdett Press, Simon & Schuster Education Group. Used by permission.

"Tabloid Culture" by Charles Gordon first appeared in the Sept. 22, 1997, issue of *Macleans* as "Are We Too Tolerant of Our Tabloid Culture" and is reprinted with permission of the publisher.

"The Magic Thread", from *Fairy Tales* illustrated by Nikolai Ustinov, Translation copyright © 1985 by Hodder & Stoughton Ltd. Art copyright © by Verlag J.F. Schreiber, Esslingen. Used by permission of Doubleday, a division of Bantam Doubleday Dell Publishing Group, Inc.

Grammar Index